AUTHOR'S NOTE

Royalties from the sale of this book will be donated to
Christian-Out-Reach-Peru
(**C**ristianos **O**brando para **R**espaldar los **Pe**rùanos)
to support relief work in and around
Puente Piedra, Lima, Peru.

For more information, please go to
www.christian-out-reach-peru.com

To: Declan & Dane

November 23, 2010

Pranksters at Play

Tales Out of School

Semper Vigilate Sobriique Estote

MEL ANTHONY

151 Howe Street, Victoria BC Canada V8V 4K5

For rights information and bulk orders, please contact:
info@agiopublishing.com *or go to*
www.agiopublishing.com

Pranksters at Play: Tales Out of School
ISBN 978-1-897435-43-4 (trade paperback)
Cataloguing information available from
Library and Archives Canada

Printed on acid-free paper.
Agio Publishing House is a socially responsible company, measuring success on a triple-bottom-line basis.

10 9 8 7 6 5 4 3 2 1a

DEDICATION

For '*mi Encantadora*', Isabel
and '*mi Alegria*', Elena
and '*mi Tesoro*', Joseph
de su abuelito, siempre – con todo mi corazòn

NOTICE

The author freely admits that St. Timothy's is modelled upon St. Mary's College, Brockville, but he advises that all of the characters and events in *Pranksters at Play: Tales Out of School* are fictitious and any resemblance to actual persons, living or dead, is purely coincidental.

The author is aware of the heinous crimes committed against so many defenceless boys in boarding schools. *Pranksters at Play: Tales Out of School* is not an apologetic for the guilty. This story is a fictionalized look back on the most contented and carefree years of his life.

ACKNOWLEDGEMENTS

The author thanks the members of *The Congregation of the Most Holy Redeemer* for the dedication, kindness and, yes, the love with which they made men of mere boys; especially for this: *Quia apud Dominum misericordia et copiosa apud eum redemptio.*

I want to acknowledge the many people without whom I would not, indeed could not, have seen this endeavour through to completion; especially Bob A., Bob F., Gretchen H., Odette M., Caroline W., and the good folks at Agio Publishing House, all of whom had more confidence in me than I had in myself.

TABLE OF CONTENTS

Prelude

As his elementary school career draws to a close, Emerson Jenks, prankster extraordinaire, plans what is to be his *grande finale*: his *pièce de résistance*.

The second Friday in June begins like any other school day. Teachers report for duty. Students arrive, on foot or peddling bikes. The grade eight girls saunter to their classroom early, skirts swaying. They bunch up near the cloakroom and giggle. Each clutches her books to her chest in a two-armed embrace. At the last possible moment, the boys in the class arrive, running and jumping, their shirttails un-tucked. Two or three – the usual suspects – are tardy. They have been waylaid by the discovery of pollywogs in the pond.

But this Friday proves somewhat different from other Fridays. The end of the school year is within sight, so the children are more keyed up than usual. Furthermore, because this Friday is a payday, the teachers are distracted. Young Master Jenks has long anticipated such favourable conditions.

Morning lessons and recess prove uneventful. But, less than five minutes before noon, Emerson's teacher acknowledges his raised hand. Seeing no reason to keep the boy from making a trip to the washroom, she dismisses him. Emerson steps from the classroom, exercises caution in retrieving the brown paper bag he has hidden, and leaves the building.

The bell sounds.

As he has done every payday, Mr. Collins, the school principal, intent on getting to the bank and back over the lunch hour, dashes across the lawn towards the parking lot. He comes up short and stares in horror at his car. Spider-web-like cracks spread out from a baseball-sized rock embedded in his windshield. Tiny cubes of glass litter the car's hood. The principal curses under his breath, throws his hands over his head and, turning on his heel, storms back into the building. Without benefit of consultation and, more consequentially, without thinking, he rings the bell a second time, summoning one and all to the auditorium.

A crowd forms. The principal rants. He raves. He describes his deep disappointment. He cautions his charges. Grave consequences await the person responsible if he does not confess. Mr. Collins pleads. He cajoles. He lectures on honesty and the dangers of stone throwing. These tactics fail. In desperation, he resorts to the hackneyed tale of how the child of a friend of a friend's cousin had his eye knocked out by a stone. This scheme fails too… miserably. The principal initiates a silent interrogation of his charges, scanning the assembly with squinty, accusing eyes. Students inspect their fingernails, or gaze up at the ceiling… or down at the floor… or at one another. Anywhere but at Mr. Collins.

Young Miss Shaw, deeply affected by her fearless leader's rhetoric and righteous indignation, suggests that the students be marched outside to see the results of so craven a delinquent's misdeed. Collins declares this a capital idea. The students parade out the door, side by side: reluctant sheep led from the cote. The principal plays shepherd; the teachers, border collies. Collins scrutinizes each face as the students pass and tries several ruses in hopes of tripping up the culprit.

"Mr. Jenks?" the principal barks as Emerson reaches him.

In response, the boy nods, slides his glasses into place and, while sidling past, replies, "Sir?" Emerson believes his prank will turn out to be even funnier than he intended.

Mr. Collins brings up the rear. Students fan out as they shuffle towards his big black Buick. The principal pushes through the silent crowd shouting, "Just look at what you've done!" It is with no small measure of bewilderment that he discovers a perfectly sound windshield.

In utter disbelief, the teachers stare at their open-mouthed leader. With a loud sniff and a scowl, Miss Shaw glares at Mr. Collins. A look of contempt crosses her face as her grade four students begin to snigger. Female students titter. Male students guffaw. The bewildered car owner does not begin to recover until one of the older boys – not Emerson Jenks to be sure – raises his hand.

"Can we go back to our games now, Sir?" the wag asks.

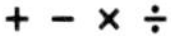

While his mates shot shifty-eyed glances at the classroom clock, eagerly counting down the seconds until lunch hour, Emerson hurried to the parking area, decorated the principal's windshield and, as soon as the bell sounded, hastened away and hid behind a hedge. From his hiding spot, he watched Mr. Collins approach his car. When the man returned to the school, Emerson raced to the vehicle and removed a battered Styrofoam ball, bits of shattered auto glass and a thin sheet of clear plastic film upon which he had handcrafted an intricate spider web design. By the time Mr. Collins rang the bell a second time, Emerson had already disposed of the evidence. The boy melted into the mob running back to the school in response to their principal's summons.

With a good deal of pride and self-satisfaction, Emerson mused upon as clever a prank as one could ever hope to carry off. The only real harm done had been the slight dent in the humiliated principal's ego. Furthermore, as planned, the perpetrator of the prank would remain forever anonymous.

Throughout the long, hot and humid summer, Emerson contemplated the prospect of beginning grade nine at St. Timothy's Preparatory School and planned how he might top that elementary school graduation prank.

Off Like a Herd of Turtles

“merson?”

No reply.

“Emerson!” Judy Jenks peered through the screen door into her kitchen, hoping to collar her missing son. The kitchen was empty. “Yoo-hoo... Emerson,” she called. “Em-er-son!”

When the boy did not answer, she entered the house for the umpteenth time that morning. She passed through the kitchen into the parlour – still no Emerson. From the bottom of the stairs, she called out, “Emerson? Are you up there, Emerson? Come down.” She paused, then added in a sterner voice, “Come on, Dad’s ready to go. We’ll be late.”

Emerson did not answer. Emerson’s older sister, Glenda, answered. She rolled over in bed and whined, “Why’d he be up here, Mom?” After a short pause, she continued, “What time’s it anyways?”

“Just past six, Sweetie,” replied her mother. “Where is that boy?”

“How should I know?” Glenda muttered just loudly enough not to be heard downstairs. She glowered, pulled the covers over her head, drew her knees up to her chin and grumbled, “How’s a person s’posed to sleep ’round here?” As an afterthought, she called out, “Mom, he’s just pulling one of his stupid stunts again. That’s all.”

She wasted her words. Mrs. Jenks had hurried off on her quest.

Behind the wheel of the family’s maroon station wagon, Peter Jenks grew increasingly agitated. “Where’d she get to?” he groaned and then wondered if he had whispered the words or only thought them. He revved the engine and thumped the horn with his fist. Three sharp blasts followed one sustained blare. “What’s the hold-up now?” the man muttered and then glanced behind him. “You passed your mother on the way out, didn’t you?”

“Nope,” replied the boy in the back seat as he looked up from his book and flipped a page. “I figured Mom was out here with you.”

Mr. Jenks drummed his fingers on the steering wheel and, with an almost silent sigh, glowered towards the kitchen door.

"Exasperated?" asked the boy.

"Exasperated?" replied his father. "Where on earth do you come up with these big words of yours?"

The boy did not answer.

"And what do you mean – *exasperated?*"

The boy removed his glasses and polished the lenses while keeping an eye on his father. "You sighed. And you're drumming your fingers. You seem… well… exasperated."

Feigning laughter, Mr. Jenks replied, "Well, I'm not. I'm just eager to be off. Aren't you?" The man shook his head as he stared at his watch. "I figured you'd be raring to go."

The boy grunted and fixed his eyes on the kitchen door.

Mrs. Jenks heard the engine and the horn. She grimaced, hung her head and sighed while saying, "He didn't go back to bed… surely?" She rushed off to her boys' room, pressed an ear to the door, cracked it open and squinted into the gloom. Only the sound of her two younger sons' rhythmic breathing could be heard. She spotted a third body curled up under the covers on a second bed.

"Oh, Emerson!" she groaned before feeling her way across the darkened room. She poked the boy's shoulder. Emerson was not in his bed. What had looked like a body, what she had thought was her son, proved to be nothing more than a pillow rolled up in a blanket.

Judy Jenks peeked into the family room – no Emerson. "Where are you?" she asked aloud. "Oh, dear!" she moaned. "Now he has me talking to myself."

She poked her head into the bathroom – no Emerson; the basement – no Emerson. "I'm reaching the end of my rope," she muttered just as a longer, more strident blast of the horn rang in her ears. She took a final peek into the parlour before dragging herself back to the car as if from the Slough of Despond.

"Emerson!" she exclaimed upon discovering her son in the back seat. "How on earth—"

"What kept you, Judy?" demanded her husband. "Come on. Let's go. We're already ten minutes late." He revved the engine as his dumbfounded wife stared at their son.

Mrs. Jenks collapsed into her seat and pulled her door closed. As the vehicle rolled ahead, she turned and stared long and hard at Emerson. The boy fidgeted with the straps on his knapsack and did not look up. "Emers…" began Mrs. Jenks. Her voice trailed off when the boy drew her attention to their neighbour's front window.

"Was that Mr. Wilson staring at us, Mom?" the boy asked as he directed her attention to the house next door.

Emerson's mysterious disappearance and miraculous reappearance faded into insignificance. "Oh, Peter," Judy Jenks wailed and pressed her hand to her mouth, "the horn. The neighbours. They'll all be staring."

"Wilson? Old George just wanted to see the boy off – that's all," replied Mr. Jenks. "St. Timothy's be prepared: Emerson Jenks is on his way. We're off like a herd of turtles." Mr. Jenks craned to see Emerson in the rear-view mirror. "Comfortable back there?" he asked.

The boy did not answer. Emerson turned and stared down the street to where Glenda, pinching the collar of her housecoat to her chin, stood and waved. The boy returned his sister's goodbye. Emerson removed a pamphlet from his knapsack, adjusted his glasses and pretended to read. Mr. Jenks turned his attention to the road while Mrs. Jenks fastened her eyes on her son. She opened her mouth to speak but decided not to interrupt the boy. Turning, she rested her head on a pillow and closed her eyes.

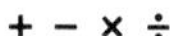

Mrs. Jenks awoke as her husband was backing the car into a parking space. Disoriented, the woman looked about. The rumble of a moving van passing between the front of the vehicle and a restaurant gave her a start. Peter Jenks turned to her and smiled. "Hey, Sleepyhead. Ready to eat? It's almost—" he glanced at his watch, "—9:15. It's time for breakfast."

All three exited the vehicle.

"Make sure the car's locked, Emerson," Peter Jenks shouted as he slammed his door. He assumed that the boy's mumbled response had been a 'yes'. The couple strolled across the parking lot. Their son lagged behind.

Inside the restaurant, Peter Jenks remained standing until his wife slid into the booth and Emerson took his seat next to her. Before sitting opposite them and without looking at the hostess, he said, "Coffee, please."

Judy Jenks noticed the hostess's slight hesitation and haughty, sideways glance. Her husband did not.

"Your waitress will be right with you," replied the hostess. The woman sounded bored to the point of tears. She had repeated those seven words a million times.

Mr. Jenks waved his menu in the air, halting the woman's retreat. "Black, no sugar," he added and smiled.

The woman's scowl registered only with Mrs. Jenks. A minute later, Peter Jenks gazed towards the kitchen and asked – just a bit too loudly – "Where on earth did she get to?"

Raising her eyes without raising her head, a mortified Judy Jenks checked to see if their neighbours had overheard.

When their server arrived, she poured Mr. Jenks' coffee while asking, "Youse guys ready tuh order?"

Mrs. Jenks cringed. Besides the screech of fingernails on a blackboard, only the word 'youse' caused her to cringe. That word, she frequently complained, made her feel like a sheep.

"I'll have the cheese omelette. Hash browns with sausage and toast. Extra butter on the toast," ordered Emerson's father and tossed the menu onto the table.

"Extra butter," repeated the waitress as she scribbled on her pad.

Judy Jenks bit her lip, hemmed and hawed and ran her finger over the prices. The waitress showed not the slightest sign of interest. The embodiment of boredom, she doodled daisies and chomped on a wad of gum the size of a golf ball. Presently, Mrs. Jenks ordered water and a poached egg on dry toast.

"Last of the big time spenders," whispered the waitress to the ceiling. To her order pad, she mumbled, "Dry toast."

The girl turned indifferent eyes on Emerson and blew a large, pink bubble which popped, eliciting a frown and loud 'tut' from Mrs. Jenks.

Emerson averted his eyes, slid his glasses up his nose and muttered into his menu.

"Better bring him the children's special—" suggested Mr. Jenks, "or we'll be here 'til Doomsday. Oh, and a refill," he added, nodding towards his all-but-empty cup. To his wife and son he said, "I'm starved," and, like a child making a Plasticine snake, rubbed the palms of his hands together. "What a day!" he said. "What… a… day!"

Mrs. Jenks rummaged through her purse without any idea of what she wanted. "You know, Peter, all that butter's not good for you."

"What?" demanded her husband and patted his stomach. "As fit as the day you married me, Judy."

"Not in a month of Sundays," muttered his wife into her handbag. To her husband she said, "Indeed!" She then studied her son's face and asked, "How are you holding up, Emerson? Is everything okay?"

Emerson flashed a feeble smile and patted his mother's hand. "Yeah, Mom… I'm fine," he answered. "Honest." He turned and stared out the window. Both parents noted their son's pensive mood and imagined that the boy was off in his daydream world again. Their every attempt to engage Emerson in sustained conversation failed.

When breakfast arrived, Mrs. Jenks warned, "Don't go dripping egg on your new blazer, Emerson. You either, Peter. They'd be impressed if you two showed up with egg all down the front of you, wouldn't they? Do those ever look good," she added and plucked a sausage from her wide-eyed husband's plate. "You don't mind do you, Dear?" She checked the sausage for flaws before taking a bite.

Twenty minutes later, Judy Jenks again set her purse on her lap and opened it. After extracting an amazing assortment of items, she found her lipstick and compact. "May I slide out, please?" she asked. "I'll go freshen up while you two finish." Emerson stood and stepped away from the table to allow his mother to pass.

"Can I go for a walk, Dad?" the boy asked. "I won't go far, Mom."

"*May I* go?" replied Mrs. Jenks. While his wife hesitated, Peter Jenks dismissed the boy with a wave of his hand. Before his mother could react, Emerson had fled to the lobby. Mrs. Jenks' eyes followed him the entire way. "I *suppose* he'll be okay," she said, tentatively.

"He's a month shy of thirteen, Judy," replied her husband. A vision of apron strings flashed in his mind. "If he can't go outside and walk around for five minutes – I mean – what can he do?"

"Six weeks," corrected Mrs. Jenks and hesitated. "I know you're right," she added. "But, Peter, it's so hard…" Mrs. Jenks stood in pensive silence for a moment then added, "I'd better go find a pay phone and call home. I want to see how Glenda is making out with the boys."

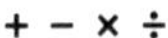

Ten minutes later, Emerson peeked around the corner of the restaurant and watched his parents leave the building. Mrs. Jenks stopped on the top step, scanning the car park for any sign of her son. Mr. Jenks skipped down the stairs, patting the pockets of his pants and, stopping suddenly, executed a smart about-face before running his hands over the front of his jacket and locating his keys. He raised his eyes heavenward, turned towards his wife and waited.

As the two adults started off towards their vehicle, Emerson ran up from behind. "Can I open the doors, Dad?" he asked with outstretched hand.

"*May I* open?" Mrs. Jenks corrected. With the keys in his possession, Emerson scampered away. He unlocked both front doors and started back towards his parents.

"Want-uh start 'er up?" asked Mr. Jenks as the boy approached.

Emerson turned on his heel and sprinted back to the vehicle.

"Make sure you don't flood it. That's all," called his father after him. Peter Jenks could not ignore the vice-like grip on his arm. The epitome of calm, he spoke to his wife. "Relax, dear. It's in park… the emergency's on. Nobody's even near us. Look, even the guy behind is backing out."

Before Mrs. Jenks could give voice to her concerns, the car engine roared to life.

"See! Told you," declared her husband.

Emerson left the driver's door open and ran to the opposite side of the vehicle. When his mother arrived, he made an exaggerated bow, opened her door and swept his hand in a wide arc before her.

"Why thank you, kind sir," said a pleased Judy Jenks and took her seat.

"You're most welcome, *Madame*," replied Emerson and pushed the door closed. The boy froze in place when he noticed that he had left his own door unlocked. He shifted his gaze to his parents; neither seemed to have noticed. He made a mental note to be more careful in future and then let his eyes sweep the parking lot before climbing into the back seat.

"Now that's what I call a breakfast," grunted Mr. Jenks and patted his stomach.

"Let's get going, eh, Dad," exclaimed Emerson.

"Well now. Look who's in a big hurry all of a sudden," replied Mr. Jenks with a chuckle.

"Let's just go, Dad," pleaded Emerson and glanced over his shoulder. "Please!"

Peter Jenks released the brake, dropped the gear lever into drive and cruised off towards the freeway.

The brawniest of three brawny truckers gestured towards the station wagon as if he wanted it to stop. Neither Mr. nor Mrs. Jenks noticed. But Emerson noticed; Emerson always noticed. The men's approach had prompted his request for a quick getaway.

Within minutes of entering the flow of eastbound traffic, Emerson's father turned and interrupted his wife's chatter. "Hon," he asked, "any idea why all these trucks are honking when they go by?"

Mrs. Jenks looked up from the roadmap she had spread across her lap. "I hadn't noticed," she replied.

"They weren't doing that before," continued Mr. Jenks. "How 'bout you, Son?"

Before Emerson could answer, an eighteen-wheeler rumbled past, its horn blaring.

"There!" said Mr. Jenks. "See what I mean? They're driving me crazy. What a dirty look I got too."

Emerson's tongue made a visible bulge in his cheek. He buried his face in some papers and pretended to read. Another semi gave the station wagon a prolonged blast in passing.

Mr. Jenks scowled. "What's wrong with those stupid—"

"Little pitchers have big ears," declared Mrs. Jenks, cutting off her husband's remark.

"But he… he… he shook his fist at me," replied her husband. "Of all the nerve!"

Judy Jenks clenched her jaws, squinted and added, "Maybe you're driving a bit too slow, or—" She received a withering glare for her pains so turned to look out the side window, her back to her husband. She felt his eyes poking her between the shoulder blades.

"What's that you're looking at, Emerson?" asked Mrs. Jenks in contrived innocence after turning her attention to her son.

"Just some stuff, Mom," the boy answered.

"Stuff!" exclaimed Mrs. Jenks and shuttered. "How I hate that word. Let me see."

Emerson passed the *St. Timothy's Preparatory School Orientation Manual* to his mother.

"Why you've nearly got this worn out," she declared. "How many times have you read it?"

"Oh, a few. I guess," Emerson answered. "It's actually pretty interesting."

"Must be," replied his mother. She flipped through the document examining its dog-eared pages and smudged ink.

"Oh man! That does it," growled Mr. Jenks as another truck passed, roaring out what sounded like an angry opening to Beethoven's Fifth. "I'm getting off this road… Right here… Right now." Mr. Jenks lifted his foot from the gas pedal and steered onto an exit ramp.

"But where are we?" cried Mrs. Jenks. The woman tossed the manual to her son and fussed with her map. "Which exit was that, Peter?"

"No idea," replied Mr. Jenks, "but I'm getting off that freeway before I go stark raving mad." A moment later he added, "I think this takes us down to the river."

The narrow road wended its way around swamps, through cedar thickets and past dilapidated barns. The smells of late summer hung in the air. Cows stood in boulder-strewn fields, forlorn within their split-rail prisons. Mr. Jenks breathed a long, slow sigh of relief and smiled. "Now that's more like it," he announced. "No more traffic, no more horns. Except on those cows over there!"

"Oh, Peter!" chided Judy Jenks in mock horror.

"Don't you get it? Cow horns... and truck horns. It's a pun," Peter Jenks explained and then laughed at his own joke.

Mrs. Jenks' groan drowned out her son's quiet grumble. In vain, she began glancing at passing road signs in hopes of discovering their whereabouts. From time to time, she cast questioning, sidelong glances at her husband. She said nothing.

The road ended at a two-lane highway. The absence of the river he had anticipated finding there proved unsettling to the driver and more unsettling to his front seat passenger. Mr. Jenks turned left and continued eastward. Within minutes, he noticed fellow travellers acting strangely. They dallied behind before passing. On coming alongside, some smiled and waved in a friendly fashion. Some flashed the thumbs up sign. A few frowned. Peter Jenks returned subtle, self-conscious nods. "I don't get it," he exclaimed.

His wife shrugged. Emerson stared into his manual, glancing up from time to time, to see how his father was holding up under the strain. "Well, it sure beats those blasted horns," Peter Jenks declared.

The man enjoyed his peace and quiet… until he heard the siren. His foot jumped from the accelerator as if it had received an electric shock. His eyes darted to the speedometer and then to the rear-view mirror. A police car, its emergency lights flashing, sped up from behind.

"Must be an accident," advised Mr. Jenks. "Better let this guy get by."

He signalled, slowed, pulled onto the shoulder and stopped.

The family waited for the cruiser to fly past. It did not fly past. When Mr. Jenks glanced back, his mouth fell open. He screwed-up his eyes and stared. The cruiser, its lights still flashing, was parked immediately behind the station wagon. The car's lone occupant exited the vehicle, pushed his cap back on his head, hitched up his pants and, without further hesitation, approached the vehicle.

"Oh dear?" grumbled Mr. Jenks.

"Oh, Peter," cried Mrs. Jenks.

"Oh-oh!" whispered, Emerson.

"You weren't driving too fast, were you, Peter?" inquired his wife.

"Please?" her husband begged. He could have sworn she had ended her statement with the word 'again'.

Out of the corner of his eye, Emerson watched the officer signal the driver to lower his window. Involuntarily, the boy held his breath.

"Problem, Officer?" inquired Mr. Jenks. His valiant effort to sound nonchalant failed— utterly.

The man in the uniform placed both hands on the car's roof, stooped forward and let his eyes run over the car's interior. "The sign, Sir," he announced at last. "Several people have complained about your sign."

"Sign?" cried Mr. Jenks. "What sign?"

The officer beckoned. Mr. Jenks stepped out of the vehicle. Mrs. Jenks joined the two men at the rear of the station wagon. Emerson could see but not hear the adults. The drumming in his ears was deafening. The police officer pointed at a large sign taped to the tailgate. White letters on a dark blue background read:

SHIP BY RAIL – BAN LONG HAUL TRUCKING.

Mr. Jenks ripped the sign loose, folded it in half, tore it in two, folded it, tore it again and continued in this fashion until his strength deserted him. He hurled the pieces to the ground and kicked them unceremoniously into the ditch. The police officer cleared his throat and levelled his gaze first into the ditch and then into Mr. Jenks' flushed face.

Mrs. Jenks cleared her throat – more loudly than the officer had. While she smiled apologetically at the officer, her husband retrieved the litter. After Mr. Jenks climbed back onto the roadside, the officer took what remained of the offending sign and swaggered back to his car. After giving the family a friendly wave and climbing behind the wheel, the man smirked, gave his head a shake and turned off his emergency lights. As Emerson and his parents stared, the officer executed a smart U-turn and sped off down the highway.

Mr. Jenks took his seat and buried his face in his hands before speaking. "That's what was going on, Judy," he wailed. "If I ever get my hands on the little—"

"Little pitchers, Honey!" Mrs. Jenks reminded her husband of their young passenger's innocence.

The man restarted the car and pulled back onto the road. He began mumbling and, from time to time, thumped the steering wheel. Mrs. Jenks stole glances at her husband. Neither parent noticed the smug look on their son's face. Several minutes passed before Mr. Jenks looked at Emerson in the rear-view mirror. "Were you out by the car back there, Son?" he asked.

The boy's heart skipped a beat and his smirk vanished.

"You didn't see anyone suspicious hanging around, did you?" asked his father.

"No," replied Emerson and exhaled. "Nobody… Nobody at all."

The trip continued in silence. From time to time, Mr. Jenks grimaced and scratched his head. He made no comment even when the missing river finally appeared through the trees. Mrs. Jenks hummed. Emerson busied himself with his orientation manual and, when he thought it safe, observed his parents.

The meeting with the police taught Emerson to anticipate complications when planning similar pranks.

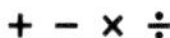

Twenty minutes later, Mrs. Jenks broke into a cheerful chatter. "Almost there," she announced and turned her attention from her map to her son. "Are you alright back there?" she asked upon noticing Emerson's grim face. The woman nudged her husband and gestured towards the rear seat.

Mr. Jenks raised his head so he could see his son in the mirror. "Looks like you lost your best friend, Emerson. What's the matter?"

Upon hearing the word 'friend', Emerson stared at the floor. He said nothing. He had a plan and he could not imagine having a better opportunity to execute it. His silence and his frown had drawn his parents' attention. Now he needed them to coax some information out of him. The boy half-moaned, half-whispered his answer, "Everything's okay… I guess."

"Spit it out," demanded his father. "What's bothering you, Son?"

Emerson refused to respond.

"You have to let us know what's wrong or we can't help," added his mother.

"Well…" Emerson replied. He stared at the floor again. "I guess I'm going to – well – miss my friends… That's all." He turned his head and gazed out the side window. "It's okay though," he added for effect.

"Oh!" groaned Judy Jenks and fell silent when she noticed her husband's stern expression. She had almost spoken the words 'my poor baby'.

"Emerson," declared the boy's father, "you'll make all kinds of new friends down here. You'll see."

"But that's not the same thing at all, Peter," argued Judy Jenks. "He's had the same friends... well... forever."

Emerson's eyes darted from one parent to the other. He said nothing while struggling to maintain the most forlorn expression he could muster.

"Anyway..." added Mr. Jenks, "there's no reason your friends can't come down to see you." He studied his son's reflection in the mirror. "Well, is there?"

When the boy's countenance remained grim, his father added, "Maybe we can bring one or two of the fellows when we come at Thanksgiving. How'd you like that?"

Emerson failed to suppress his delight. A smile crept across his face when his mother added, "You know, Emerson, Thanksgiving's not that far off!"

"You're making this way too easy," Emerson mumbled.

"What was that?" asked his father.

"I said, do you really think so?" replied the boy.

Upon seeing the joyful expression on Emerson's face, the boy's parents sighed: the father in relief, the mother in commiseration. They glanced at one another and smiled. Neither noticed their son's efforts to conceal a smirk. Neither noticed the twinkle in his eyes.

A few minutes later, Emerson blurted out, "Dad, I guess you'll have to ask him, eh?"

His father's face registered confusion. "Ask who what?"

"Ask whom?" interjected Mrs. Jenks. This grammar lesson went unheeded.

"Ask the headmaster if my friends can visit," explained Emerson.

"Oh, I think you can manage that on your own," responded Mr. Jenks. "I mean... you've got that meeting when we get there." He checked his watch. "When the headmaster asks if you have any questions, that's the time to bring it up, eh?"

"I guess," responded Emerson and turned to look out the rear window. The corners of the boy's mouth started to curl into a grin. He concealed the grin with his hand.

"Nearly there, Son," declared Mr. Jenks. The station wagon rolled onto the main street at the western edge of the city. "They said ten minutes east of town. Hey, we're still in pretty good time too."

With little more than ten minutes in which to prepare for his meeting with the headmaster, Emerson picked up the orientation manual and continued his silent study of the school's floor plans.

As they continued eastward, out of the city, the last in a line of great, grey limestone mansions, sentinels along the river, dropped from view. "Just look at that," exclaimed Mr. Jenks and pointed over an open field and across a wide expanse of sparkling blue water. "That's New York State over there," he announced. "A hundred and fifty years ago—"

Judy Jenks interrupted the impromptu history lesson. "Oh my goodness!" she cried. "It's so… so big." Agape, the woman pointed to several huge, red-brick buildings surrounded by a high, brick and wrought iron fence. "Oh, Peter, he'll never find his way around a place like that. I had no idea—"

"Relax, Judy. That's not St. Timothy's. It's a psychiatric hospital. And even if that was the school—"

His wife corrected him. "If it *were* the school—" she said.

"Okay! If it were the school, Emerson would know the place, top to bottom, inside a week. Right, Son?" Emerson glanced up, mumbled a non-committal reply and returned to his studies.

Mrs. Jenks' chatter ceased and she began to fidget. Five minutes later, she pointed left again. "That must be it," she cried as a large limestone building came into view.

"Gotta be!" replied her husband.

"Slow down, Peter. Turn right here," shouted Mrs. Jenks. The driver ignored his wife's comment and proceeded past the narrow tractor trail to which she had pointed and swung left between the school's stone gateposts. The car entered the deep shade beneath twin rows of tall maples that flanked the long gravel drive.

"Oh!" exclaimed Mrs. Jenks. "How beautiful! Like a tunnel."

"A cathedral," declared her husband and craned to look up into the interlacing branches.

Emerson stared up the drive. Through the inverted 'U' formed by the two rows of maples he could see the building's dark brown doors standing stark against its ivy-covered limestone. He noticed four steps leading to a landing and a steep, broad staircase climbing from there to the entrance. His eyes were drawn to a round, multi-paned, rose-shaped window above the doors. The building's red tile roof stood out against a clear, blue sky. At either end of the old structure were newly-built red-brick and glass additions.

Having reached the end of the lane, Mr. Jenks drove halfway around a grand curving driveway encircling a well-clipped expanse of grass in the centre of which was a manicured flower garden. He parked beneath a giant elm that stood guard just to the left of the main stairway.

Emerson's father switched off the engine and, for several seconds, stared ahead in silence. Finally, he turned to his son, swallowed hard and then said, "Well, my boy… we're here!"

Emerson leaned forward, draping his arms over the back of the front seat. His eyes darted about, taking in the scene, absorbing every detail. Mr. and Mrs. Jenks stepped from the car, joined several people on the lawn and, hand-in-hand, gazed up at the front of the massive main building. Mrs. Jenks stole several glances towards the car while she and her husband spoke to one another in whispers.

"Are you sure about this, Honey?" asked Mrs. Jenks. "Maybe if we wait another year he'd—"

"—Judy, Judy, Judy! You worry too much. The boy'll be fine. Just wait and see. He's going to love it here."

"I'm not so sure, Peter," added Mrs. Jenks. She bit her lower lip and shook her head. "We never even thought about him missing his friends. I just don't know—"

"Let's not panic. At least not 'til after he's talked to the headmaster, okay?"

"I suppose," replied Mrs. Jenks. The woman sounded doubtful. She continued glancing towards the station wagon. "It's just that he seems so frightened," she continued. "I know my son, Peter. Just look at him. The poor kid's too scared to get out of the car." Peter Jenks rubbed his wife's back, hoping to reassure her and calm her ragged nerves.

Judy Jenks did not know her son half as well as she imagined.

Emerson was neither a poor kid nor frightened. His decision to remain in the car was purely strategic. He watched several boys playing flag football on the broad front lawn. Between and around half a dozen other parked vehicles, at least a dozen others ran and romped, engaged in some form of tag. All were dressed in rough play clothes and created a racket much louder than Emerson thought St. Timothy's would tolerate. He shrugged. "All those guys have been here before," he said aloud. "That's for sure."

Groups of three to six people congregated on the lawn. In each was a boy dressed, like Emerson, in a dark blue blazer, a white shirt, grey slacks and a narrow school tie. New kids and their families, concluded Emerson with a nod.

Three boys, Emerson noted, sniggered and snorted while standing in a line at the foot of the main stairway. They too were dressed in blue blazers and grey pants. Repeatedly, the tallest punched his two companions on the shoulder and laughed. The victims' protests only invited more frequent jabs. Boss-man and his toadies, Emerson determined. "They look like the Three Stooges in schoolboy outfits," he muttered, smiling at the image that had popped into his mind.

Emerson recognized only Headmaster Fitzroy. The man had visited the Jenks' home several times in the past year. The short, dark-haired gentleman stood talking to a man, a woman and a young boy. The headmaster's efforts to extricate himself from the encounter were being thwarted at every turn. When the man took a step backwards, his companions stepped forward. When he half-turned and began to walk away, they followed. When the headmaster stopped, so did the father, mother and son.

Emerson shifted studious eyes from the headmaster to the stooges. When it was possible for Fitzroy to see them, the three boys stood ramrod straight with their hands clasped behind their backs. When the headmaster's back was turned, they tittered and talked, talked and tittered and tried to body check one another off balance. Emerson considered all that he saw, pursed his lips and nodded. "Yep, pretty much what I expected," the boy muttered and smiled.

First Impressions

Young Emerson Jenks shook his head in disbelief as he evaluated the headmaster's performance. The man's unsuccessful attempts to shake off his guests proved especially amusing. The boy watched as a tall, redheaded, freckle-faced student hurried from the building. The three stooges snapped to attention and, after the boy spoke to them, exchanged half-chagrined, half-worried looks. The young fellow approached Fitzroy from behind, tapped him on the shoulder and whispered in his ear. The headmaster glanced at the latest arrivals with a hand raised to his mouth and nodded. He excused himself and, relieved of his burden, crossed the lawn, preening himself as he approached Mr. and Mrs. Jenks. The redheaded boy ushered the other family towards their vehicle with a grace that belied his years.

"Mr. and Mrs. Jenks," said Mr. Fitzroy, "so very sorry to have kept you waiting." He extended his hand. "I just had to get r— I mean— to see the Fredericks off." The two men shook hands.

"Not a problem," replied Mr. Jenks. "If you're not quite done…"

The headmaster glanced towards the Fredericks' car before dismissing the offer. "No, no, young Andrews appears to have everything in hand. Now tell me, how was your trip?"

Emerson's parents exchanged pleasantries with Mr. Fitzroy. Yes, they had enjoyed a safe trip. No, they had had no difficulties finding the school. Yes indeed, the buildings and grounds were lovely.

"I'm so glad to hear you say that," the headmaster said. "First impressions are so very important after all." Fitzroy, conspicuous in his craftiness, stole a glance at his watch. "And Emerson?" he asked.

"Still in the car," replied Mrs. Jenks as she stooped slightly and waved to her son. Some signal must have passed from the headmaster to the students near the stairs, for the tallest boy crossed the lawn, took up a position at Mr. Fitzroy's side, his back turned towards the infantile antics of his two friends. Nothing but the headmaster's signal escaped Emerson's keen eye.

"While I'm with Emerson," declared Fitzroy, "Meddows here will give you the grand tour. Meddows… Mr. and Mrs. Jenks." The boy shook Peter Jenks' hand. "Mr. Meddows is in fourth year. Right, Meddows?" Meddows confirmed the fact with a slight nod and focussed his eyes on his tasselled loafers. "He'll be happy to show you around. Won't you, Meddows?"

"Pleased to meet you, Ma'am," said Meddows. "And you too, of course, Mr. Jenks, Sir. If you'll follow me, please, we'll start over there in Disraeli Hall." Meddows pointed to his right, drawing the Jenks' attention to the red-brick addition to their left. "I'll show you the gym and auditorium first," the boy explained. "We'll just—"

"Oh, Meddows. Make sure Mr. and Mrs. Jenks get a bite to eat, would you?" called Fitzroy. The station wagon reached, the headmaster opened Emerson's door, stooped down, placing his hands on his knees. "Well now… There you are," he exclaimed. The surprise in his voice suggested that he thought Mrs. Jenks might have lied to him. "Ready for our wee chat, are we, Jenks?"

Emerson slid out of the car, shook Mr. Fitzroy's outstretched hand then followed him up the steps.

The man stopped and shouted. "Meddows! Meddows, I say!"

Meddows stopped, turned and cocked his ear towards the main entrance.

"Make sure you have the Jenkses back to my office by—" Fitzroy drew out his pocket watch and stared at it, "—one o'clock, say. And Meddows…" The headmaster looked around. "Now, where did Andrews get to? I say, Meddows! Remind Andrews to ring the lunch bell at one-fifteen sharp."

"Sir," replied Meddows by way of acknowledgement.

Mrs. Jenks asked about the addition at the opposite end of the old building. Meddows explained that Gladstone Hall housed the faculty. "It's off limits 'less yuh've got— sorry —unless *you have* written permission, Ma'am."

Mrs. Jenks had no real interest in the building and missed Meddows' response. Not even his grammatical gaffe registered with her. Her attention was fixed on her son as he mounted the stairs. With foreboding, she watched Emerson and Mr. Fitzroy disappear through the school's cavernous front entrance. "My poor little boy," she muttered and stepped into Disraeli Hall followed by her husband. Before Meddows could follow, he heard his name being called yet again.

Mr. Fitzroy had stepped out of the building, followed by Emerson, and shouted, "Meddows! If Mr. Jenks will trust us with his keys—" the man laughed a great horsy laugh, "—have a couple of the fellows haul young Mr. Jenks' things up to the dorm. There's a good lad." As if for the first time, the headmaster noticed Meddows' two companions. He took three or four steps towards the pair and, with a snap of his fingers, said, "Burns and... and... ah..."

"O'Neil," the second boy replied.

"O'Neil," repeated the headmaster. "That's right," he added as if O'Neil's ability to recall his own name was somehow praiseworthy. "You and Burns there, cart this young man's belongings up to the dorm for him." As he spoke he patted Emerson on the shoulder.

"Sir," Burns and O'Neil responded together.

Mr. Fitzroy, with a hand pressed to the middle of Emerson's back, guided the youngster inside once more. Together, they climbed yet more stairs and passed through a second set of doors into a foyer. Emerson thought the entryway a gloomy affair. The noonday sun, apparently the room's sole source of illumination, penetrated just a few feet inside the building. The air felt heavy and cool. Emerson stopped and, straining his eyes, tried to make out the features of what had to be a spacious, high-ceilinged room. The boy noticed four recessed doors, two on each side wall; all were closed. Ahead, through an archway and across a wide hall was a double doorway through which he could see a row of tall, heavily-draped windows high up on the wall opposite. The floor plan indicated that that doorway led into a chapel. He closed his eyes and breathed deeply. A strange but not unpleasant odour permeated the space.

"What's that smell, Sir?" asked Emerson.

Fitzroy tilted his head back, closed his eyes and drew a deep breath. A seraphic smile formed on the man's lips as he exhaled. "That's the smell of St. Timothy's," he replied. "That's incense mostly… and beeswax from the candles, of course… and altar wine and years and years of paste wax… hardwood floors, you know. You two'll get used to that smell in a hurry," he added. "Everyone does."

Emerson did not know what the headmaster meant when he used the words 'you two'. He had failed to notice another student standing behind the headmaster in the darkest part of the foyer. The boy stared down at the floor.

"Jenks… Fredericks," stated Fitzroy. "Fredericks… Jenks." The boys acknowledged one another with nods but said nothing. "You'll be classmates— and cubicle-mates, too, if I'm not mistaken," advised the headmaster. Neither boy understood exactly what the man meant by the word 'cubicle'; they soon would.

"What's that say?" asked Fredericks, pointing to the school crest set into the mosaic tile floor.

"You should be able to catch the gist of the thing," replied Fitzroy.

Fredericks shrugged.

"A riddle, wrapped in a mystery, inside an enigma," exclaimed Emerson and stared up at Mr. Fitzroy, smiling a sly smile.

"An enema?" cried Fredericks with a gasp.

"Enigma!" shrieked the headmaster. He almost added the words 'you dolt' but managed to catch himself. "I suppose, Jenks," he continued, "that it's an enigma of sorts." To Fredericks he said, "Look that word up, Fredericks. Look them both up. Enema— indeed!"

While Fitzroy handed Fredericks his first assignment, Emerson squinted down at St. Timothy's school crest:

SEMPER VIGILATE SOBRIIQUE ESTOTE.

Emerson had seen the words on the cover of the orientation manual and now read them aloud. "Let's see! Hmmm… always vigilant and something… sober?" He looked up.

"Not bad, Jenks" admitted Fitzroy. "It's Latin, of course— from the Bible, you know. Here at St. Timothy's, we've always translated it as *Be forever vigilant and sober*."

"Really?" replied Emerson. "Vigilant, Sir? *Semper vigilate!* I think I can manage that, Sir."

The headmaster waved towards two of the foyer's four doors. "The sacristy's on our left and the vestry's to our right," announced Fitzroy. Neither boy was familiar with the word 'sacristy' or 'vestry' either. "And, ahead of us we have our chapel," Fitzroy added with a nod. The headmaster plucked his watch from his waistcoat pocket, brought it close to his face and angled it towards the shaft of sunlight. "My, my, my!" he muttered. "We're running a bit late. Well now, Jenks," he added, "it's time for our wee chat, eh?"

Leaving Fredericks to ponder the motto, the man led Emerson down a dark corridor, through a doorway and onto a stairwell landing. "Chapel landing," Mr. Fitzroy announced as he pushed the chapel door open.

Emerson looked over the pews to the altar. The view confirmed that the chapel had a main aisle and a side aisle which led to the foyer. On the landing, opposite the rear door, stood a life-sized statue set into a deep, raised alcove.

"St. Timothy," explained the headmaster when he noticed how Emerson, apparently awestruck, stared up at the imposing presence.

Emerson eyed the lifelike sculpture, sidled past it and followed Fitzroy upstairs and along a hallway: grey walls, greyer floor, even greyer ceiling. At the end of the hall they turned a corner, continued for another twenty paces and stopped before a set of oak doors. Along the way, Mr. Fitzroy chatted. Emerson only half listened. He did notice, however, that the headmaster was fond of saying that St. Timothy's made men out of boys like him.

Mr. Fitzroy pressed the thumb latches and swung his office doors open. "Go right ahead, Jenks," said the man. "No need to be nervous."

Emerson approached the doorway, stopped on the threshold, screwed up his eyes and peered right and left. Like the rest of the building, the room was poorly lit and filled with shadows.

"Nothing to be afraid of, Jenks," advised Fitzroy. "We just need to run over a few of the ground rules. It shouldn't take more than half an hour."

Emerson's eyes swept the room.

The headmaster smiled ruefully, nodded and stepped past his young guest. "Don't worry, Jenks, your parents won't leave without saying good-bye." Like a tennis player making a backhand lob shot, he waved Emerson forward.

Emerson moved quickly to the centre of the room and turned full circle. A high-backed, red leather chair occupied the space between a large rosewood desk and the room's only window. A small, straight-backed, wooden chair had been positioned at the right side of the desk. Emerson did not have to ask where to sit. Several bookshelves stood against the walls. Armchairs were scattered about the room. There was a single door on the side wall to the left of the desk. When Emerson spotted a small, antique roll-top standing alone in the corner, to his far right, he grinned a gratified grin and stepped forward. He had anticipated finding that desk somewhere in the headmaster's office. So much depended on it being there.

"Sit anywhere you like, Jenks. Make yourself comfortable," Fitzroy stated. He turned and closed the doors.

Emerson moved the small chair to the left side of the desk and took his seat. He sniffed the air and detected the smell of tobacco smoke. In vain, he scanned the room for signs of an ashtray. *He smokes but doesn't want anyone to know*, the boy observed. Emerson figured he should be able to make use of that information at some point.

The headmaster's eyebrows rose when he noticed that his guest had moved the small chair. He muttered, walked across the room and stepped behind the desk. He turned on his desk lamp, fussed with some papers while contemplating the unprecedented turn of events and then took his seat. He clasped his hands together and stretched his arms out over his blotter. "So, Jenks, you want St. Timothy's to make a man out of you, do you?" asked the headmaster.

"A man, Sir? Oh, yes, Sir. I'd like that, Sir," answered Emerson.

Fitzroy was taken aback but nonetheless pleased. "That's just great," he replied. "Well, let's get started, shall we?" The man rubbed the palms of his hands together while Emerson removed his glasses and polished the lenses. From where he sat, he had a clear view past the headmaster to the roll-top desk.

Fitzroy slid his glasses up and down his nose as if he was unsure whether he could see better with or without them. He peered over the top of the frames and droned on about the school's history before beginning to review the rules. "We operate on the honour system here, Jenks," he advised. "That means—" The man stopped in mid-sentence. "Jenks?"

he added with alarm. Emerson did not respond. He slid to the edge of his chair and opened wide his mouth and eyes. He fixed his gaze on the roll-top. Fitzroy glanced into the corner too. "Jenks? Is everything alright?"

"Are there many ghosts here, Sir?" asked the boy without changing expressions.

"Ghosts!" cried Fitzroy and eased himself from his chair. "Of course not, Jenks. There's no such thing as ghosts."

"Then who's that, Sir?" asked Emerson and pointed towards the roll-top.

The headmaster gawked at the old desk. He looked back at his guest and said, "It's just the poor lighting in here... Plays tricks with the eyes, you know."

"I really don't think so, Sir. I can see the old fellow quite clearly," said the boy and got to his feet.

"The— the— the old fellow?" stuttered Fitzroy, exhibiting more interest. He took three or four tentative steps towards the old desk and inspected the corner, but failed to see anything unusual.

"Oh yes, Sir," replied Emerson. "He's right there by that roll-top. Can't you see him, Sir? He's twirling a feather pen around and he's got on a vest with buttons all down the front."

The headmaster staggered backwards, bumping his chair. He had to clutch the edge of the desk for balance. His heart beat faster and rose in his throat at the mention of the pen and the vest. His stare shifted between the corner and the strange boy. Mr. Fitzroy found himself unable to say a word. His mouth, suddenly bone dry, begged for water. In slow-motion, Emerson swivelled his head to his left. The headmaster's eyes followed the boy's gaze until both host and guest stood staring at the single door on the room's side wall. Fitzroy's fingers moved spasmodically as he scratched his clammy palms.

"It's okay now, Sir," announced Emerson. "He's gone. Passed right through that door there."

Fitzroy stood close to his desk with his eyes fixed upon the door.

"You were saying something about the honour system, Sir?" suggested Emerson.

Every year, the headmaster sent orientation manuals to new students. A couple were read from cover to cover. A few were thumbed through for highlights. Most were glanced at and discarded. But Emerson had read the manual over and over again. He went so far as to examine its photographs under a magnifying glass. That is how he knew about the roll-top and could describe the quill pen and the multi-buttoned vest of St. Timothy's first and long-dead headmaster.

"Ah… yes, Jenks. Yes— as I was saying." Mr. Fitzroy took his seat and cast another long, tentative look at the roll-top. "As I was saying—" another glance into the corner, "—we have an honour system here. Students are…" He took a fleeting look at the door on the side wall. "Students are expected to—"

"Oh, no!" cried Emerson leaping to his feet. He stared at the room's main entrance for several seconds. "Not now, you guys!" he shouted. "We'll be twenty minutes. Half an hour maybe." As Emerson spoke into thin air, Mr. Fitzroy sprang to his feet and stepped behind his chair. He gripped its headrest with both hands. His mouth fell open as the boy continued in conversation with their unseen visitors.

"Okay," Emerson said. "Thank you." He turned, sat and stared into the headmaster's ashen face. "It's alright now, Sir. My friends will come back later."

"Friends?" declared Fitzroy. "These… these… these ghosts are your friends?"

"Yes! Well… I mean no," replied Emerson. "Not exactly, I suppose. You see, Dad likes me to call them 'friends' just so Mom and— well, other people don't get so… well… so all freaked out and stuff." No response from Mr. Fitzroy. "Every time my mother hears the word 'ghost'… well, she breaks down and cries."

"Oh, my," gasped Fitzroy. "Your parents know all about the… the… I mean… about your friends, do they?"

"Oh, of course, they do, Sir. I'd never keep anything like that from my parents, Sir," replied the boy.

"No. I suppose not," continued the headmaster with quick glances at the roll-top and the room's three doors.

"They said they wouldn't bother us again, Sir. My friends, I mean," Emerson added. "I don't know about that old man though." Emerson jerked his thumb towards the door on the side wall. "You were going to tell me about the honour system, Sir." The headmaster's eyes darted about the room resting on the roll-top, the doors and the boy in turn. "You *are* alright, aren't you, Sir?" Emerson inquired.

"Fine, Jenks… fine," answered Fitzroy who looked anything but fine. "I guess it's just that I've never…" Fitzroy used a manila folder as a fan. "It's just that I've never met anyone who saw… and well… *talked* to ghosts. That's all."

"*Friends*, please, Sir?" begged Emerson. "'Specially 'round my mom, eh?" Emerson paused for a moment to give his message time to sink in. "It came as quite a shock to my parents too," added Emerson. "At first, we found it all but ineffable, Sir."

"Ineffable?" repeated the headmaster. "You know what 'ineffable' means, do you, Jenks?"

"Oh yes, Sir," answered Emerson. "It means—"

"That's okay," Fitzroy interrupted. "I know what 'ineffable' means." The headmaster drew his watch from its pocket. "Oh my," he cried. "It's getting rather late."

The interview lasted longer than planned. Mr. Fitzroy spent an inordinate amount to time glancing into shadowy corners and staring at doors. His train of thought went off the rails several times and he had to back up and restart many of his sentences. Emerson did his best to keep the man on track.

"So, do you have any questions for me, Jenks?" asked Fitzroy, rising as he did so.

"I did, Sir, but… well… my Dad, you know… he told me to ask about the ghosts… Oops, sorry. I mean my friends. We're always supposed to say friends, eh? But I guess… well…" Emerson hesitated.

"I see," interrupted Fitzroy. "Your Dad wanted—" The headmaster moved from behind his desk and the boy leapt to his feet. "Let's just go see if your folks are back yet, shall we, Jenks? I'm eager to talk to your Dad, you see."

"Of course," replied Emerson. "May I ask what's in there, Sir?" he said and nodded towards the single door on the side wall.

"That's just my sleeping room," answered Fitzroy. "Why do you ask?"

Emerson already knew about the headmaster's sleeping room. It was marked on the building's floor plan. At the mention of the sleeping room, the boy arched his eyebrows and shivered as if a chill had run through his body. "It's just that that's where that old man... Oh, never mind, Sir. It's not important."

Fitzroy's mouth fell open as he stared at his bedroom door. A tingling electric shock raced up and down his spine. Wide-eyed, he watched Emerson cross the room, open the doors and step into the corridor.

+ − × ÷

"Well, Emerson, that wasn't so bad, now was it?" asked Mr. Jenks. Without waiting for an answer, he continued. "So then, Headmaster, have you decided to keep him or—" The expression on Fitzroy's face caused Mr. Jenks to stop in mid-sentence.

"Oh, we'll keep him, Sir," replied Fitzroy. "No doubt about that. We've a very bright young man on our hands, Mr. and Mrs. Jenks. Very bright indeed."

Mrs. Jenks smiled a proud smile. "He has a very active imagination too. Emerson's a good boy— a quiet and sensitive boy. You'll not have the slightest trouble with him. Will they, Emerson?"

Emerson gave his mother an evasive shrug.

"Imaginative," repeated Fitzroy with a smile. He nodded towards the boy. "Indeed, indeed! But, time is getting on," he announced and beckoned his guests towards the foyer. Emerson latched onto his father's arm. Mrs. Jenks walked beside the headmaster, her hand resting on his forearm, chatting non-stop all the way to the front entrance. Her captive could not break into her monologue. Mr. Jenks and Emerson followed close behind.

When they reached the main doors, the headmaster finally interrupted Emerson's mother. "Now, Ma'am, Emerson will be just fine. The new boys learn the ropes quickly, Ma'am. You needn't be concerned."

"Emerson has been a bit... well... *preoccupied*, Mr. Fitzroy. Especially today," said the woman. "He's been reading that manual you sent us over and over—"

Emerson tugged on his mother's sleeve. The woman looked down at her son. "What?" she whispered.

"Well, I'm sure that Jenks— Emerson, I should say, will be quite alright, Ma'am," replied the headmaster and beckoned the family outside.

Emerson stood at the head of the stairs as Mr. Fitzroy escorted the two adults to their car. The gentleman opened and closed Mrs. Jenks' door while Mr. Jenks walked to the driver's side of the vehicle. Over the station wagon's roof, Mr. Fitzroy addressed Emerson's father. "Have a safe trip home now. Burns returned your keys, I hope."

Mr. Jenks dangled his keys between his thumb and forefinger. "Oh, Mr. Fitzroy! Did Emerson happen to mention about his friends?" the man asked.

Fitzroy thought Mr. Jenks spoke the word 'friends' more loudly than advisable. A quick glance at a sobbing Mrs. Jenks confirmed his worst fears. He watched the woman hold a handkerchief to her eyes and then blow her nose. The headmaster leaned over the car and, in a conspiratorial whisper, answered, "Yes, he did, Mr. Jenks. Indeed! Yes, his… ah… *friends…*" As he whispered the word 'friends', Fitzroy tapped on the roof of the car above Mrs. Jenks. "I'm not quite sure what to make of them," he added with a wink.

Why the headmaster tapped on the roof and winked remained a mystery to Mr. Jenks who tilted his head to one side and stared. "Make of them?" he repeated at last. "I don't see that there's much to be made of them. Pretty straightforward, don't you think?"

It was the headmaster's turn to stare. "I see," he replied, thoughtfully. "Well… you do seem to take all this in your stride, I see," he added as he massaged his chin. The man's mouth popped open. "Oh, now I see. Ah, perhaps you're right. Downplay the whole thing. Right! Splendid idea! Ignore it, eh? What do you think, Sir?"

"Well," answered Mr. Jenks, "I think…" He decided it was probably best not to say what he was thinking. "I'm sure you know best," he said. "You've had so much more experience with this kind of thing, I suppose."

"Well, sometimes the younger boys have a few little adjustment problems… at first, I mean." Fitzroy caught a glimpse of Mrs. Jenks out of the corner of his eye. She was still weeping. "But these here, ah… these—"

Emerson's father did not let the headmaster finish. "We'll just leave all this in your capable hands. I'm sure you don't want us butting in, eh?"

"Indeed," answered Fitzroy. "Not that you'd be butting in, of course." In a whisper he added, "If the problem persists—" another glance at Emerson's mother, "—we could have him see our doctor." The headmaster turned to look at Emerson.

"What?" barked Mr. Jenks. "A doctor!"

The headmaster quickly refocused.

Mr. Jenks continued, "I don't think a doctor will be needed. Do you… really?"

"Well, not right away, of course," stammered Fitzroy and cleared his throat. "I only meant if this thing… ah… *persists*. As I said… we'll downplay the whole thing. How will that be?"

Mr. Jenks stared at the ground, scratched the back of his neck and grimaced. "Downplay it," he repeated. "I guess." To avoid further eye contact with the headmaster he inspected the interior of the station wagon. "Emerson!" he exclaimed. "They forgot your guitar."

The boy started down the stairs.

"Oh, I'll take that off your hands, Sir," Fitzroy said and stepped around the back of the car. The two men shook hands one last time as the headmaster took possession of the instrument.

Mr. Jenks climbed into the station wagon, started the engine and let the car roll back so his wife could wave to their son. Mrs. Jenks rolled down her window as Emerson hurried down the steps to give her a hug and a peck on the cheek. The station wagon started forward.

"Bye, Mom! Bye, Dad! See you at Thanksgiving," Emerson shouted and waved wildly as the car rounded the circular drive and started down the lane. The handkerchief Mrs. Jenks had been using to dry her tears fluttered as she held it out the window. Emerson and the headmaster watched as the vehicle turned onto the highway. Neither of them looked away until the flapping handkerchief disappeared from view.

Headmaster Fitzroy tried to hand the guitar to Emerson. Emerson ignored the effort. Fitzroy drew his watch from his waistcoat and moaned, "Oh, my, I'm late. We'll talk again soon, Jenks." Again, he held the guitar case out towards the boy.

Emerson pointed to Disraeli Hall and asked about the building. Fitzroy gave a brief explanation, turned and started off towards the stairs. To further delay the man's escape, Emerson asked the same question about Gladstone Hall. "Mr. Fitzroy, whose room is that, Sir?" Emerson pointed up at the faculty wing.

Fitzroy followed the boy's gaze and noticed a venetian blind swaying in a window. "That's Professor Warneke's lodgings, Jenks. Why do you ask?"

"I thought I saw a man watching us from up there, Sir. That's all," answered Emerson.

"Yes... well, that's quite possible, Jenks," replied the headmaster. "Professor Warneke arrived last night."

Emerson took another long, lingering look at Professor Warneke's window. For a moment, a man's face appeared. It was not the same face Emerson had noticed earlier. It was the face of a younger, shorter, thinner man. The boy's eyes met those of the stranger. It was not Emerson who looked away first.

Emerson finally took possession of his guitar and then watched as the headmaster jogged up the long flight of stairs, shaking his head, consulting his pocket watch and mumbling. The boy listened as the man lamented the lateness of the hour. The White Rabbit, thought Emerson and shook his head as Mr. Fitzroy disappeared into the building.

Emerson carried his guitar towards the footballers who continued running helter-skelter upon the lawn. He stopped and began watching the game. The boy failed to see Mr. Fitzroy return to the main entrance and peek out. The man rolled his lower lip between his thumb and index finger. "I'll have to keep an eye on that one," he muttered.

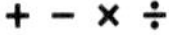

Emerson had no interest in football. As he watched the game, he concentrated on his first meeting with the headmaster and mused about what pranks might flow from it. He did not hear footsteps approaching.

"Jenks!" demanded Meddows. Emerson turned and stared up into the boy's face, then leaned to one side and glanced past him and, as expected, saw Burns and O'Neil standing well back, elbowing each other and tittering. Without a word, Emerson turned his attention back to the game.

"I'm Meddows," announced Meddows. "And I'm a senior."

Emerson refused to look at the older boy. "Good for you, Meddows," he replied.

"I said… I'm a *senior,* Jenks," repeated Meddows. He assumed the tone of a doctor who has been mistaken for an orderly.

"So?" said Emerson.

"So!" cried Meddows. "*So?*" He looked towards his toadies and shrugged, as if he wanted them to confirm that he had heard correctly.

"Sorry… I guess I should've said, *so what,*" added Emerson.

"Ah! I get it. We've got ourselves a smartass, guys," declared Meddows and looked back over his shoulder. "I guess somebody needs an attitude adjustment, eh? Whatcha think?" The stooges snorted and grinned in response. "You're makin' a very bad first impression, Jenks. I guess we're gunna have tuh teach yuh some manners," threatened Meddows.

"Is this where I'm supposed to act scared?" asked Emerson, calmly, without taking his eyes off the game.

"If yuh ain't scared now, you're soon gunna be," growled Meddows. Before the boy finished speaking, a bell sounded. Its echo had not died away before the football players disappeared inside. Emerson moved towards the main doors with Meddows and his toadies close on his heels. "So you play guitar, do you, Jenks?" asked Meddows.

Emerson stopped. Meddows stopped. The toadies stopped. Emerson looked down at his guitar case and then back at Meddows. "Good guess, Meddows… but it's a tuba."

While Meddows tried to stifle his friends' inane laughter, Emerson skipped up the stairs and re-entered St. Timothy's. The Meddows Gang chatted before dashing into the foyer. As the three boys passed, Emerson, who stood, shrouded in deep shadow, addressed them.

"Hey! I guess we got off to a rough start, eh, guys?" The three senior students came up short. "Sorry…" continued the new boy, "guess I should've said it's a tuba… *Meddows.*"

Without a word the older boys entered the chapel.

Thus began prankster Emerson Jenks' new life at St. Timothy's.

+ − × ÷

Mrs. Jenks remained uncharacteristically quiet during the first hour of the drive home. She had stopped crying soon after St. Timothy's dropped from view, but she had not stopped worrying about her son.

Mr. Jenks' mind occupied itself with the headmaster's bizarre behaviour. "Did you happen to notice anything different… anything sort of weird, I mean… about Mr. Fitzroy?" he asked his wife. The woman pondered her husband's question. "I mean… after Emerson's interview."

"No, I don't think so," replied Mrs. Jenks. "Why?"

"Well… he thinks Emerson missing his friends is a problem or something," said her husband. "And a serious one too."

"Really?" Mrs. Jenks spoke with more than a hint of astonishment in her voice.

"Really," repeated Mr. Jenks. "I'm serious. At one point there he even suggested that their doctor talk to the boy."

"Doctor!" cried Emerson's mother.

"Well, that's what I've been wondering about," admitted Mr. Jenks. "You'd think Emerson was the first kid who ever showed up there missing his friends or something."

"That's only natural, isn't it, Honey?" asked Mrs. Jenks. "Missing his friends, I mean."

"Why, of course, it is. And that's what surprises me," replied her husband.

"Well… maybe they're just being extra careful?" mumbled Mrs. Jenks. "But a doctor? Really!"

Mr. Jenks concentrated on the highway. From time to time, he frowned and shrugged. Mrs. Jenks pressed her pillow against the side window and rested her head on it. Peter Jenks listened to his wife's breathing grow shallow and more regular. He peeked at her several times. Her eyes remained closed. He continued to think about his day. "That thing with the sign… now that was really weird," he mumbled.

His wife sighed. "Probably just some stupid kid horsing around, Hon," suggested Mrs. Jenks without opening her eyes. "You know how bold some kids can be nowadays."

"You're probably right," replied Mr. Jenks and sighed too. "But what I'd really like to know is why they keep picking on us."

Temporary Accommodations

The young man made a valiant effort at stifling a yawn. He massaged the back of his neck and grimaced as his eyes wandered about his new room, coming to rest on the bed. "Like a rock!" he grumbled.

He stooped down and slid his hand under the mattress, probing for the solid boards that he knew must lie beneath. He discovered only a board-hard box spring. An unsatisfactory first night's sleep had followed the previous day's tedious train ride. The mattress and incessant snoring – not his own – had conspired to rob him of a decent night's sleep. He frowned at an older man – the snorer – who stood looking out the window.

"Tell me, Sir…" asked the young man, "how long have you taught here?"

This question, like every other he had asked since rising, went unanswered. The gentleman to whom he spoke, an imposing figure at six-foot-four and 280 pounds, filled one of the room's two windows. He stared out towards the school's front entrance, silent and motionless, save for his fingers with which he twisted and twirled the ends of his great, bushy, white moustache.

The young man walked to the room's other window and cautiously raised the blind. Lush, green foliage brushing the windowpanes blocked his view. He lowered the blind, strolled across the room and inspected his reflection in a full-length mirror. His loafers gleamed. The creases in his slacks were crisp. His powder blue sweater vest and white shirt were spotless. He adjusted his tie, nodded his satisfaction, removed a navy blue blazer from his closet and began giving it a thorough brushing. This flurry of activity failed to distract him from wondering what he could have done to offend his new roommate.

At the window, the older man rocked on the balls of his feet, shook his head and grumbled. He wore a tired-looking, double-breasted suit. Its jacket, for want of buttons, hung open displaying a well-worn waistcoat.

His trousers, clearly not the suit's better half, were more ragged still. The ensemble possessed a slept-in look, wrinkled and stained with frayed cuffs. His shoes could not recall their last polishing. In every respect, the older man was his roommate's opposite number.

St. Timothy's newest teacher was younger, shorter and thinner. He was meek and mild-mannered – many would describe him as naïve. His attire was immaculate. He cut a fine figure, well turned-out and impeccably groomed. Nobody would describe the older fellow as meek or mild, and certainly not naïve. At a single glance anyone would conclude that he was anything but clean-cut.

"Sir?" stammered the younger man – he avoided looking at his companion. "I was hoping… I mean you said… ahem… you'd give me… well… a few pointers. You know, I've never taught before."

There was no response.

"I'd appreciate…"

The older gentleman released the blind which banged against the glass and casement before striking the sill. The chaotic clatter and crash rattled the younger man's nerves.

"Humph, indeed!" grumbled the older man. "The very idea!" He crossed to the door, pressed his back to the wall and paced the room's width, counting as he went, "Six, nine, twelve and fifteen… at most." He repeated the exercise, estimating the room's length, and elbowed past his mesmerized roommate with no hint of apology. "Twenty… maybe twenty-one," he grumbled. "Listen here, Whittingly-Wendles," he continued, "this just won't do. Why… the very idea, Sir!"

The smaller man looked about. "The room, Sir?" he asked. "Oh, it seems plenty big, Sir."

"*Plenty big?*" exclaimed his companion. "What on earth do you mean? The place is a hovel, Sir. Humph! If you think this is in any way workable, Sir, well then—"

"But, Sir—"

"Listen to me, Whallaby-Whattles," the older gentleman butted in, "this room's not meant for two. Can't you see that, Sir? Is that not perfectly clear?"

"In university…" The man addressed as Whallaby-Whattles decided not to describe the tiny room he had shared in residence. His inner voice warned him not to argue with someone in such a blustery mood.

"Humph! Just because you're the new man, they've no right to shove you into this… this closet." The big man returned to the window and gave the blind cords a mighty tug. The slats clicked and clacked together. "Look at that sorry scene, would you, Sir?" he demanded. "They get grubbier every year."

The young man approached the window but his roommate's bulk blocked his view.

"Do you believe in karma, Whelderby-Whittles? Or reincarnation and all that? Do you think we're being punished for sins from our former lives? Hmmm! Well?" The big man turned to face his roommate.

The young man was not Whittingly-Wendles nor Whallaby-Whattles nor even Whelderly-Whittles. The dapper fellow was Probationary Professor Wilfred Willoughby-Wallows, M.A. (*summa cum laude*). He was St. Timothy's newly appointed Greek and Latin man.

His roommate, Cyrus Warneke, tugged on the ends of his moustache and continued his rant. "If there's any truth in that eastern nonsense we must have done some evil deeds." The big man licked his fingertips and vainly attempted to get his bushy eyebrows to lie flat. "I can't imagine what evils I could have done. Perhaps I was Attila the Hun or one of those Caesars. Ah! To deserve such a fate!" Warneke finished by solemnly pronouncing, "This school would be such a fine place… if it weren't for all the blasted children running about!"

Wilfred Willoughby-Wallows could not answer. Stunned, he stared at Warneke and tried to determine if the man was mad. Then his face lit up. "Oh, I get it, Sir," he cried out and then laughed. "You're pulling my leg, Sir, teasing the new fellow. Well—"

"—I am not pulling your leg, Whitterly-Whar… oh, drat," he said. "They're devils, Sir. Demons and golems. You'll be of the same opinion inside a week. You and your romantic, naïve notions about our high calling! I still say we're being punished." Warneke returned to the window. Looking back over his shoulder he added, "You'll find that what Mr. Dickens said about—" he hesitated, frowned, cleared his throat and continued, "—about some place or other, I can't recall exactly where at the moment. Anyway, what he said fits this place to a tee: a fairy-land to visit, but a desert to live in... Or something like that."

Some are drawn to teaching by a love for learning. Some are motivated by concern for the malleable minds of children. Some, recalling the generosity of their own teachers, enter the classroom intent on inspiring excellence. Cyrus Warneke paid dues to none of these groups. Cyrus Warneke's parents had threatened to separate their only son from a generous allowance if he refused to make something of his life. Their words of warning drove him into Engineering, but in short order, he convinced his teachers he had neither interest in, nor talent for, buildings, bridges and the like. Besides playing whist and listening to classical music, his only interest had been reading. He transferred to the English Department and, without much effort, graduated top of his class – the man lacked industry not intelligence. Directly out of university, Cyrus Warneke installed himself at St. Timothy's.

Warneke removed a razor from his medicine cabinet, walked to the door and opened it. He stopped and stared at his roommate. The big man grunted, shook his head, stepped into the corridor and closed the door behind him.

+ − × ÷

Willoughby-Wallows strolled to the window. He observed the footballers, then watched parents and students standing about on the lawn. His attention was drawn to a maroon station wagon which rolled up the drive and parked. A man and a woman exited the vehicle. Willoughby-Wallows checked the time: 11:57. Bored, he used the heel-to-toe method to pace off the room's length and breadth. On discovering its true dimensions – 20 by 28 feet, he muttered aloud – his eyes fixed upon the door through which his roommate had disappeared. He scratched his head, half amazed... half amused.

Noticing that the door to Warneke's medicine cabinet had been left ajar, Willoughby-Wallows approached it, glanced over his shoulder, opened the mirrored door and peeked inside. The shelves were chock-a-block with shampoo. Willoughby-Wallows had never dreamed of there being such a collection outside a beauty salon. Such variety! He returned the door to its original position, walked to his desk, picked up a book, sat on the edge of his bed and began to read aloud: "*It is incumbent upon the newcomer to establish and maintain positive working relationships with his fellows.*" Willoughby-Wallows read the words and laughed aloud. "Incumbent upon? Positive relationships?" he said aloud. The Greek and Latin teacher checked the book's title: *Tips for Teachers – Everything you need to know before entering the classroom.* Willoughby-Wallows' mother had given him the book in celebration of his first teaching job. He tossed the volume on the desk and fixed his eyes on his bed. The pillow appeared exceedingly enticing and reminded him of just how exhausted he felt. He kicked off his shoes and stretched out on the covers. Inexplicably, the mattress seemed softer than he remembered. He closed his eyes and events of the previous eighteen hours began to dash and dance about in his head.

He recalled meeting Warneke at the train station in Montreal. The gentleman said little on the trip. In fact, thinking about it, Willoughby-Wallows realized he had been snubbed. From the station, they shared a silent cab ride to St. Timothy's. The young man bristled as he recalled how, on their arrival, Warneke had leapt from the taxi and jogged up the front steps, shouting, '*Right-oh, pay the man, won't you, Son.*' He recalled how the headmaster had seemed nervous when explaining that the two men would be bunking together. He recalled how, shortly thereafter, Warneke had transformed himself and talked on and on. Willoughby-Wallows recalled that the big man had even ignored his requests for directions to their room. Willoughby-Wallows thought about how the English master offered to show him the ropes and demanded details about his studies and his tastes in food, music and literature. It was 2:15 in the morning before the young man finally felt his head sink into his pillow. These thoughts and more traipsed through Willoughby-Wallows' mind as he hovered somewhere between wakefulness and sleep.

+ − × ÷

"No, no, no!" shouted Warneke upon re-entering the room. He placed a foot on the edge of Willoughby-Wallows' bed and shook him awake. "No *siestas* here, Sir. We're not on the Mediterranean, Waverly—I mean, Sir."

Willoughby-Wallows rolled off the bed and onto his feet. "What—what is it, Sir?" he asked groggily as he patted his hair into place.

"Sleeping in the middle of the day, Sir," the English master added, "is the worst of bad habits! Don't you know that? It's such a waste of time and a sure sign of sloth. We frown on sloth here, Sir. Don't want to start off on the wrong foot now, do you, Sir?"

As Warneke applied copious amounts of cheap *eau-de-cologne*, Willoughby-Wallows wandered over to the window. He watched as two young men removed suitcases from the station wagon and carried them into the building. "Sir, is there any way to tell the newcomers from the... the... the... returners?"

He has a Master's degree, the nincompoop, and he lets a word like 'returners' cross his lips, thought Warneke. To Willoughby-Wallows he replied, "That's easy, my dear fellow. Just look..." Warneke tapped the corner of his eye. "And listen..." He pinched the lobe of an oversized ear and pulled it away from his head. "There's nothing like looking and listening, Wallerly-Willers."

"Willoughby-Wallows, Sir," the younger man said.

"Pardon?" said Warneke.

"Willoughby-Wallows, Sir! Wouldn't it be easier if you just called me Wilfred... or Wilf, Sir?"

"*Wilfred!*" exclaimed Warneke. He stared open-mouthed at his companion. Had Willoughby-Wallows suggested that he be called Napoleon, Warneke could not have acted more shocked. The older man rolled his eyes and then narrowed them, conveying disbelief and utter disdain. "Wilf!" A hint of derision entered his voice. "Never!" he cried. "That will never do. Informality, Sir, leads to familiarity and familiarity breeds contempt, you know. We frown on contempt here at St. Timothy's." If Willoughby-Wallows hoped Warneke had finished his dissertation on the use of first names, his hopes were soon dashed. Warneke had stopped only to draw breath. "My name's Warneke... here in the lodgings and in the refectory, I mean," the big man continued. "When students are around you must say Professor Warneke or just plain Professor or something like that. Shows respect! Understand? These ruffians need to learn some respect. And if we don't teach them... why... who will?"

Willoughby-Wallows caught himself staring, then flushed and looked away.

"Wilfred? Wilf? Lord help us," exclaimed Warneke. "And you're Whitterly— oh drat. What is it with these silly hyphenated names?" asked the big man. "I don't get it. I can't see the sense in having two last names. What, was your father a Wallows and your mother a Willoughby or something? One of those suffragettes, I warrant."

"*Suffragettes?*" cried Willoughby-Wallows. "What is that supposed to mean?" Before the word 'mean' crossed his lips, the young man regretted the remark. His mind hearkened back to *Tips for Teachers*. He glanced at Warneke and decided that the man had taken no offence and that his rant had run its course. Willoughby-Wallows tried to introduce a more agreeable topic. "Actually, Sir," he advised, "my mother was a Stanley-Jones from—"

"—Lord, love a duck!" cried Warneke and raised a hand to his forehead. "I don't recall asking for the family history, Sir. Or perhaps I'm mistaken?"

Willoughby-Wallows averted his eyes, shuffled to the window and gazed out over the grounds. A few of the football players, some of those playing tag and all the adults had disappeared. Of the several vehicles there earlier, only the maroon station wagon remained. The scene cast a spell on the young man. His eyelids grew heavy and his mind began to wander. He flinched when he felt a hand on his shoulder. Warneke tugged his roommate off balance, spun him around and pushed him to the centre of the room. Willoughby-Wallows had to flail his arms about, windmill fashion, to maintain his balance.

The big man's body once more filled the space before the window. He clasped his hands behind his back and stared outside. Less than a minute later, he jerked the blind's cords and lowered the shade. "Light's bothering my eyes," he complained. "Oh, while it's fresh in my mind…" Cyrus Warneke marched to Willoughby-Wallows' dresser, picked up his clock, opened the top drawer and stuffed the alarm under a stack of neatly folded underwear. "You woke me with that blasted contraption this morning, you know?" he grumbled. "And the ticking nearly drove me insane."

A pair of Willoughby-Wallows' underwear peeked at him from the corner of his dresser drawer. The new teacher had never met anyone who behaved so badly. "You self-centred, old curmudgeon," Willoughby-Wallows muttered as he rearranged his belongings.

"What was that?" asked Warneke over his shoulder.

"I said, *sorry, Sir! Won't let it happen again, Sir.*"

"Ah… I should certainly hope not," replied Warneke. He returned to the window, inserted his hands between two slats and pulled them apart. He peeked out through the diamond-shaped gap. "Not a parent in sight," he reported. "But, little wonder, I suppose. I'm not a parent myself, understand, but after you pound the rudiments of the language into so many hard heads for so long, you can see why their mommies and daddies gallop off into the sunset, *toot-swit* as the Frenchies say, after pawning their boys off on us."

Willoughby-Wallows had stopped listening. He read his book, wondering if he would find anything relevant therein.

Warneke glanced over his shoulder. "Wantingly-Wardles!" he cried. "Would you pay attention, Sir… please? I'm trying to teach you something. If you don't want my help just say so."

Willoughby-Wallows stood, closed *Tips for Teachers* and studied its spine and back cover, thinking he may have missed something of value there. He prepared to drop the book on his desk but worried about what Warneke might say about the bang. The young man tucked the book under his arm and struggled to hear his roommate's description of activities on the lawn. He tilted his head to one side and shook it. It felt as if his ears were stuffed full of cotton batten.

"The wild savages have returned," announced Warneke. "I thought we might be spared their screeching for the rest of the day… But alas, it's not to be. They call that game *Run Sheep Run* by the way."

"Uh huh," mumbled Willoughby-Wallows absentmindedly. He had abandoned all hope of seeing what Warneke was talking about and taken a seat.

"And the ruffians with the football… Why they've not been relegated to the sports field I have no idea," added the English master. "Our headmaster can't handle the boys, you know. Spoils them with kindness, Whittingly…"

"Uh huh."

"Just look at them tear about. Too bad all that energy can't be put to better use," moaned Warneke. "Truly, youth is wasted on the young."

"Uh huh," muttered Willoughby-Wallows.

"Oh, Lord," exclaimed Warneke, "more football players. And how they're dressed? You'd think they feared embarrassing any vagrants hanging 'round the place. Those are the *returners* as you call them."

The English master turned and found Willoughby-Wallows fast asleep. The young man's left arm rested on his lap. The other hung over the armrest, almost touching the carpet. His head had rolled to one side. Warneke picked *Tips for Teachers* from the floor and read the title. He chuckled and slipped the book into his jacket pocket. Smiling, he rubbed his palms together. His plan was working better than he had hoped.

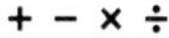

Ten minutes later, Warneke used *Tips for Teachers* to slap his roommate on the sole of a shoeless foot.

"What..." shouted the younger man as he sat bolt upright in his chair.

"You must try to get to bed earlier," Warneke cautioned and dropped the book into his companion's lap. "You won't get to nap around here once classes start."

Willoughby-Wallows stretched and yawned. He felt woozy and not at all well.

Warneke returned to the window and drew back the blind. "I thought I should wake you so you could freshen up before the meeting. The bell's going to ring in..." The English master plucked a pocket watch the size of a hockey puck from his waistcoat pocket and stared at it. "You have about ten minutes," he added.

"Oh, thank you, Sir," replied Willoughby-Wallows. "I appreciate that, Sir." The young man ran a comb through his hair, straightened his tie and popped a breath mint into his mouth. With a dismissive wave and a gruff 'bah', Warneke declined the candy Willoughby-Wallows offered him. He turned back to the window.

"Now what the heck's going on down there?" exclaimed Warneke. "I thought all the parents had cleared out already."

"What's happening?" The young man's curiosity had gotten the better of him.

"Our fearless leader's down there talking to some fellow over the roof of that big old boat. Oh, and there's little Winthrop or Perceval… some double-barrelled name no doubt, too big for the kid I'll warrant. He's standing on the stairs taking in the show… Harold Lloyd glasses and all." Warneke began to laugh. "They look like two double-O-sevens plotting a caper." He laughed again. Willoughby-Wallows tried in vain to squeeze between the English master and the casement. Warneke made no effort to accommodate him.

"Now what?" groaned Warneke. "Oh Lordy, the kid's brought a guitar. If I have to listen to one more pathetic rendition of *Kumbayah*, I'll go mad. Drooling down my chin mad, I tell you." The English master turned his head towards his roommate and added, "To survive here, without getting ulcers I mean— pay attention, Wibbilly-Wobbilly —you must always remember what the great man said. Old G.K. once wrote that one must keep one's temper in this madhouse."

Willoughby-Wallows knit his brow and fixed a puzzled stare on the big man's face.

"You've never read Chesterton, I see," Warneke muttered in a clearly disapproving manner. "Ah well… more's the pity." He turned and gazed out the window.

"Well, there they go," Warneke reported. "The last of them have hit the road. Mommy's waving a hanky the size of a flag out the window." Warneke checked the time again. "The headmaster's desperate. Our silly meeting's in less than five minutes and the kid's holding him up. Oh my, my, my… that young lad's doing it on purpose. By golly! He's having the old man on. Well, I never…"

Warneke let the blind drop. It clattered onto the sill as he turned his back to the window and walked away. Willoughby-Wallows and the professor became entangled as they tried to two-step around each other. The younger man started right as Warneke, ignoring traffic flow convention, headed left. Willoughby-Wallows zigged back just as Warneke zagged in front of him.

"May I have this dance?" cried the English master and grabbed his companion by the elbow. He shoved Willoughby-Wallows to one side and squeezed past.

The young man made his way to the window and raised the blind. He peered down onto the lawn. His eyes met those of a young, rather undersized boy. The youngster was dressed in the school's blues and greys and wore round, black-rimmed glasses. The way in which the youngster stared up at the window without blinking caused Willoughby-Wallows to avert his eyes and back away. He felt as if he had been slapped.

"Well, it's time we were off," announced Warneke and moved towards the door. Willoughby-Wallows stepped into his loafers and grabbed his coat. He tried slipping into his jacket with *Tips for Teachers* in his hand. This manoeuvre proved more difficult than expected. As he looked back to see why his arm could not locate the jacket's sleeve hole he ran full into Warneke.

"Careful there, Son," exclaimed the older man.

"Sorry, Sir." Willoughby-Wallows made a last-minute wardrobe adjustment. "Shouldn't we be going, Sir?"

Warneke stood with one hand on the doorknob and, with the other, scratched his chin. His eyes surveyed the room.

"Is there a problem, Sir?" inquired Willoughby-Wallows.

"Oh, it's nothing," answered Warneke.

"No, Sir. What's the matter, Sir?" insisted the new professor. He scanned the room, but he had no idea why.

The English master hesitated. "I was just reconsidering… about the size of this room and all. You know… I might have overreacted a bit."

Willoughby-Wallows nodded. "I have to agree with you there, Sir. We'll be very cozy in here. It's a nice big room and comfortable too. Even for the two of us. Besides, Sir, this might only be my temporary accommodations anyways."

"Temporary? Ah, perhaps, my boy, perhaps," Warneke said with a slight sigh. He licked his finger and scratched a bit of breakfast from his lapel, then turned and opened the door.

"And now that you've been kind enough to tell me about my alarm clock—" Willoughby-Wallows coughed "—you'll hardly know I'm here, Sir."

"Indeed, indeed," Warneke replied, laughing. "I'm quite sure you're right about that too, my young friend."

The two men stepped into the hall. Willoughby-Wallows started down the corridor but stopped when he realized he was unaccompanied. He turned and watched as his roommate tugged on a long, heavy chain until a brass key popped out of his pants pocket. Warneke stooped and inserted the key into the door lock.

"Oh, don't lock it, please, Sir," pleaded Willoughby-Wallows. "I don't have my own key yet, Sir, and I won't be able to get back in."

"That *is* a problem," Warneke replied as he locked the door. He rattled the knob, stuffed the key into his pocket and added, "We'll solve each little difficulty as it comes along, eh? But anytime you need my key—" he patted his pocket, "—you only need to ask."

Willoughby-Wallows stood motionless. Warneke placed a huge hand on his companion's slender shoulder, spun him around and, with a hand on the small of his back, hustled him off down the hall. "Our esteemed colleagues await us," declared Warneke. "Let us not disappoint. You'll find this meeting... well... *educational*, I suppose."

As the two men reached the entrance to the main building, a bell sounded.

"We need to hurry, Whittley-Winslow," advised the English master. "It wouldn't look good, our being late for the first meeting of the year, now would it?"

Like a shore tender tied to a frigate, Wilfred Willoughby-Wallows shuffled along in Cyrus Warneke's wake as the older gentleman hurried down the stairs and through the basement corridor towards the school's auditorium.

Meetings, Bloody Meetings

Warneke kicked a doorstop into place and ushered Willoughby-Wallows into the auditorium with a salaam, saying, "After you, my esteemed young friend."

Willoughby-Wallows entered the room, sniffed the air and frowned. A dank, musty odour permeated the space.

"Well, how 'bout that? First ones here," announced Warneke.

An otherworldly voice sounded out of the gloom. "Not quite, Gentlemen."

Willoughby-Wallows peered into the darkness, but saw no one.

"Good day, Professors," the disembodied voice greeted the men.

"*Goo-tun-tog* to you, too," grumbled the English master.

"And you," the voice continued, "must be our new Greek and Latin man."

Before Willoughby-Wallows could reply, Warneke dragged him into a corner, just back of the door. "Baumgartner!" he explained. "Von Baumgartner, the old geezer insists. German master… been here forever."

The two men looked up as the fluorescent tubes hummed and flashed before filling the room with light. Two men had entered.

"Just you watch this, Waggly— I mean, Sir," continued Warneke. "Sheep, I say! I could tell you where they'll sit. Pathetically predictable, my boy. Every last one of them."

Willoughby-Wallows watched the two gentlemen arrange chairs as others arrived. Many, upon entering the room, peeked behind the door and acknowledged Warneke, almost as if they expected to find him there.

"Fong, Smithers… Jim," Warneke greeted his fellows.

Willoughby-Wallows stared at the professor.

"What?" the big man asked. He sounded indignant.

"Jim?" asked Willoughby-Wallows. "I thought—"

"—Yes, I know. But that's Professor Darling. Just think how that would sound," growled the English master. As if imitating a play-by-play announcer, he continued, "Now just watch how most of them huddle together along the aisle, halfway down. They want to *appear* engaged without actually getting dragged into all the nonsense. Now, Baumgartner there and Bent—"

"—*Von* Baumgartner, is it not, Sir?" suggested Willoughby-Wallows.

"Listen and learn, would you, Sir," Warneke cried. "Von Baumgartner, indeed! That makes me what then, *the Earl of Essex*? Now, where was I? Baumgartner and Bentley like to sit off by themselves. They just want to get back to whatever arcane pursuits fill their dreary little lives. Oh! And just wait 'til you see the shepherd of the sheep in action, Sir!"

Willoughby-Wallows had stopped listening when, to his surprise, a woman entered the auditorium, walked to the front of the room and began assembling a flip chart near the stage. The lady was tall and slender. Her jet-black hair was pulled back, rolled up in a tight bun and, seemingly defying gravity, clung to the back of her scrawny neck. Under a red bolero vest, she wore a white blouse with lace trimmed collar and cuffs. A pencil-thin, white belt held up her black skirt. The skirt had no pleats and fell to her ankles. The woman, true to type, wore sensible shoes.

"Who's the young lady?" asked Willoughby-Wallows.

"*Young lady!*" cried Warneke and coughed. His face registered amazement. "Young lady? Why, Sir, I had no idea you possessed so droll a sense of humour. My boy, that withered old stick is Miss – or should I say Missed – Leticia Strupples." Warneke observed Willoughby-Wallows observing the woman. "Remind you of anyone?" the older man asked.

"Pardon, Sir?"

"Strupples," answered Warneke. "She doesn't remind you of anyone?"

Willoughby-Wallows hesitated. Warneke's manner suggested he should be able to see a resemblance to someone famous. "I can't really say she does, Sir."

"Behind her back," explained Warneke, "the students call her *Olive Oyl*. But she's much skinnier than Popeye's beanpole of a girlfriend. We're in for some free entertainment, my boy. *Young lady!*" Warneke elbowed the new teacher in the ribs. "Ha, ha, young lady! That's a good one!"

Just then, the headmaster entered the auditorium, closed the door and, while proceeding to the stage, called for order.

"Oh, Captain, my captain," whispered the English master. "It's show time, my boy." Warneke checked his watch and crossed his arms over his chest. "And only twelve minutes late," he added.

"Ahem! Welcome back everyone. Welcome back," shouted Warneke's shepherd of the sheep. "Let's get started, people. Professor Warneke and Mister… Mister…" began Fitzroy and rummaged through his notes.

"Willoughby-Wallows, Sir," the new teacher declared. He stepped forward, bobbed his head and raised his hand. He resembled a prize-fighter being introduced in the ring. He felt like a schoolboy asking to use the toilet.

"Of course," continued Fitzroy and shuffled his papers. "I… I…"

Strupples rose, clapped her hands and shouted, "Come now, Gentlemen. That's no way to greet our new colleague!"

"I told you, boy, free entertainment," croaked Warneke. "Here we go."

"Sir," continued the lady, addressing Willoughby-Wallows, "please tell us about yourself. Everyone's just dying to hear."

"Pray be brief," whispered Warneke to his blushing companion.

Willoughby-Wallows blundered through an impromptu autobiography.

"Five minutes well spent," complained Warneke when his companion retreated to the corner. "I said, be brief."

"Thank you for that, Sir," responded Fitzroy. With a flourish, he stroked the first item from his agenda and, lowering his head, levelled an icy stare over his glasses towards Strupples. "I guess you beat me to the punch," he added.

The woman mumbled what may have been an apology.

The headmaster paused to consult his notes. "Mr. Willoughby-Wallows. Yes, yes!" he added. "Here it is. Well, then, let's continue." He eyed the flip chart and turned back to Strupples. "We— all of us I mean— shall try to keep this meeting short and snappy."

"Amazing," whispered Warneke, "how in trying to be short and snappy that man can speed through a thirty-minute meeting in a mere three hours."

"Professor Warneke!" cried the headmaster. His words came out sharp and half a pitch too high. "Please take your seat." He beckoned. "Professor and… and… Mr. Wing… and your friend too… come."

Willoughby-Wallows started forward, but, to his amazement, felt himself yanked backwards. Warneke had a firm grip on his collar.

"No, no, we're quite comfortable right here," shouted the English master. "Carry on, Sir, I beg of you. Proceed! Bad back, you know…" The man's voice trailed off.

Fitzroy stared at Warneke, inhaled deeply and puffed out his chest. He clamped a hand on either side of the lectern, leaned forward and thrust his chin in the English master's direction. Stony-faced, Warneke stared back. Willoughby-Wallows' face turned crimson and he wished he had never met the big man. Like gunfighters in the old west, Fitzroy and Warneke faced off across the room. Like frightened townsfolk, the audience hunkered down in anticipation of a shootout. Willoughby-Wallows worried that he might be in the line of fire. Fitzroy had a bad habit of avoiding eye contact. Without considering the consequences, he glanced down at his notes.

"Check and mate," muttered Warneke for Willoughby-Wallows' benefit.

Eager to re-engage, the headmaster looked up, but the showdown was over. Fitzroy realized he was a beaten man. "Well, where was I?" asked the headmaster and, after a short pause, he began rattling off teaching and non-teaching assignments. Before he revealed the job he planned to award to Warneke, he faltered, and balked. "Professor Warneke… ahem… I have you down for… um… dormitory supervisor." Fitzroy stiffened.

Staff members looked either down at the floor or up at the ceiling. Some examined their nails and engaged in discrete whistling. The silence grew awkward in the extreme. Warneke said nothing. Fitzroy said nothing. Willoughby-Wallows said nothing but shivered when he felt a chill spread throughout the room. Strupples turned and stared at the English master.

"Well, then…" Fitzroy continued. He sighed with relief. "That's that, I guess. But before we have tea, I'd just like to say…" The headmaster rambled on about the teacher's high calling and, in doing so, referred to the newly revised Policy Manual.

Strupples assumed that his mention of the Policy Manual was her cue to usurp the man's authority. She bounded to her feet, pointer in hand, and inflicted upon her captive audience a detailed account of her committee's summer work. Two absent instructors missed a most stimulating forty-five minutes. Several audience members became so enthralled that they had to close their eyes to shut out distractions. Headmaster Fitzroy sprawled across the lectern, his head face down on his arms. He resembled a Raggedy Andy doll.

Just twenty minutes into her lecture, the audience mistook Strupples' pause for breath as the end of proceedings and rewarded her with restrained applause. Some started to stand. Leticia Strupples was having none of it. She tapped her pointer on a metal chair and uttered the three words dreaded most by all who must attend such meetings. "And in conclusion…" she stated.

"Meetings, bloody meetings," whispered Warneke. "Hell, I'm sure, will be one eternal meeting. And *that woman* will be the chief tormentor."

Strupples continued, exhausting her material some thirty minutes after exhausting even her three unnamed co-conspirators. She then beckoned those reluctant, reticent gentlemen to stand with her and, upon prying the last free of his seat, led the group in an affecting bow. Polite applause ensued.

Fitzroy stirred, raised his head and said, "Thank you for that, Madam. Very good… yes, well… If no one has any questions…" His eyes swept the room. "Good! I think we can—" A brisk movement at the back of the auditorium caught the headmaster's eye.

+ − × ÷

Warneke took one giant step forward and begged pardon. "We need to have just one minute to confer," he explained and turned to Willoughby-Wallows. He placed his hand on the young man's shoulder and raised the other, palm outward, toward the audience. He resembled a traffic cop.

Like compliant drivers, Fitzroy and the others waited. Warneke placed his ear a few inches from Willoughby-Wallows' mouth. Traffic remained at a standstill. All eyes remained fixed upon the two men. Warneke pursed his lips and squinted as if considering some great secret.

"What on earth are you up to, Sir?" whispered Willoughby-Wallows.

Warneke nodded and shrugged.

"Sir?" demanded Willoughby-Wallows and cast a questioning glance towards the headmaster.

"Well, that's no problem," Warneke loudly exclaimed. Then, so only Willoughby-Wallows could hear, he whispered, "Do you or do you not want your own room, Son?"

"Oh, yes, Sir, I do," Willoughby-Wallows answered with an enthusiastic nod. "Absolutely!"

"Beg pardon?" shouted Warneke. He cupped a hand behind his ear and leaned towards his roommate.

"I said, *yes. Yes, I do!*" repeated Willoughby-Wallows more loudly.

No one heard the question. Most heard the reply. Everyone saw the young man nod. Warneke pushed his companion back into the corner and then paced halfway down the centre aisle. "There is one small item… if I may, Sir. It's hardly worth mentioning. I'll get through this quickly so we can go and eat." Warneke knew the audience had grown restless and hungry. "Right-oh then! It's about the dorm, Mr. Fitzroy. You see, I have so many other responsibilities and, well… with helping out young Mr. Wither… my friend here… well… Mr… or… my young, um, colleague and I were just discussing—" Warneke glanced at Willoughby-Wallows. "—Weren't we, Sir?" he asked. "Well, the long and the short of it is… we were saying… it would be a capital idea to have this gentleman… younger you know and more in common… with the… the youngsters, I mean. He's very eager to contribute, Sir. And I really don't mind— "

"—What is it that you want, Professor?" Fitzroy interjected.

"Oh, not I, Sir. You've got me all wrong, Sir. It's my young friend here, Sir. You see, he presumed *he'd* be supervising the dormitory. He's very disappointed, Sir."

"Well, why didn't he just say so?" exclaimed Fitzroy and looked at the clock. "I don't have any objections if you don't. It's all settled then? Right!" He jotted down a note. "How good of you… Walloughby-Willows. That's the spirit," he added. "I did get your name right, didn't I? Of course I did," he muttered. "No objections anyone?"

"No objections, Sir, none at all. Thank you, Sir. Let's go eat," cried Warneke and headed for the exit as the rest of the teachers stood to go.

Willoughby-Wallows stepped in front of the big man and whispered, "How could you, Sir? How… how… how dare you!"

"*Mind?* Me… mind? Never! And, there's no need to thank me. No need at all," shouted Warneke over the clang and clatter of chairs.

Willoughby-Wallows had a hundred things to say. But, when he tried to speak, no sound crossed his parched lips.

The ever-helpful Warneke came to his rescue. "We've no objections at all, eh? I say! What? Capital and all that. Right, my lad?" He slapped Willoughby-Wallows on the back in an affectionate, a filial, a not quite fatherly fashion. "I believe tea is served," he added.

The crashing and banging of chairs ceased and the staff stampeded towards the exit. Warneke tugged Willoughby-Wallows in front of the doors. Like cows being shooed away from a breach in a fence, the leaders of the charge veered away. The herd followed: bedlam.

"But, but… wait!" cried Willoughby-Wallows.

But too late. No one heard his protest.

"Tea is served. A chance to mingle and welcome our new professor," shouted the headmaster. He turned on his heel, squeezed through the opening in the stage curtains, passed into the students' locker room and fled the scene.

"Don't worry, my boy," advised Warneke. "You'll love it up there."

"Up there?" was Willoughby-Wallows' wild-eyed retort. "Up where, Sir?"

"Why up in the dorm," exclaimed Warneke, the very picture of innocence. "You can't very well supervise the boys from my lodgings now, can you? I'm going to miss you. Barely got settled in, what?" With another *right-oh*, the English master beat a hasty retreat.

St. Timothy's new Greek and Latin man thought his feet had been fastened to the floor. He watched Warneke hurry off, unaware that he had been left blocking the doorway.

Jim Darling squeezed past with a quiet, "Excuse me, Sir?" The man's escape sparked a wholesale evacuation. Like water from a breached dam, the teachers spilled past Willoughby-Wallows into the corridor and dispersed. As they passed the new teacher they pretended to have misplaced glasses and pens. They hurried by as if he were a leper. Leticia Strupples patted Willoughby-Wallows' arm.

Only Professor von Baumgartner stopped for a word. "Watch him, Sir. That man wears a belt and suspenders."

"What, Sir?" inquired Willoughby-Wallows. He was already confused and the old man's comment baffled him.

"*Once Upon a Time in the West*, Sir."

Willoughby-Wallows frowned.

"Henry Fonda?" added the German master.

The Greek and Latin man's face pleaded ignorance.

"Never mind," continued von Baumgartner. "Just don't trust him… We'll chat later."

The lights went out. The door swung closed. Willoughby-Wallows found himself both literally and figuratively alone in the dark. The new dormitory supervisor's head swam as he turned to leave the room. He felt terribly tired and weak. He walked like a motion-sick man departing the rollercoaster.

+ − × ÷

On his way past the staff refectory, Willoughby-Wallows stopped and peered inside. He felt no inclination towards food or idle chatter. He jumped and clutched at his heart when Miss Strupples tugged on his sleeve.

"You must wait for tea," she told him. "We need to talk." The woman dragged him further down the corridor and out through a doorway into the afternoon sun.

"Miss Strupples—" Willoughby-Wallows began.

"—Leticia," corrected the woman. "We're not all as stuffy as that, that Warneke. Do I call you Wilf or Wilfred?"

"Whichever, Miss Strup…" The woman wagged a boney finger under her companion's nose. "I mean Leticia," said Willoughby-Wallows.

"Much better," she exclaimed and led the young man into the back lane. Strupples removed a slim, silver case from her vest pocket and held it out to him. Willoughby-Wallows, managing to disguise his shock, declined. "What was that awful man—" Miss Strupples stopped to light a cigarette, "—up to in there?" she asked. Her head disappeared in a puff of blue-grey smoke.

They walked across the grass towards the steam plant – St. Timothy's people called it the powerhouse. Its smokestack towered over everything for miles around. "Was he twisting your arm, Wilf?" inquired Strupples.

"Twisting my arm?" gasped Willoughby-Wallows. "Oh, no! Worse than that. You see, I had no idea what he was up to. I didn't even know there was a dormitory supervisor."

"Then, why'd you volunteer?" demanded Strupples.

"Volunteer! I didn't volunteer! Professor Warneke, he… he… he volunteered me."

"What?" demanded Strupples.

"He just let on I was asking him to."

"What?" the woman repeated, hardly able to believe what she was hearing.

"It wasn't 'til the very end that I figured things out," Willoughby-Wallows continued. "But by then it was… well… too late."

"Oh, that scoundrel," grumbled Strupples and stamped her foot. "Never trust him, Wilf, never," she added as she took the young man by the arm and began hauling him back the way they had come.

"We'll just see about this," she added as they stepped through the doorway onto the stairwell landing.

"Where are you taking me?"

"To see Headmaster Fitzroy," explained Strupples. "We'll get this straightened out right now."

Her companion dug in his heels and caught hold of the banister. Strupples pulled harder. Willoughby-Wallows held on for dear life.

"I really don't want to cause anybody any trouble," he pleaded, recalling *Tips for Teachers*.

"Nonsense, Wilf," the woman replied. "Mr. Fitzroy will just have to take this up with that… that old reprobate."

"I think, Miss Strupples…" Willoughby-Wallows replied, grunting in his vain effort to free his arm. "Well… Mr. Fitzroy doesn't seem… well, you know…"

"Um..." grunted the woman. "You're probably right." She released her grip. Willoughby-Wallows massaged his arm. "But, remember what I said. Under no circumstances trust that awful man."

The woman propped the door open with her foot and waved her arms about to dissipate the cigarette smoke. She looked like a large bird attempting to take flight. "I'm not supposed to smoke in here," she explained. "Well, go along and eat."

Willoughby-Wallows headed for the refectory.

"Wilf," Miss Strupples called after him. He turned to see the woman leaning into the building, holding her cigarette outside. "Someday, somehow, someone's going to pay that brute back. You just mark my words. A day of reckoning is coming."

As Willoughby-Wallows approached the staff refectory, the last of the diners left. Like rats scurrying down the dimly lit corridor they vanished at his approach. Willoughby-Wallows surveyed the remains of the feast. Cups, saucers, scrunched-up paper napkins and luncheon plates littered the tables. The serving trays had been given a thorough going over. The scene reminded him of a fairground the morning after the circus leaves town. As he gleaned remnants from the table, he heard Professor von Baumgartner's voice. Turning, he saw the old man sitting in a shadowy corner.

"Go ahead. Get your tea. I was just thinking you might not show up at all," announced the German master. "You must think us unfriendly?"

"Pardon, Sir?"

"The fellows... They're avoiding you," replied von Baumgartner.

"Do you think so?"

"Oh, no! I *know* so. It's your... your close relationship with the English master."

"*Really?*" exclaimed Willoughby-Wallows.

"Really," repeated the German master. "You've been with us less than twenty-four hours and you're already a victim of his dirty tricks. As I said, be very careful especially around Warneke. Dirty tricks are a way of life here."

"I see what you mean, Professor. But I'll be seeing a lot less of him," explained Willoughby-Wallows. "I have to move up to the dorm soon, I guess."

"Warneke's pulled another fast one and there's not a thing to be done about it," the old fellow continued. "And let me tell you, he's just the worst of a bad lot. Now, let's drop this *sir* and *professor* business, eh? My name is Rolf. Call me Rolf, please. And yours again... is..."

"Oh! Wilfred, Sir, but Wilf, if you prefer," he answered while searching the table for something to eat.

"Let me see... I think I prefer Wilf. And remember, Wilf, my name is not sir," von Baumgartner added. "I should have warned you about Warneke... Wilf," the old man continued. "But I'm afraid I didn't get to you in time."

"You're not the only one, Rolf. Who wanted to warn me, I mean."

"Leticia has spoken to you then, has she?" asked the old man. "Good! That's very good. She's trustworthy, Wilf, but a little too... well, how should I put it? Excitable. She suspects that Warneke's the only one. And that's rather unreasonable, of course. And oh, how she resents him."

"She does, Sir— I mean, Rolf. She suspects him, I mean. She told me as much."

Von Baumgartner stood and made for the door. "I'll leave you now, Wilf," he said. "But do keep a sharp eye, okay?" He winked, checked the time, turned and shuffled off down the corridor.

As Willoughby-Wallows ate, he thought about what Warneke had done. Four words his mother had often used entered his mind and he repeated them aloud. "Of all the gall!" he muttered.

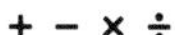

As Willoughby-Wallows approached Warneke's lodgings, he noticed a student standing opposite his old room. With a shoulder against the wall, the fellow stared into what the new dorm supervisor took to be a Science text. Beside the lad, stood several pieces of furniture. The boy tucked his tie inside his blazer and ran his fingers through his bright red hair.

"Mr. Willoughby-Wallows, Sir," announced the boy, "I'm Andrews, Sir. Head Student, Sir." Willoughby-Wallows' eyes had locked onto the furniture: his furniture. "Oh, I'll have all that put back in storage for you, Sir. No need to worry yourself about that stuff, Sir."

Andrew's repetitions of the word 'sir' threw the man off stride. "Ah… Andrews, is it?"

The boy nodded.

"I see…" said the Greek and Latin man.

"The professor, Mr. Warneke, that is, Sir. He asked me to take your belongings up to the dorm, Sir. So I rounded up a couple of the fellows and they— they should be finished by now, Sir."

Willoughby-Wallows stared from the boy to the furniture and back.

"You did want your stuff— your belongings, I mean— moved, didn't you, Sir?" The head student received no response.

"It's alright, isn't it, Sir?" asked Andrews. "I mean, I haven't done anything wrong, have I, Sir?"

"No, no… Of course not, Andrews, of course not." Willoughby-Wallows patted the boy on the shoulder. "It's just that I didn't expect such… such efficiency, I suppose." His eyes were fixed on Warneke's door.

"Shall I show you up to your rooms, Sir?" asked the head student. "I'd be happy to, Sir."

Willoughby-Wallows' imagination fastened on the word 'rooms'. He thought it sounded promising. As he followed Andrews down the hallway he asked, "Somebody'll bring my dresser along, will they?"

"Oh, no, Sir. What I mean, Sir, is you'll not need it, Sir. Maybe once you see your new lodgings, Sir, you'll understand better, Sir."

"But my clothes?" exclaimed Willoughby-Wallows and pointed towards what had been his dresser.

"Ah!" replied the boy. "Your clothes, Sir… Well, they're already up there, Sir." He pointed at the ceiling. "Mr. Warneke packed everything in your suitcases for you and—"

"I see," Willoughby-Wallows grunted. He glowered at Warneke's door. "Is the professor in?"

"Yes, Sir. But he told me to wait for you and to make sure nobody disturbed him."

Andrews started towards the exit with Willoughby-Wallows close behind.

"Tell me, Andrews, about our roles. You know, head student and dormitory supervisor. What are we supposed to do?"

"Well, Sir… Oh! Before I forget, Sir. Professor Warneke asked me to make sure to tell you— I'm not quite sure what he meant by this, Sir— he guesses you won't be needing his key any time soon. Does that sound right, Sir?"

Willoughby-Wallows was too stunned to reply.

Andrews chose to postpone wondering about the new teacher's strange behaviour and began to answer his earlier question. "We have to ring the bells and keep the students from getting out of line. We're policemen really, Sir. Dorm's closer if we use this staircase, Sir."

They started the long climb.

"I have a room at the senior end. You get two rooms at the junior end."

"Two rooms?" asked Willoughby-Wallows.

"Yes, Sir," replied Andrews. "There's a laundry collection area and a place for trunks separating the two dorms. The guys who'll be graduating get private rooms on the second floor… except for me, of course."

Andrews and Willoughby-Wallows arrived at the dorm supervisor's quarters. The boy pulled a key from his pocket. "This is yours, Sir. If I may… a piece of advice, Sir?" he whispered while holding up the key. He surveyed the surrounding cubicles for possible eavesdroppers. "I'd use this, Sir, and I wouldn't let it out of my sight."

The young teacher stared at the key. He did not think to ask Andrews the reason for the warning. Indeed, it did not even register that the boy's words were a warning.

"Well, thanks, Andrews," he said and pocketed the key.

"Welcome, Sir." The boy turned and started back through the dorm.

"Oh, Andrews?" called Willoughby-Wallows. The boy turned and waited. "I didn't catch your first name, Andrews."

"My *first name*, Sir?" replied the head student with a hearty but short-lived laugh. "Oh, excuse me, Sir." Andrews clamped a hand over his mouth. "Sorry for laughing, Sir, but you don't need to know that, Sir. I'm Andrews, Sir, and I can't have you calling me anything else, especially in front of the guys, Sir. Good-bye, Sir."

Wilfred Willoughby-Wallows opened the door and entered his new lodgings. He discovered why Andrews had not had the dresser carried up. Through a door on the back wall to the very small front office, he could see an even tinier sleeping area. His baggage was stacked on the single bed that took up half the room.

"Well, at least Warneke won't keep me up half the night with his snoring and his other nonsense," mused the new dorm supervisor.

And thus began a new phase in the life of Wilfred Willoughby-Wallows, St. Timothy's Preparatory School's newly appointed Greek and Latin professor, probationary.

St. Timothy, I Presume

Meddows masked a smouldering indignation. Even when Emerson's second mention of a tuba threatened to fan coals of resentment into full flame, the older boy kept his emotions in check. Emerson paused to ponder the meaning of so cool a response and then followed the three older students through the chapel doorway. Pandemonium greeted him. Over thirty new boys milled about in confusion at the junction of the chapel's main and side aisles. Their eyes pleaded for help from the sniggering, snorting and scowling older students who hogged space on their pews. Veteran students beckoned newcomers to sit, only to push them away when they responded. The drill was a hackneyed first day ritual at St. Timothy's. Faces glowed crimson with either hilarity or humiliation.

Emerson sized up the situation at once, lowered his eyes, charged through the throng and made straight for the nearest pew, brandishing his guitar case as a knight would his lance. The bench's dumbfounded occupants ceded ground and Emerson slumped down onto the seat. As the boy twisted and turned in an effort to stow his guitar beneath the pew, he felt a sharp jab in the ribs. Looking to his left, he discovered Burns and, next to him, Meddows. The two boys' threatening looks disappeared when a loud, angry voice filled the chapel.

Andrews had entered through the back doorway. He shouted, "Enough already!" Those familiar with protocol donned angelic masks and exhibited excellent deportment. New students froze in place and gawked, unsure of what else to do. The head student, ignoring the melee, save for a 'tut-tut' in passing, made his way to the pulpit.

"This is the chapel," he announced. "Forget that and you'll regret it. That's a promise, Gentlemen." The redheaded boy unfolded a sheet of paper and added, "If you're not new here you'd better be sitting one pew back of where you sat last year. If you've forgotten..." He did not need to finish. A score of boys stood and shuffled to their proper places, leaving the two pews at the front empty. Andrews shook his head as he scribbled each offender's name in his notebook.

As Meddows passed Emerson, he stepped on the boy's foot. "Sorry, *Jenks*," he growled.

"Meddows!" cried Andrews. "I've got my eye on you, Meddows. And you too, Burns. I'd advise you to stay well clear of your friend there, Burns."

Meddows played the innocent. His toady smirked. The head student continued. "You guys who tried to put one over on me… don't try it again. I know who you are." He slapped his palm with his little black book. "I have no intention of letting you embarrass me." Andrews paused. "Okay then… seating assignments."

He scanned his list and called out, "Albertson… first pew, right side."

No one moved.

"Al-bert-son!"

A short, plump boy emerged from the scrum and raised his hand. Andrews beckoned. To a chorus of subdued snorts, Albertson slunk forward, genuflected and started to sit down.

"Other right, Albertson… and tuck in your shirttail."

A loud, short-lived bark of a laugh rose from the back pew.

"Reynolds, was that you?" demanded Andrews.

Several helpful students leaned to the side to give Andrews an unobstructed view of their friend. Repentance registered on Reynolds' face, betraying his guilt.

"Come see me after lunch, Reynolds," ordered Andrews as he jotted down a note. Albertson used the distraction to slide to the end of his pew.

Andrews continued seating the newcomers. "Condon, first pew, left side." Andrews called out another five names. Five more boys left the huddle and took their seats. "Jenks, third row, right side."

When Emerson had taken his newly assigned seat in the pew bordering the chapel's side aisle, Andrews continued. "Sitting there means you're the new sacristan, Jenks. Burton, the fellow, there, at the other end of your pew…" Emerson, wondering what a sacristan was, leaned forward, looked past three boys and acknowledged Burton's wave. "Show Jenks the ropes, Burton."

"Now listen up, people," warned the head student after everyone was seated. "You new fellows in particular. When a warning bell sounds, you follow the others straight here. If I catch you straggling in late..." Andrews scanned the room. So many faces having turned from cherry red to pasty white confirmed that his Captain Bligh-like reputation was established. "When I dismiss you... like this..." continued Andrews and knocked on the pulpit, "you'll file out in two rows. Orderly rows. You new fellows here in front will leave first. You others know the drill." Andrews rapped again, stepped into the aisle and cried, "C'mon, let's go."

The boys spilled out of the pews and formed a ragged queue behind their leader. On reaching the basement corridor, students jockeyed for position near the refectory doors.

"Hinerman," called Andrews after stepping into the large room, "you have table one. Johnson, you're at table two." Soon, a senior student stood at the head of each table. Andrews addressed those remaining in the corridor. "The head of your table reports all problems to me. Understood?"

They seemed to understand. He began calling out table numbers and students' names. "We'll chant *Te Deum*," ordered Andrews when he had finished.

New boys gawked at their tablemates as the Latin hymn rang out. At the word 'amen', there was a thunderous racket as over one hundred boys dragged chairs from under the tables and the newcomers began talking.

"Quiet!" Once more Andrews' voice rose and silence fell. "Who gave you permission to speak?" he demanded. "When I knock, you'll lift your chairs and keep the noise down to a dull roar. You new fellows, you have one week to learn *Te Deum*. The head of your table will tutor you." He rapped on his table and a harmonious hum replaced the crass cacophony. From their seats, Andrews and his assistant enjoyed an unobstructed view of the diners.

Emerson's contemplation of the seating arrangements was interrupted when his neighbour tapped him on the shoulder. Turning, he looked into a massive chest, then up into a broad, swarthy face and a toothy grin. He marvelled that he had not seen this boy earlier. The giant seemed to have materialized out of thin air.

"I'm Guardiano," the boy announced as a student waiter set lunch on the table. "Minestrone," announced the big boy after peeking into the terrine. "Hate it!" His gaze and his hand shifted from the soup to the sandwiches. "You play guitar, huh?" he asked Emerson before stuffing one half of a sandwich into his mouth.

Emerson considered repeating his tuba quip but thought it unwise to antagonize this particular boy. "A little," he answered. "You?"

The boys' three tablemates snorted and then stared at each other in silence before breaking into scornful laughter. Guardiano's face glowed red and he bowed his head.

"What?" demanded Emerson and stared from face to face.

"Angelo Guardiano! Play guitar? He can't even play the hi-fi," the head of the table explained to the amusement of the others. They subdued their laughter to avoid drawing Andrews' attention.

Guardiano's head slumped forward and the boy said nothing. Emerson opened his mouth to defend his neighbour but he was distracted when someone poked him between the shoulder blades. He turned his head and his attention to the table behind him. A boy wearing a puzzled grin pointed across the room and shrugged. Emerson's eyes swept to his left and came to rest on Meddows who sneered, pretended to strum a guitar and, using his chin, gestured towards his two friends. The expressions Burns and O'Neil wore conveyed something between amusement and intimidation. Emerson looked away and stared down at his empty plate.

Minutes later, Emerson turned to Guardiano. "If you'd like to learn guitar, I'll teach you," he offered.

Guardiano squinted, thinking hard.

"Anybody can learn," Emerson added. "I taught my sister… and a couple of friends of mine."

To say that their tablemates were sceptical about the big boy's ability to learn guitar would be a gross understatement. Their hooting died a quick death when they felt Andrews' steady, suspicious and disapproving gaze settle upon them.

"It's Jenks, right?" asked the boy at the head of the table. Emerson nodded. "I guess I shouldn't laugh, Jenks. Maybe you can teach Guardiano something." The boy surveyed his audience, winked and with the timing of a polished stand-up comedian added, "After all… I saw a bear ride a bicycle once."

"Ah, don't let 'em get to you, Guardiano," advised Emerson. "Like my dad always says, you never know what you can do 'til you try."

A smile replaced Guardiano's pained expression. "Yeah! You're right, Jenks." His tablemates had never heard the boy speak with such determination. "When can we start?"

"How 'bout right after lunch?" suggested Emerson.

The big boy looked into the eyes of the others at the table. Grim determination registered on his face. "I'll show you guys. *You'll* see," he said. Guardiano and Emerson's tablemates clamped their mouths shut, snorted and shook their heads. Soon, the three boys were discussing their summer exploits and prospects for the coming year. Emerson and Guardiano said little.

Emerson had lost his appetite. He had too much information to digest to think about food. When a waiter placed a pan of variegated-brown mush smelling of cinnamon on the table, Emerson decided it must be dessert. The boy opposite him began to speculate about what, besides apple, might be in the cobbler. When the pan was passed to him, Emerson spooned his share into a bowl and slid the treat in front of Guardiano who was already scrapping his own bowl clean. "You can have mine," said Emerson.

"Hey!" pleaded the speculator as he turned open-mouthed to the head of the table. "I turned 'im off it, eh. That dessert's mine."

According to the long-established rules at St. Timothy's, the boy was correct – technically speaking. However, the head of the table had to pause and review the sequence of events – he had been in his new role no more than thirty minutes after all. Before he could adjudicate the conflict, Guardiano made the point moot.

"Wanted to wrestle for it, did yuh, Fleming?" Guardiano asked.

The boys might have argued had Andrews not knocked on his table and stood. Students wolfed down everything edible and scrambled to their feet when Andrews rapped a second time. After a prayer, the head student announced, "Free time 'til dinner. 'Cept for you new guys. You come with me."

"Meet me in the chapel," Emerson whispered to Guardiano. "We'll start practicing right away."

The students were in full flight to the scullery, returning dirty plates, bowls and spoons. Meddows' toadies rushed off empty-handed. Meddows gathered up their dishes and tried to squeeze into the queue behind Emerson who used Guardiano as a buffer.

The newcomers rallied around Andrews outside the scullery. "I've gotta show you where to be for first class tomorrow," explained Andrews. He led the way to the third floor and pointed out the new boys' homerooms. "You're on your own 'til dinner," he announced and sprinted away towards the common rooms and his Monopoly game. Emerson coaxed six boys into accompanying him to the top of the stairs leading to the chapel. When he detected no sign of danger, Emerson dashed down the steps. When he entered the chapel his new friend stood and smiled.

"Guitar's right here," declared Emerson and stooped down to look under the pew. If the guitar had been where he had stowed it, Emerson would have been surprised. He dropped to one knee, peered along the floor and announced that the guitar was missing.

On hands and knees, Guardiano stuck his head under the benches to make sure Emerson was not mistaken. "Uh, where'd it go?" he wondered aloud.

"Maybe somebody put it out there," Emerson replied and pointed to the side doors. Guardiano set off on a fool's errand. Emerson tagged behind. Meddows and his boys were not waiting in the foyer as Emerson had suspected. Guardiano searched for five minutes before convincing himself that the instrument was indeed missing.

"Sorry 'bout that, Guardiano," confessed Emerson. He stretched his arms out wide, palms up, and shrugged. "No lessons 'til we find my guitar."

"But who'd want'uh take your guitar?" asked Guardiano. The pained expression that Emerson had noticed at table returned. "C'mon," exclaimed Guardiano, "Never mind, it'll turn up. Let's go down to the river."

As they reached the foot of the front stairs they heard a voice call out, "Over here, guys. He's out front." Meddows poked his head through a window and sneered down at the two boys from the top floor. He was not alone but it was impossible to tell who or even how many others were with him.

"What d'yuh want, *Meddows?*" demanded Guardiano.

"Nothin' from you, you empty-headed donkey," roared Meddows.

"I ain't no donkey!" replied Guardiano.

Meddows and his entourage hooted, indeed howled, with laughter. Emerson shook his head and, placing a hand on his companion's shoulder, tried to turn him towards the river. Guardiano brushed the hand away.

"What?" he cried as he stared up at Meddows. "What's so darn funny, eh? C'mon down here and say that."

"Forget it, Guardiano," answered Meddows. "Hey, Jenks! Does tuba boy want his horn back?" Meddows disappeared for a moment, then shoved the guitar case out the window and jeered. He pulled the instrument inside and began to regale his friends. When, a minute or two later, the boy's head reappeared, Emerson alone remained below. Guardiano was missing.

"Ha!" snorted Meddows. "Your new friend's already vanish—"

A huge hand fell on Meddows' shoulder and he disappeared from Emerson's view even as the word 'vanish' fell from his lips. He found himself on his tiptoes, nose-to-nose with, and looking into the bulging eyes of Angelo Guardiano. The boy had a two-fisted grip on Meddows' lapels and no intention of letting go.

"Who yuh callin' a donkey, Meddows, and where's my friend's guitar?" demanded the much bigger boy.

"L–L–Let go," stammered Meddows. "You're hurtin' me. Let go, eh." His head turned left and right, as he looked for assistance. Not one of his companions offered to intervene. The bravado they had displayed while at a distance fled the scene the moment Guardiano stormed into the dorm. The big fellow lifted Meddows off the floor and shook him from side to side.

"Burns, give 'im the stupid guitar! Quick!" Meddows croaked.

A few minutes passed before Guardiano rejoined his friend at the main entrance. He carried the guitar in one hand.

"Better make sure everything's here," suggested Emerson and set the case on the lower landing.

"Oh, it'll all be there," assured Guardiano. "Meddows ain't *that* stupid."

Emerson could not help but smile. "So, Guardiano… the river?" he asked. "Or do you want a couple of chords to work on?"

As he followed his companion towards the auditorium, Emerson made a suggestion. "Listen… I know everybody uses last names 'round here but how 'bout I just call you Angelo? When we're alone, I mean? And you can call me Emerson."

"Um… okay… I guess," replied Guardiano but a look of doubt crossed his face. A second later, the boy grinned. "Yeah, that'll be lots better. Sure… Emerson."

+ − × ÷

By the following Friday evening, the newcomers' initial confusion was a thing of the past. Responding to bells had become second nature. Every student and every member of the staff crawled into bed that night feeling tired but looking forward to Saturday: the first free day since their arrival.

The following morning, Mr. Fitzroy toiled at his paper-strewn desk and lamented the absence of his secretary. Professor Warneke remained in bed. Miss Strupples prowled the halls in search of the two teachers who had missed her opening-day lecture. Those gentlemen, accompanied by Professor Darling, were far away enjoying restaurant coffee and a hearty laugh at the woman's expense. Mr. Willoughby-Wallows marked assignments and prepared his lessons. Andrews watched Reynolds remove St. Timothy from his nook. Reynolds could look forward to spending a good portion of his day washing and drying the school's patron saint.

Guardino sat in the auditorium with his stubby fingers wrapped around the neck of Emerson's guitar. "D,D,D… G,G,G… D,D,D… A-seventh," he repeated. The tip of boy's tongue protruding from the corner of his mouth bore witness to his powers of concentration. Meddows and his toadies were holed up in their classroom discussing what to do about Emerson Jenks and how to neutralize Guardiano.

"I've watched 'im close," reported Burns. "That Jenks is bein' plenty careful."

"And stupid Guardiano's never more than two steps behind 'im," added O'Neil.

"Careful or not, I'm gunna get 'im... and get 'im good," stated Meddows. "But first... he's gotta trust us, see? So no stupid stunts 'til he steps in our trap. Got it?" As Meddows said 'got it', he poked Burns on the shoulder.

"Ow, c'mon, eh! That really hurts, Meddows," complained his number one toady.

"What trap?" asked O'Neil.

"The one we're gunna cook up right now," answered Meddows. "We need a prank Jenks can have a good part in."

"Then we'll fix 'im real good, eh?" added Burns. This merited a second jab to the shoulder. "Man, I wish you'd stop doin' that," the boy whined.

"Shut up!" ordered Meddows. "We've gotta play this first one straight. He's gotta think we're legit, see? After, when he ain't expectin' nothin', then we'll get 'im. But not 'til then though." Meddows looked to his crew for signs of agreement. In anticipation of more pain, Burns backed away. "Got it?" asked Meddows and ground his right fist into the palm of his left hand.

By Sunday afternoon, the gang had only the most important detail of its plan to arrange. At dinner, Meddows passed a note to Emerson. It requested a truce and a parley. When Emerson glanced at Meddows, the older boy returned a pleading look and mouthed the words 'after dinner', 'auditorium' and 'alone'.

Emerson arrived for the meeting and pressed his ear to the door: not a sound. He pushed against the door and peered through the crack into darkness. He propped the door open with the doorstop he found on the floor, took a deep breath, stepped into the room and dragged his hand along the wall, searching for a light switch.

"Leave 'em off, Jenks." Emerson heard Meddows' voice but could not see him. "You're safe. We're alone... promise," advised the older boy. "Unless you brought your muscle along, that is."

Emerson did not respond. He stalled for time to let his eyes adjust to the darkness.

"You got guts," added Meddows. "Me and my boys like that." The boy paused. "We thought you might wanna join our crew. Interested?"

Despite Meddows' promise, Emerson suspected that someone else lurked in the shadows. He remained near the exit. "Got something in mind?" he asked.

"Just a little prank on a couple of the new guys. Somethin' to give 'em a scare… that's all," answered Meddows. "We could use your help."

"What would I have to do?" Emerson inquired. "I don't need any trouble from Andrews, eh?"

"One condition first, Jenks. You say nothin' to nobody whether you throw in with us or not," demanded Meddows. "You gotta promise."

"Sure, I promise," replied Emerson. "I'm no squealer."

"Not even your pal Guardiano, eh?" added the older boy.

"Not even Guardiano," replied Emerson. "Cross my heart. If Guardiano finds out anything, it'll be one of you guys that'll spills the beans, not me."

"Okay, here's the plan. Tonight," explained Meddows, "O'Neil's gunna make sure there's a big hold-up in the showers. The older guys ain't stupid so they'll take off. But the new guys'll hang around, eh?"

"Yeah?"

"O'Neil makes sure some new kid's late so he'll have to sneak back in the dark. Me and you'll meet in the chapel and pretend we're prayin' right? Just in case somebody wonders what the heck we're doin' in there."

"Okay," muttered Emerson.

"When the lights go out me and you'll take down St. Timothy and I'll take his place," explained Meddows.

"And what am I supposed to do?" asked Emerson.

"You stand across from me and hold my flashlight," replied Meddows. He passed a beam of light over Emerson's face.

"Hey! You're not allowed to have that," cried Emerson as he threw up his hands and turned his face away.

Hidden by the darkness, outright contempt registered on Meddows' face. He turned off the light. "When our mark comes up the stairs, I'll groan and when I do you'll shine the light on me, okay. But yuh gotta be fast and you gotta hit me right in the face or it's no good— soon as I start moanin', eh?"

"Yeah, right! Then the kid screams and Andrews comes running," muttered Emerson. "Just great!"

"Andrews will be tied up on the other stairwell and O'Neil is gunna have the super held up over in the shower room," replied Meddows. "But if the kid does make a lot of noise, we scatter and it's every man for himself."

"We make our own plans in case something goes wrong, right?" asked Emerson.

"Yeah, but don't worry. The kid'll prob'ly be too scared to yell. By the time he opens his mouth, me and you and Burns will have 'im calmed down," declared Meddows.

"Burns! How'd Burns get in on this?" demanded Emerson.

"Oh, I forgot. Burnsy'll wait on the landing right above us. He'll whistle if anybody comes down that way."

Emerson rocked his head from side to side. "No way to get Andrews out of the way?" he asked.

"Not a chance," replied Meddows. "Andrews'll smell somethin' fishy soon as you try. Yuh never get nothin' past Andrews."

After a pause, Emerson spoke. "Okay… I'm in, Meddows. But Andrews'll be the problem if there is one."

"One more thing," added Meddows, easing himself down off the stage. "If we pull this thing off… perfect-like… and if there's time… we'll get the mark to take my place, eh? Tell 'im somebody else is comin' along. If he goes for it, we'll leave 'im standin' there like a dummy 'til Willoughby-Wallows or Andrews finds 'im."

"Got it all figured out, eh, Meddows?" Emerson chuckled as he spoke.

Meddows ignored the comment. "Okay then," he continued as he walked towards the exit. Emerson gave the boy a wide berth and let him pass. At the door, Meddows stopped, turned and spoke. "See yuh tonight, Jenks. In the chapel."

Emerson hurried to the door and listened to Meddows' retreating footfall. He heard the boy climb the stairs to the common rooms and then turned towards the stage. "One thing's for sure… we have to watch those guys," Emerson warned as Guardiano slipped through the curtains. "Stay clear of the showers tonight, okay?"

As the two boys left the auditorium, Emerson stooped down to remove the doorstop. He stared at it, tossed it in the air, caught it and slipped it into his pocket. Emerson slapped Guardiano on the back and said, "I really do appreciate all your help, my friend."

+ − × ÷

After evening prayers, Andrews signalled the beginning of 'grand silence'. Anyone caught talking between now and tomorrow's breakfast would soon be waxing hardwood floors – or worse: St. Timothy's many toilets always need scrubbing. The students had only twenty minutes to get to and from the showers and into bed. Not being tucked in before lights-out was as serious as getting caught chatting before breakfast.

Without going to the dormitory first, O'Neil hurried straight to the shower room and turned off the main hot water supply. On discovering the water problem, experienced students fled. The less observant remained. Presently, Willoughby-Wallows found what was wrong and put it right. When the first arrivals entered the showers, O'Neil hid their slippers and house coats.

Albertson, of shirttail infamy, was the last to finish the evening ritual. He discovered his dressing gown missing and took several minutes, even with O'Neil's kind assistance, to locate the item. When Albertson finally left the locker room, less than a minute before lights out, O'Neil approached Willoughby-Wallows. "Do you have a minute, Sir?" asked the boy and began pouring out his homesick heart.

Meddows and Emerson had arrived at the chapel from opposite directions, knelt down several pews apart and listened as the dormitory-bound students stampeded past. When the lights went out, the boys stepped onto the landing. Emerson held the door open and provided light while Meddows removed St. Timothy from his nook and carried him into the chapel. Meddows removed two altar boy soutanes he had hidden behind the statue. "These'll make us harder to see in the dark," he explained as he and his co-conspirator slipped the jet-black, ankle-length garments over their heads.

Under cover of darkness, Burns took up his post one floor above. He heard movement and saw a glimmer of light below. "Meddows and Jenks," he whispered to himself as he exhaled in an effort to reassure himself and calm his ragged nerves. But, just in case it proved to be Andrews, the boy prepared to race back up the stairs. Not just Emerson, but Meddows' toadies also harboured suspicions about the true thoughts and intents of their leader's heart.

On the darkened landing, with his back to the chapel door, Emerson unbuttoned his soutane. He succeeded in resisting the temptation to use the penlight to check on Meddows. Emerson was comforted by the thought that if he had the misfortune of being caught, Meddows would surely share his fate. Emerson knew that the older student could not escape the landing and leave him stranded without his knowing it. Both boys checked their breathing and waited.

When Emerson heard someone approaching, he bent low and set the penlight on the floor. Having counted the stairs earlier, he knew there were twenty steps between landings. As the mark climbed, shuffling quickly towards him, Emerson silently counted off the steps. When he reached fifteen, Emerson kicked the penlight, sending it skittering across the landing, shoved the door open, stepped into the chapel, slammed the door and jammed his doorstop into place.

Three-quarters of the way up the darkened staircase, Andrews heard a metallic clatter. He heard the chapel door open and close. His flashlight illuminated the stairwell as he dashed to the door and pushed hard against it; it refused to budge. He rammed his shoulder hard into the door. To his surprise, it would not open. He turned the beam of light on the floor. Stooping down, he picked up the penlight.

Meddows also heard the metallic clatter and the sound of the door. Before he could react, the stairwell was flooded in noonday brightness. His soutane-shrouded body froze in place and he gazed down upon Andrews. The boy's heart beat so loudly he was afraid the head student could hear it. He clenched his jaws so tightly he feared cracking his teeth. Meddows watched the beam of light as it darted about the landing and saw Andrews bend down to pick up the flashlight. In St. Timothy's nook, he shrunk back and, for real on this occasion, prayed for a miracle.

The boy cautioned himself not to move. He heard an inner voice ordering him to not even breathe.

While Andrews wasted precious seconds assaulting the door, Emerson darted through the chapel's side entrance, stripping off his soutane on the way. He tossed the garment in the general direction of the sacristy and, in almost total darkness and without the slightest sound, he raced headlong down the corridor towards the far stairwell. During the afternoon, Emerson had practiced his escape until he could make the trip with his eyes closed. In his stocking feet, the boy braked on cue and slid sideways for a few yards, regained his traction and sprinted up the stairs. Speed, silence and good luck, he hoped, would carry him safely to bed. When Emerson reached the junior dormitory, he was badly startled. He discovered someone waiting for him on the landing.

"Who's there?" croaked Emerson. With his heart in his throat, he found speaking difficult.

"Everything go okay, Jenks?" whispered Albertson.

"Perfect," answered Emerson. "How 'bout you?"

"Before the lights went out, I ran like the wind— just like you told me," reported Albertson. "You should've seen Andrews' face when I told 'im I heard scary noises by the chapel."

"You did good, Albertson," admitted Emerson. "But you can't say a word about all this. Meddows will come after you if he finds out."

Albertson laughed. "Andrews was so hot he forgot to write me up for being late."

"Better get to bed," Emerson advised. "Someone'll be along any minute. And remember! Keep your mouth shut."

Outside the chapel, Andrews passed his light over the stairs and landing. The beam darted and danced about until it fell upon a pair of size eleven sneakers where the base of a statue should have been. Andrews let the beam creep upwards, illuminating Meddows' knees, then his chest and finally his face. Where St. Timothy had rested unmolested for almost a century, Meddows stood still, his head tilted back, his eyes clamped closed, his jaws clenched tight.

"St. Timothy, I presume?" declared Andrews.

Meddows opened his eyes and looked down. "Nope," he replied.

(Later, in a show of bravado, he bragged to his friends, "I should've been able to come up with a better line than that, eh?")

"Got a good explanation, Meddows?" asked the head student as he fanned himself with his notebook.

"Nope," answered the boy.

"Didn't think so," Andrews replied with a long sigh. "Make sure you come and see me in the morning." Meddows did not move. "You can get down now, Meddows. And get to bed."

Meddows eased himself to the floor and started up the stairs, retreating like a whipped dog.

"Oh, Meddows, wait a sec," called Andrews. "Your flashlight— "

"—Oh! That's not mine, Andrews," replied Meddows without the slightest hesitation. "We're not allowed to have flashlights. Remember?"

"Give me that soutane, Meddows," demanded Andrews as he pocketed the contraband. Meddows complied without comment and the head student went off in search of the boy's partner-in-crime. He found only Emerson Jenks' discarded soutane, the doorstop and the most innocent of the night's pranksters: St. Timothy himself.

The following morning at breakfast, there was no knock to end grand silence. Andrews' eyes and those of his assistant scanned the silent room for any evidence of mirth. No one had to be reminded of the dangers inherent in a smirk, smile or snort of laughter. Albertson, Burns, O'Neil and Emerson Jenks avoided eye contact with Meddows and with one another. Andrews watched to see if Meddows would single out his accomplice by looking once too often or a second too long. But Meddows was no fool. At the end of the meal, Andrews sounded the dismissal. The students departed in perfect order and spoke only when well beyond the head student's hearing.

"What the heck were you thinking, Jenks?" croaked Burns as he hurried past Emerson on his right.

"Meddows is gonna kill you," cautioned O'Neil as he barged by on the left.

Emerson smiled as he climbed the stairs and saluted St. Timothy before proceeding to his classroom.

After morning classes and lunch, Meddows and his crew confronted Emerson as he and Guardiano left the refectory. "We gotta talk, Jenks," growled Meddows. He glared at Guardiano. "Alone!"

"You're darn right we have to talk," replied Emerson. He placed a hand on Meddows' chest and pushed. The boy, totally unprepared for such an affront, stumbled backwards, caught his balance and stared at Emerson in amazement. Dumbfounded, Burns and O'Neil stepped away and gawked. Emerson turned to Guardiano. "Wait here, Guardiano? I have to talk to these bozos for a minute."

Emerson paced quickly down the corridor. Burns and O'Neil followed on his heels. They were not about to miss the confrontation. Meddows hesitated and then joined the parade.

"No smart stuff, Meddows," called Guardiano after him, "or else!"

The gang reassembled at the end of the hall. The conversation took a very different turn than Meddows had anticipated. "You did that on purpose, Jenks," he declared.

"What were you thinking, Meddows?" demanded Emerson. "You nearly got us all caught. So don't go blaming us for your own stupidity. Anybody with half a brain could tell the guy coming up those stairs wasn't some new kid. Just look at Burns, eh?"

"Yeah, just look at me," bragged the toady. He did not pick up on Emerson's backhanded compliment nor had he any idea of what Meddows was supposed to see in him.

Meddows, taken aback by Emerson's observation, stood in silence with his mouth open. He noticed that Burns and O'Neil seemed impressed with the new boy. The observation irked him.

Emerson continued, "Look, Meddows, you said if anything went wrong we were on our own, right? Well, things went wrong— so we took off. Burns heard Andrews coming and he took off, right, Burns?"

Burns nodded. For perhaps the first time in his life, Meddows found himself unable to speak.

"I told you Andrews would be the problem but, oh no…" Emerson paused for effect. "I figured if I made enough noise I'd distract whoever it was and you'd light out of there." Emerson continued to weave his spell.

"But you just stood there like a dummy. What did you expect? Duh, if I just stand here smiling he'll think I'm St. Timothy or something?"

"Yeah, Meddows!" Burns grumbled.

"Shut your trap, Burns," demanded Meddows and thumped his toady on the shoulder.

"Don't go hitting me just 'cause you screwed up and got caught," whined Burns.

"Yeah," added O'Neil. "You messed up, Meddows, not us three."

Sensing a mutiny in the making, Meddows decided to back off. "I still say it was all Jenks' fault," he growled, though his voice betrayed a trace of doubt.

"Say whatever you like, Meddows," Emerson said and beckoned to his buddy. "But I'll tell you what. I'll sure think twice before pulling another prank with you as a partner."

Before Meddows could reply, Guardiano reached Emerson's side.

"Beat it, you two!" Meddows ordered his toadies away. They slunk down the hall side by side. "We'll talk later. I gotta go see Andrews again," their leader called after them. "You better watch it, eh, Jenks," Meddows added before shuffling away to keep his noon-hour date with the head student.

As Emerson and Guardiano started back down the corridor, Emerson drew a deep breath. "So," he whispered, "that seemed to go rather well, Angelo, don't you think?"

That's Stroud Island, Sir

At 6:55 P.M., the bell echoed throughout St. Timothy's and rolled across its grounds. In the common rooms, boys tossed notes with polite requests, like *PLEASE DO NOT TOUCH* or threats such as *TOUCH AND DIE*, onto unfinished board games. Athletic types scampered from the gym and handball courts and made straight for the classroom corridor. With the head student and his assistant waiting to close the study hall doors at 7:00 on the dot, no one dared be late.

The bell also summoned the teachers to the year's first regular staff meeting. Von Baumgartner heard it ring while he waited in the auditorium, Strupples from the entrance to Disraeli Hall. All but two of the other members of the teaching staff were in the main building, on their way from the faculty wing, when Andrews sounded the clarion call. They all wanted the meeting to begin and end on schedule. At 7:00, only Warneke, Willoughby-Wallows and Mr. Fitzroy were missing. Heads turned when, at 7:01, someone entered the room. Hopes ran high that it was the headmaster, so Warneke's arrival proved disappointing. The English master parked himself in his favourite corner, observed his peers and chuckled. Von Baumgartner scowled at his watch. Others read or marked assignments. The headmaster had a well-established and well-deserved reputation for arriving late for almost everything. When, only a few minutes later, the bell sounded a second time, the teachers questioned one another with their eyes and answered with shrugs. They consulted their watches, stood and milled about.

"Oh, for heaven's sake, stop fretting," shouted Warneke. "It's just some silly ass playing with the buzzer."

Willoughby-Wallows was leaning back in his chair with his feet on his desk when the first bell rang. But he did not hear it. He continued reading Ovid until a sense of alarm, a premonition of sorts, swept over him prompting him to check the time: 7:05! The young man slammed his book shut, scrambled to his feet and raced out of the dorm to the classroom corridor. Alarm blossomed into panic when he found the corridor deserted. At 7:06, he rang the bell and heaved a sigh of relief.

Within seconds, both Andrews and his assistant stepped from the study halls into the corridor.

"What's wrong, Sir?" asked the head student. "What's the bell for, Sir?"

"You were supposed to ring it, Andrews," chided Willoughby-Wallows.

"Pardon, Sir?" replied Andrews. He looked to his assistant for support. "But I did ring it, Sir… right on time, Sir."

"Well, why didn't I hear it then?" demanded Willoughby-Wallows.

To the boy, the dormitory supervisor appeared incredulous. "I couldn't say, Sir," responded the puzzled head student. "But I rang the bell, Sir."

The discourse was interrupted by tittering. A few younger students had wandered into the hall. A half-dozen graduating students had hurried up the stairs from the second floor.

"Back to your desks. Back to your rooms, you guys," ordered Andrews. The audience retreated. "You see, Sir. They all heard it, Sir."

Willoughby-Wallows did see but he did not understand. He took another glance at his watch and gulped. "Oh, man! I'm late," he cried and fled, leaving Andrews scratching his head. Huffing and puffing, the young professor reached the auditorium at 7:10. He heard nothing from within so cracked the door open and surveyed the room. He, but no one else, was happy that Fitzroy was still absent. He entered the room, looked behind the door and nodded to his former roommate. Warneke responded with an unmilitary-like salute. The Greek and Latin teacher sat beside von Baumgartner but could not engage the old man in conversation. The German master was preoccupied with his watch. Strupples sat alone – front row centre. The others too had claimed their usual seats. Willoughby-Wallows sat and wondered how he could possibly have missed hearing the bell. It hung on the wall no more than ten paces from his door.

At 7:20, by the clock, von Baumgartner stood, slammed his book down on his chair and declared, "Well, if none of you will fetch him, I shall," and stormed out of the auditorium.

The German master became intrigued by muffled thumping as he approached the headmaster's office. He could hear dread oaths and pleas for help. On rounding the corner, the old gentleman stopped and stared. A length of stout cord stretched across the corridor, from the office door handles to the base of a radiator. If staring could sever a rope the headmaster would have been set at liberty at once. Von Baumgartner, ignoring Fitzroy's shouting and banging, plucked the rope as one plucks a harp string. A note, somewhere in the range of middle C, sounded. The old man cried out, "Mr. Fitzroy, Sir! Are you alright, Sir?" and beat upon the door with both of his fists. Fitzroy's hammering abated but the tempo and intensity of von Baumgartner's barrage increased. "Are you in there, Sir!" the German master shouted.

"Rolf! Is that you, Rolf?" answered the headmaster. "What's going on out there?" Fitzroy heard only von Baumgartner's incessant banging.

"Scotty— Mr. Fitzroy! I say. Is that you in there?" demanded von Baumgartner.

"Of course it's me in here, man. Let me out of here."

After minutes of mayhem, von Baumgartner, by dint of approaching apoplexy, was forced to rest. He gasped for air while doubled over, his hands on his knees. He panted and, in a state of helplessness, stared from the door to the radiator and back.

"Professor—" demanded Fitzroy, "what in the name of heaven is going on out there?"

"Why..." the old gentleman replied between fits of coughing, "you're... you're locked in there, Sir."

"I know I'm locked in, man," bellowed the headmaster. "But how?"

Von Baumgartner related the state of affairs in detail. The words 'door handles', 'radiator' and 'rope' cleared away most of Fitzroy's confusion. He tried to interrupt the old man to say as much. Von Baumgartner's need to finish his tale did nothing to diminish the headmaster's frustration.

"Untie it, Rolf?" he ordered. "Don't you have a knife on you? Or something?"

The German master patted all of his pockets. Before responding in the negative, he ran his hands over the front of his jacket again. Even a policeman would have concluded that von Baumgartner was not carrying a concealed weapon. "I'm terribly sorry, Sir, but I do not," answered the German master.

The headmaster's patience, the virtue he revered and recommended to the boys so often, vaporized in the blink of an eye. "Rolf!" he pleaded. "For the love of Pete, man— please, would you just go and get help."

Von Baumgartner plucked a last, pitiful note on the cord and returned to the auditorium where, to the amusement of the staff, he related his adventure. A question about Fitzroy's whereabouts sparked the old fellow's memory. He had returned for a knife.

Strupples slipped past the German master and hurried to the headmaster's office followed by most of her peers. She sized up the situation in a moment, removed a jackknife from her vest pocket and cut through the knot. The Science professor threw Fitzroy's office doors open, ending her ruffled headmaster's incarceration.

"This nonsense has to stop," declared Mr. Fitzroy. "I'll see an end to it. I swear—"

"Now, now," chided Strupples. "Boys will be boys. And no harm's been done, Sir."

"No harm!" cried Fitzroy, striding down the hall. "*No harm*, you say?"

+ − × ÷

"Can we get started now? Gentlemen... Miss Strupples, come, come," shouted the headmaster as he herded his staff into the auditorium. The wall clock read almost 7:40. Fitzroy fidgeted with his tie and ran his fingers through his hair. "Please, people, take your seats," he continued. "The sooner we begin this, the sooner we'll finish." Fitzroy glanced into the back corner and saw Warneke standing there. The man was grinning. The headmaster cleared his throat and made as if to invite the gentleman to take a seat. In the end, he decided to stick to his agenda. "We have only four items..." he announced, holding up a sheet of paper to a chorus of groans. "Unless..." He looked around for any late additions to his list of items. His offer met with silence. "Okay, then— here we go."

After dispatching three trivial matters in short order, Fitzroy began to hem and haw. All but one member of the assembly knew why. "Ahem! Last of all..." muttered the headmaster. "If we get through this quickly..."

The 8:00 P.M. bell, signalling the end of first study hall, interrupted the man's statement. Fitzroy and several others paused to stare at their watches. When the bell's echo faded away, the headmaster finished his sentence, "If we get through this quickly, all of us can be on our way." He fumbled with his papers and, in spite of knowing they were empty, searched his pockets.

"It's Stroud Island time again," Fitzroy declared. He did his best to say the words with a smile. Everyone but Willoughby-Wallows groaned and tried to eradicate the memory of Stroud Island from his or her mind. Even so, the Hydra raised its ugly heads. "We need six volunteers. Anyone?" asked the headmaster and looked up. Eyes glazed over and even louder groans were heard.

"What's Shroud Island, Sir?" inquired Willoughby-Wallows. The young man looked from colleague to colleague wondering why they seemed less puzzled than he.

"Oh, I am sorry, Mr..." replied Fitzroy. "That's *Stroud Island*, Sir. Stroud's a school tradition."

"Shroud's a better name for the place," interjected Warneke and laughed.

Others found humour in the remark; Mr. Fitzroy did not. He ignored the English master and continued his explanation. "We take the boys to the island every fall. Everybody has a great time. You know... they swim, picnic, play games." The groaning turned to moaning at the mention of games.

Willoughby-Wallows became even more puzzled. He shrugged. "Sounds like fun to me," he stated. "I think I'd like to go."

"Now, that's the spirit," Fitzroy responded. This time, his smile was genuine. "Thank you, Willer... I mean, a... a... Sir." He made a notation on his agenda.

Warneke hooted with glee. "Lamb to the slaughter," he roared.

The others in the room wished they were chameleons. They shielded their faces with their hands and wished with all their hearts that they could disappear. Willoughby-Wallows observed his fellows with trepidation. His inner voice shouted a warning: *Recant! Recant, you fool!* But he ignored the voice's wise counsel.

"Come, come. We can't send this young man off all on his own," exclaimed Fitzroy in a vain appeal to pity. "Come now, everyone... Anybody at all?"

No one blinked. The teachers felt themselves being drawn irresistibly towards a flashing sign upon which Dante's immortal words appeared: *Abandon all hope ye who enter here*. Each determined to resist Fitzroy's pleadings, harangues, threats and bribes until the six weakest succumbed.

"Oh! Come, come! We can't disappoint the boys now can we?" whined Fitzroy in a vain appeal to guilt. Members of the staff, arms folded across their chests, answered with a stony silence.

+ − × ÷

"Sir?" Warneke spoke as he stepped from his shadowy domain. All eyes focussed on him. "I have all our names here," he explained and held up a royal-blue velvet bag by its golden drawstring. "We can pick names to see who has to go."

"Capital," shouted Fitzroy. "We'll have a draw. Come right up here to the front, Sir."

As Warneke advanced, he waved the bag above his head.

"Last year we took almost two hours to settle this," cried the headmaster over the low grumble that had filled the room. "This'll take just a few minutes. Warneke," he continued, "hand me that bag."

The headmaster opened the bag wide, held it towards Warneke and invited the big man to draw the first name. "Wait," declared Warneke and reached into his pocket. "Just to assure everyone that everything's on the up-and-up..." He handed the headmaster a slip of paper. "Tell them what that says, Sir?" he instructed.

"Warneke!" Fitzroy shouted as he waved the paper over his head. "It says Warneke, everybody... see!" The headmaster popped the paper into the bag and shook it the way an enthusiastic bartender shakes a martini. "Go ahead, Sir," he ordered.

As Warneke reached out, Fitzroy pulled the bag away. "Wait now! Gentlemen and Miss Strupples, remember now—" he warned, "if your name gets pulled I'll have no excuses. Understood?" He shook the bag again and continued, "Okay, professor."

Members of the audience slid forward on their chairs and leaned towards the stage. The Greek and Latin professor's inner voice howled. As Warneke's hand neared the bag, Willoughby-Wallows, like a drowning man grasping for an oar, snatched at his last chance of redemption. "Just a minute, Sir," he shouted as he bounded to his feet. "I'd like to withdraw my offer, Sir! And… and… take my chances in the lottery."

Before the Greek and Latin instructor's issue could be addressed, the German master spoke. "You can't expect me to go… not at my age," he shouted.

"What about me? I had to go last year," cried Bentley.

"Come, come, Gentlemen!" shouted Fitzroy as he pounded his fist on the lectern. "Has anyone got a better idea? Maybe I'll just appoint six of you?" he threatened in a not-so-vain appeal to fear. "I though not. So… now we need six names." Again, he held the bag out to Warneke.

The big man's hand disappeared into the bag and then emerged holding a slip of paper. Warneke waved it about as if it was stuck between his finger and thumb before looking at it. His voice rang out, "Strupples!" He reached back into the bag as mock congratulations burst from the crowd.

Fitzroy shouted, "Quiet, please. Quiet! We still need five more winners."

"*Winners!*" cried Strupples in astonishment.

Warneke withdrew his hand. "Fong!" He pulled out a third name, "Wiggly-Widows!" A fourth draw followed. "Darling! I mean, Jim." The fifth name belonged to von Baumgartner. The old man started to his feet but the headmaster warned him back.

Fitzroy held out the bag so the final name could be drawn. "Just one more and we'll be out of here," he cried, giving Warneke a nod. "Absolutely capital, this!"

"Sir," said the English master, "give me the bag and you draw the last one."

"No need, Sir," replied the headmaster. "You're doing just fine."

Warneke hesitated and then shoved the first five slips of paper into his jacket pocket, plucked a sixth from the bag and stared at it. Dismay swept across his face. His arms dropped to his side. His head fell forward. His colleagues began to snigger as the big man stood before them defeated, motionless. Fitzroy had to stifle a laugh. Suspense grew as several silent seconds passed.

"Go ahead, professor," demanded the headmaster. "Come now. What does it say?"

Warneke waited a moment before he whispered, "Fitzroy!" He passed the slip to the stunned headmaster with one hand, retrieved the bag with the other and headed to the back of the room. The audience began to mumble and mutter as word of Fitzroy's fate spread from those in the front row to those near the back of the room.

The headmaster inspected the paper. A single word, in capital letters, leapt off the page: FITZROY. No one spoke. No one smiled. No one laughed. No one dared laugh. The headmaster's mouth opened to protest but he thought better of it. Instead, he announced, "The trip is scheduled for a week today. Oh, and you, I mean we, who are going will have to meet to discuss the details. You can go."

Save one, the entire audience, in shock, remained seated. In great haste, Warneke headed for the door.

+ − × ÷

A thought struck Strupples when she reached the auditorium's exit. She glanced into Warneke's corner. He was not there. She scanned the room. Warneke had disappeared.

The English master entered his room, locked his door, leaned against it and stared at the ceiling. He raised his hands over his head, snapped his fingers and danced across the floor looking for all the world like Anthony Quinn in *Zorba the Greek*. With a cigar clamped between his teeth and a three finger glass of Jameson Irish Whiskey in his hand, he emptied the contents of the velvet bag onto his desk. One-by-one, he read the names aloud. "Fitzroy, Fitzroy, Fitzroy, Fitzroy and another Fitzroy," he repeated. With the papers, he constructed a miniature funeral pyre in his ashtray. After several more Fitzroys, five from his jacket pocket, he laughed and declared, "Ah, there you are, Warneke, you sly old dog." He stopped reading the slips of paper but continued to build the tower, gloating all the while. "One Warneke to two hundred Fitzroys… not bad odds," he chuckled. He struck a match and held the flame first to his cigar and then to the papers. With an agility that belied his age and size, the English master did a buck-and-wing across the carpet to his hi-fi, dropped the needle onto an LP, pushed the start button and cranked the volume to high. After a few cracks and pops, Handel's *Messiah* rattled every loose object in the room.

As Warneke celebrated, Strupples arrived at his door. She debated whether or not to confront the man. The smell of smoke distracted her. She knocked just as thumping bass notes and thundering hallelujahs staggered her. Shaken, she stepped back. "What's the use?" she grumbled and stormed off vowing revenge. Hotter than the fire that burned in Warneke's ashtray was the resentment burning in her bosom.

Warneke did not hear Strupples' knock. He was lending his voice to Handel's hallelujahs as he waltzed to his bed. He removed a length of nylon cord from under his pillow and made a mental note to visit the incinerator at the earliest possible opportunity.

After chapel, Andrews caught up to Willoughby-Wallows as he headed to the showers. "Sir, I found out why you didn't hear the bell, Sir. After you left… I went up to the dorm and… well, Sir… both bells up there were stuffed full of toilet paper, Sir. So nobody would have heard—"

"Toilet paper! I see," replied the Greek and Latin professor. "Who would do a thing like that, Andrews?"

Andrews blinked. "Why… just about anybody, Sir," answered the incredulous head student. The boy's freckled face reddened. "It's been done before, Sir," he explained. "Lots of times."

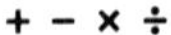

A week later, after morning mass, the head student announced that classes were to be cancelled for the day. "We're off to Stroud Island. Usual assignments, everyone. Older guys help the new kids. And no nonsense, eh!"

Once outside the chapel, the boys chattered in anticipation of a sunny, fun-filled day. Smiling and shaking his head, Andrews overlooked the boys' many breaches of protocol.

Three buses pulled up to the school's back door on schedule. The students loaded food and drink aboard and clamoured for the best seats. Willoughby-Wallows, short pants flapping about his pale, sparrow-like legs, dashed to the last bus and hurried past Miss Strupples who stepped aboard behind him. She had determined to make sure none of the lucky lottery 'winners' missed out on the trip. As he made his way to the rear seat, the Greek and Latin professor fussed with his fly rod, landing net and creel – those three universal symbols of hopeful anticipation. Little did he know how thoroughly his hopes for a day of fishing would be dashed.

The yellow and black procession snaked its way around the buildings towards the school's front gate. As the buses approached the main drive, most of the students – but none of the faculty – waved to Professor Warneke. The big man stood on the lawn, a nine iron in his hand. As Strupples glared at him through the back window of the third bus, he lobbed a ball high into the air and blew the furious woman a kiss.

When the buses arrived at the docks, Mr. Fitzroy excused himself. He explained that he had some urgent, unfinished business to conduct and hurried off with the senior skipper. Strupples appointed herself acting headmaster and assigned tasks to the other teachers. Despite their obvious disinclination to comply, they did so. The Science teacher personally supervised the students as they carried food from buses to boats. The headmaster returned and, in passing, gave instructions to staff members on the first two boats before boarding the third vessel. Strupples walked the dock looking for strays and then stepped aboard the lead boat. As the crew readied to cast off lines, the skipper jogged down the dock, calling for Mr. Fitzroy. The headmaster stepped ashore and waved.

"Telephone— they said it's urgent," the gentleman announced. "This way, please, Mr. Fitzroy."

Strupples poked her head through an open deck hatch as the headmaster hurried past her towards shore. "Hurry back, Sir," she cried. "Hurry or you'll miss the boat. We're all ready to go."

The headmaster followed the skipper to the ticket office where they shook hands. Fitzroy kept his end of the bargain by presenting the man with a pint of rum. The skipper jogged to the boats, explained that the harbourmaster had ordered him off the dock and made weigh. Fitzroy watched the three vessels edge out into the river and swing their bows into the current before running down the dock, dramatically gesturing for the boats to return.

Willoughby-Wallows' eyes drank in the beauty of the islands. Vast, smooth granite sheets sloped down to the water's edge. The leaves hinted of the coming crimson and gold spectacle of autumn. Sumacs were already turning blood-red. The weather could not have been better nor the students more enthusiastic. The only boy not elated was Emerson Jenks. While the others sang *Ninety-nine Bottles of Beer on the Wall* and endless verses of *The Quartermaster's Store*, Emerson thought only of the pranks he could have planned had he known about Stroud Island sooner.

The boats entered a shallow bay and approached its deserted wharf. The students rejoiced to see that they would have the island park to themselves. Willoughby-Wallows felt a tug on his arm. "Wilf," shouted Strupples over the clamour being made by the students. She had a boy in tow. "Wilf, get to the tower as soon as we're ashore. Young Mr. Connors here will show you the way."

"Tower?" gasped Willoughby-Wallows.

"They jump off it," explained Strupples. "It can be a bit dangerous."

"Golly," he replied with a gulp. "How'm I supposed to stop them?"

"No, no," instructed Strupples. "You just make sure no one is forced to jump. That's all. You know… no teasing and double-dog-daring, eh?"

The boats bumped the dock and the crew hopped ashore to secure lines. Connors dragged Willoughby-Wallows off the boat, along the dock, up the rocks and across the island. Even so, two students made the tower before them. The Greek and Latin professor stared up twenty feet to the top of the beacon as the two boys climbed its ladder. He fought off an attack of vertigo as he peeked over the edge of the cliff. Thirty feet below, the river raged and roared between Stroud Island and the mainland. He gasped and stumbled back as two bodies flashed past. The boys hit the churning water feet first, their arms held stiffly by their sides, and disappeared. Slack-jawed, Willoughby-Wallows scanned the water's surface for signs of the two daredevils. In answer to his prayers, the duo surfaced thirty feet downstream. They swam to shore, climbed a steep path and raced back to repeat the death-defying feat.

Over two hours later, Fong finally found the blackfly bitten Greek and Latin teacher. "Where've you been all morning?" Fong asked. "We've missed you."

"Here. Supervising attempted suicide," answered Willoughby-Wallows. "I don't know how these kids do it. They scare me half to death, Mitch. I can't swim, you know."

Fong looked up at the tower and down at the water. "Swim?" he said with a laugh. "You'd probably break your neck when you hit the water. Anyways, we have to chase everyone back for lunch now. We'll split up and meet at the far end."

Willoughby-Wallows ordered his dozen jumpers to the picnic shelter, then strolled along the river to the far end of the island. He found Fong waiting. "That wasn't so bad, Mitch," declared Willoughby-Wallows and turned to go.

"Whoa!" cried Fong. "Where do you think you're going?"

"To eat," answered Willoughby-Wallows.

"Not quite yet, my friend," replied Fong and pointed to a massive chunk of rock hardly large enough to be called an island. A channel, twenty feet across and two feet deep, separated it from Stroud proper. "We wade across here," explained Fong as he kicked off his sandals and began to roll up his trouser legs.

"You're kidding!" declared Willoughby-Wallows. "Why?"

"There's a small island with a beach down at the other end. We have to check it out. It's not far."

"No sense in both of us—" began Willoughby-Wallows. Fong's expression prompted the younger teacher to remove his sandals. He followed his companion into bone-numbing, heart-stopping cold water. "Remember, I can't swim," warned Willoughby-Wallows.

"I suggest you try not to fall in then," replied Fong.

"Lordy— how do they stand the cold?" complained Willoughby-Wallows. Fong pushed on to the far shore and his companion, ooching and ouching, stumbled along behind. Two trips through the icy water proved easy going compared to the trek through the swamp. The last of the season's blackflies savaged both men.

After lunch, the students formed two teams for *Capture the Flag*. The game had no set rules so generated endless griping and grousing, debates and accusations of cheating. Teachers were expected to adjudicate disputes. As near as the adults could make out, one team pretended they were wild boars while their opponents imitated fox-threatened hens. The boys raced hither, thither and yon, and screamed for the entire afternoon while the unenthusiastic umpires pulled out tufts of their own hair. As always, when the boars and hens were called to dinner and their arguing ended, the game was declared a stalemate.

As shadows fled eastward and the western sky turned red, the adults patrolled the landing area as carefully as guards patrol a prison exercise yard. Strupples and the four other staff members had to ensure that none of their charges escaped into the woods. That would only prolong their stay on the island.

"I wish the boats would come," said Strupples with a long sigh. "This place is starting to feel like a penal colony." These words marked the beginning of an episode that lived on in infamy as *The Great Stroud Island Duck Hunt.*

Twelve mallards paddled about near the dock. Clearly, they were conscious of the two-legged predators harassing and haranguing them. The ducks scorned their tormentors. One belligerent bird badgered the boys by approaching to within five feet and quacking. A student with primitive hunter-gatherer instincts hefted a rock the size of a five-pin bowling ball, ran the length of the dock and launched the missile. Eleven ducks, heeding the adage about discretion and valour, engaged in a hasty discussion and redeployed to the far side of the bay. Their mate, long-suited in bravery or short-suited in brainpower – there is a fine line between fearlessness and folly – displayed more bravado. He dawdled until he deemed it too dangerous to delay his departure a moment longer, then paddled away unaware that death was about to drop dangerously near, if not upon him. The duck dodged left then doubled back, managing to manoeuvre to the very spot the rock chose to enter the water. His timing proved impeccable – tragically impeccable. At the last possible moment the duck unfolded his wings to take flight. Several pounds of Precambrian granite splashed down near or on the incautious bird. Water shot into the air and rained back down on the rippled surface of the water. No one ever fully explained what happened to the duck. Every eye turned shoreward at the crucial moment of impact.

When Strupples saw the granite orb rocket skyward she shrieked and ran to the dock. She broke through the crowd just in time to witness the last of the air bubbles rise to the surface and disturb a few floating feathers. The Science teacher did not need the little grey cells of a Hercule Poirot to solve the mystery. Everyone heard boys screaming, "Ballard brained a duck! Ballard brained a duck!"

The boatmen with their lone passenger, the apologetic Mr. Fitzroy, arrived to find Ballard chest deep in icy cold water and calf deep in the ooze beneath it. Under Strupples' watchful eye, the boy's feet felt about in vain, trying to fish out the mallard's mortal remains – if there were any mortal remains to recover. Some witnesses claimed the duck was a goner. Others insisted the mad mallard had, in the confusion of the moment, made good his escape.

The stench of slime and decay emanating from Ballard made him a pariah to both his schoolmates and his teachers the entire way home. Never again did those who witnessed the event hear the term 'lucky duck' without remembering that year's Stroud Island trip.

+ – × ÷

The teachers supervised the boys until the leftovers were deposited in the kitchen. Locking up should have marked the end of their trying day. But their trials were far from over.

Fong pushed his door open and slammed it shut behind him. A metallic clatter stopped him in his tracks. He turned to find his doorknob missing. He peeked through the crack under his door and discovered the outside knob – the knob with the slide bar – resting upon the corridor floor. Shaking his head in disgust, he began to ponder his most likely means of egress.

Von Baumgartner entered his room, made his way to his desk and gave the chain of his teller's lamp a tug. The light did not come on; his clock-radio did. Rock and roll blared from the box at over ninety decibels. He tried to shut it off. Every control knob was missing. When the old man's attempt to smother the sound with a pillow failed, he reached behind his desk and removed the plug. The racket continued. By the time von Baumgartner located the radio's newly arranged and well-hidden power source, neighbours were pounding on his door.

Darling snapped his wall switch up and down only to discover that his ceiling light no longer functioned. Both his floor and desk lamps had blown bulbs. He noticed that someone had tampered with his bed, tutted loudly and grumbled, "Short-sheeted. How childish!" In frustration, he tugged at his bedding without noticing the monofilament fishing line attached to the bedspread. The line loosened the tape that held a clear plastic sheet to the ceiling. The plastic sheet fluttered open and enough rice and confetti for a dozen June weddings rained down around the astounded gentleman.

Strupples spent twenty minutes removing two rolls of duct tape from her door. She wasted another hour searching in vain for a second prank: a prank that did not exist.

Fitzroy, after a rare day off, panicked when he tried to enter his office. He pushed on the doors which opened about six inches before gently closing again. The headmaster recalled Emerson Jenks' ghost stories and slapped his forehead in self-derision. He pressed an ear to the door but heard nothing. "You can't get out of there without facing me," he shouted and pushed on the doors – harder this time. His second attempt to force his way into his office was met with greater resistance. "Look here! I'm way too tired for this nonsense," he declared. "Let's end this now, shall we?"

No one responded. The man backed up six feet and ran at the doors. On contact, two thick shock cords snapped and the doors sprang open. After hopping halfway across the office on one foot, Fitzroy lost his balance, ricocheted off an armchair and tumbled to the floor.

Willoughby-Wallows, who had locked his door, was the only member of the Stroud Island supervisory team to escape Warneke's attention.

The English master arrived first to breakfast the following morning. When von Baumgartner entered the refectory, Warneke greeted him with a hearty, "And how are we this fine morning?"

Willoughby-Wallows ignored a similar greeting and shook his head as he passed Warneke. Strupples, approaching like stormy weather, came up short at the end of the English master's table.

"Hark! What light through yonder window breaks?" quoted Warneke and raised his coffee cup in a toast. Strupples delivered a tongue lashing that would have flayed a thinner-skinned man. Warneke sat, serene in silent superiority. He waited for the woman to stop for breath before saying, "Dear Madame, is that any way to behave in the presence of gentlemen?"

Strupples laughed a derisive laugh. "Oh, don't you dare *Dear Madame* me. If you ever acted like a gentleman—" she stammered and raised her nose in the air. "A gentleman, Sir, would show a lady more respect." The other men, enjoying the free entertainment, began to titter. "And you—" growled Strupples, turning on her male companions. "You are no better than he is. It's no wonder not one of you has found a woman stupid enough to marry you."

Shamefaced, the men turned to their breakfasts.

Warneke stood and broke the ensuing silence. "Allow me to apologize, Miss Strupples. If I've offended," continued the object of the woman's disdain, "it's only because I was unaware there was a lady anywhere hereabouts!" The woman found herself unable to speak, so the English master continued, "And you do err, Ma'am... we gentlemen are not *unmarried*." He swept his hand in a wide arc. "We are *wife-free*."

Miss Strupples struggled to find words capable of expressing her feelings. She sputtered for a moment then cried, "You, Sir, are a lout... an evil, vile man... a... a..." She ran out of invective and breath and said no more.

"Goodness!" declared Professor Warneke in a voice intended for all to hear. "Is that any way for the most attractive woman at St. Timothy's to behave?"

Little Green Apples

After *The Chapel Landing Affair*, Emerson put to rest any concerns he had about Meddows out-pranking him. He figured he had the older boy sized up well enough, that he represented no serious threat. Meddows had capitulated, thought Emerson. In this, Emerson erred.

Meddows took to ignoring the new boy. He did ask after Mr. and Mrs. Jenks but only occasionally and for reasons Emerson could not quite fathom. Meddows, day by day, grew more determined to settle the score. There was no need to hurry. It was still early in the year, early in the race. Emerson Jenks was going nowhere. The older boy knew, as does any good prankster, that one cannot afford to frighten away his mark. Accordingly, he backed off.

When a school is home to more than one hundred boys and has a kitchen full of food, either the boys or the food need to be locked up. The boys of St. Timothy's had to roam free, so the kitchen was declared off-limits and secured under lock and key. These precautions deterred but did not eliminate raids on the kitchen. Each year, despite threats of severe punishment, two or three enterprising fellows who seemed destined for a career in crime found ways to circumvent security.

Only one food item was in seemingly endless supply. St. Timothy's orchard was blessed with big, old trees that produced small, mealy apples and newer, smaller trees that produced plump, juicy fruit. Bins of apples lined the root cellar walls. A bushel of apples, free for the taking, sat outside the kitchen. From Labour Day until the end of picking and packing, a walk to the orchard was all that stood between a hungry student and the freshest fruit anywhere. The refectory tables saw a steady flow of apple pie, apple cobbler, apple cake, baked apples, apple-pan-doughty and, on rare occasions, apple strudel. There was sweet apple cider, apple juice, apple jam, apple jelly, apple butter and applesauce by the barrel.

One might ask why, with such a glut of apples, any student would raid the apple orchard next door? Everyone knew that the severest punishment awaited any student caught stealing. If peaches, plums or even pears were available, one might understand a fellow's willingness to run the risk. But why would anyone in a school chock-a-block with apples purloin his neighbour's fruit? Meddows asked himself these questions, came up with very good answers and set about planning a prank.

On the first Sunday of October, Meddows joined Emerson and Guardiano as they stood in the queue at the mail basket, waiting to post their weekly letters home. "Did you tell your folks hello from me, Jenks?" Meddows asked and nodded towards Emerson's letter.

"Nope," replied Emerson. "Why?"

"'Cause my folks ain't comin' on Thanksgiving," answered Meddows, "and I thought I'd wangle an invite out to dinner from yours."

"We'll see," Emerson replied and shrugged.

Moments later, Emerson heard someone call Meddows' name. Burns jogged up, intent upon mailing his letter, and barged into the line beside his buddy. Meddows did Burns a favour by pushing him back into the hallway before Guardiano saw to the task.

"Whatcha think you're doin', Burns," grumbled Guardiano and jerked his thumb towards the end of the long queue.

"But we gotta talk, Meddows," whined Burns. "C'mon!"

With a shrug, Meddows handed his letter to Emerson and pointed to the mail basket. He and Burns moved off for a *tête-à-tête*. Burns whispered and gesticulated. Meddows signalled his friend to hush. With their foreheads almost touching, they moved further down the hall. Emerson tapped the letters against his palm and observed Meddows and Burns out of the corner of his eye. He posted the letters, instructed his friend to keep an eye out for him and approached the two conspirators.

"What's up?" Emerson asked.

"Get lost, creep," demanded Burns.

Emerson stood his ground. Burns shoved him away. Emerson waved off Guardiano's swift advance.

"Go on, beat it," ordered Meddows. "Scram!"

Meddows placed his fist against Emerson's chest and pushed. Later, he admitted that it had been a stupid thing to do. Guardiano slapped a giant maul over Meddows' hand and squeezed. Burns took several quick steps back as his friend howled.

"Uncle. Uncle!" Meddows cried and hopped from foot to foot as he vainly tried to free his fingers from Guardiano's powerful grip.

"Hold on, Guardiano," cautioned Emerson. "Don't hurt him, eh." The big boy eased his hold, but did not let go.

"Yeah, listen to Jenks, man," cried Meddows. "Let go! You're still hurtin' me."

"Yeah, don't," demanded a wide-eyed Burns.

Emerson waited a few seconds then said, "Better let him go, Guardiano."

Guardiano gave Meddows' hand one final, bone crushing squeeze: a reminder to the enemy of his brute strength.

"See you later," said Emerson to his friend. Guardiano backed away as far as the entrance to the stairwell and gave Emerson a look that asked if he was sure? Emerson nodded and Guardiano, after a show of reluctance, headed to the auditorium to practice guitar.

"Man!" moaned Meddows, nursing his hand. "Yuh better keep Quasimodo there on a chain, Jenks."

"Yeah, right!" Emerson ignored the slur cast upon his friend. He repeated his question as if the hand-squeezing incident was ancient history. "So, what are you two guys up to, eh?"

Meddows turned and walked away, opening and closing his hand and looking back at Emerson. Burns followed. After they turned the corner and started down the stairs, Emerson followed. He listened to the echo of their footsteps as they skipped down the stairs. Flight by flight, Emerson scurried down the steps after them. At the base of the stairway, Emerson peeked around a corner and watched the boys pace along the basement corridor. He trailed behind the two seniors until they entered Disraeli Hall. The boys' carelessness amused him. They had not looked back once. "*Semper vigilate!*" Emerson muttered. "Yeah, right!"

Emerson arrived in the student recreation building just in time to see the shower room door swing closed. He tiptoed down the hall and laid an ear to the door. Just as he was beginning to make out what Meddows was saying, Burns pulled the door open, lunged at and collared the eavesdropper. Meddows helped his toady haul Emerson into the locker room. He held the startled, stammering boy by the collar. Burns left to make sure Guardiano was not lurking about. He found the big boy plucking the strings on Emerson's guitar and returned to Meddows with the news.

"Spyin' on us, eh, Jenks?" accused Burns. "Let's teach 'im a lesson, Meddows."

"What do you think you're doin', Jenks?" barked Meddows. He sounded more annoyed than angry. "What'll we do with 'im, Burnsy?"

"I dunno," answered Burns. "But we gotta teach 'im a lesson."

"Maybe… no! What if…" Meddows hemmed and hawed while massaging his chin.

Emerson, not yet fully recovered from his fright, stuttered, "I… I… I won't tell… honest. I ain't no— no squealer."

Meddows looked at Burns. Burns stared back. They turned their eyes on Emerson who gawked first at one boy and then the other. Meddows scratched his head. "Well, I guess…" he began.

Burns interjected. "Oh, no! No way, Meddows. No way! Forget it!"

"Ah, c'mon, Burnsy," pleaded Meddows.

"If he's in then I'm out," threatened Burns. "Remember that statue thing? Anything goes wrong and he'll squawk like… like a…" Burns waved a dismissive hand and stormed off.

"Thanks a lot, Jenks," grumbled Meddows as he headed for the door. "Wait up, Burnsy. Ah, c'mon," he shouted. Burns did not wait up.

Emerson ran after Meddows. "I'll do it," he cried and tugged on the older boy's arm.

Meddows swatted Emerson's hand away then turned and grabbed his shoulder. A menacing scowl covered his face. "Do what?" he demanded. "Just how much did you hear, eh?"

"N–n–nothin', I swear! I didn't hear nothin'," Emerson stuttered. In his state of shock, all his mother's grammar lessons abandoned him. "But I know— you guys were up to somethin'. And I know I could do it way better than that stupid Burns."

"Fat chance," replied Meddows. "You're way too puny and wimpy, Jenks. Besides—"

"—Bet I can," bragged Emerson.

"Well..." Meddows considered the offer, dragging out the word 'well' and stroking his chin again. "I guess we could talk about it. But not here." Meddows directed the younger boy outside.

"Okay, here's the plan, Jenks..."

Emerson listened to all Meddows had to say. He would analyse the prank later to see if he could turn it back on its creator.

+ − × ÷

The following Saturday evening, Emerson, as he was instructed, sat with the TV room crowd. Meddows slipped in and nudged him from behind. Emerson did not turn. The older boy leaned forward and whispered, "Locker room. Two minutes." He waited a few seconds before leaving.

As arranged, the two boys met and donned dark pants and sweaters. Meddows pulled the collar of his black turtleneck up over his nose. He placed a black toque on his head and pulled it down until it covered his eyebrows. Incredulous, Emerson had to avert his gaze to hide his amusement. The two boys exited the building, circled the gymnasium, passed between the hockey rink and the handball courts and, after checking to see that no one was about, raced across open ground to the powerhouse.

From the darkest corner of a handball court, Burns watched the pair's progress. From deep in the shadow of the smokestack, Guardiano observed the two nearly invisible boys until they passed through a hedge. He kept a sharp eye on Burns' hiding spot until the boy slunk out of the shadows and returned to the school. Two minutes after Burns quit his post, Guardiano abandoned his position. Before entering the main building, he cast his eyes in the direction in which Emerson had gone and considered disobeying his friend's instructions not to follow. Finally, he walked slowly towards the auditorium, still worried about his friend's welfare.

Meddows and Emerson slipped past the root cellar and tennis courts, mere shadows in the starlight. Before Emerson stepped through the hedge, he took a quick look back to where Guardiano was hiding, drew a deep breath and resigned himself to the fact that, for better or worse, he was now totally on his own. The two boys dashed to the school's outdoor shrine. Meddows led the way through the thick brush behind the structure. Emerson followed. The evening's breeze made more noise than the two boys. They finally reached the school's property line and scurried down a disused tractor trail until they reached the end of a ramshackle fence that ran along the edge of the neighbour's property. From there, they crept along the base of an even higher, eighteen-inch thick stone wall that ran along the back of the orchard.

For several seconds, Emerson stared up at the top of the wall, unaware that Meddows stared at him. "Okay," whispered Meddows, "you wait here. I'll toss the apples over to yuh. Now, I'm gunna need a boost."

Emerson continued eying the wall. Up close, it appeared a much more intimidating obstacle than it had from a distance. "But… uh, Meddows…" he mumbled.

"What?" demanded the older boy. "Yuh ain't gunna chicken out on me now, are yuh?"

"No way! It's just… well… I mean… how are you going to get back out?"

"Through the fence," growled Meddows in frustration and pointed back the way they had come. "Once you've got the bag, yuh jus' hightail it back to the corner. I'll meet yuh there."

"But—" began Emerson.

"But nothin'," Meddows replied. "You just do what I say. And be quiet about it. If anything goes wrong, you're on your own. Just take off. Don't worry about me. We'll meet up back in the dorm."

"But, Meddows. Why not just go in through the fence in the first place?" asked Emerson, recalculating the wall's height.

"Too noisy, stupid. The old girl would hear me before I got anywhere near them apples. Look… are yuh gunna boost me or not?" Emerson did not answer. "Did yuh even remember the bag, Jenks?" asked Meddows. Emerson pulled the sack from his pocket. Meddows stuffed it under his sweater then pressed his hands against the wall. He lifted his leg high. Emerson cupped his hands under the raised foot.

"On three," mumbled Meddows, "and if anything goes wrong, yuh better keep your trap shut. One, two, three!" Meddows pushed down with his foot. Emerson lifted up with all his strength only to have his fingers slip apart under his companion's weight.

"Ah, c'mon, Jenks," Meddows croaked. "We ain't got all night."

"You're way too heavy, Meddows," whined Emerson.

"Oh, man! Told yuh," chided Meddows. "C'mon. Let's get outta here." In disgust, Meddows yanked his turtleneck down, pulled off his toque and started back towards the school.

Emerson shifted his gaze several times from his retreating accomplice to the top to the wall and back. "Wait, Meddows, wait," called Emerson as he ran after the older boy. "You can boost me over, right?"

"No way, Jenks."

"Yeah, way!" insisted Emerson. "Boost me over."

"No way! When I say no, I mean no. Let's just get outta here. I'll go get Burnsy."

"Come on, Meddows. Boost me. I can do it," pleaded Emerson. "I swear."

Meddows took half a minute to reply. "Look, Jenks, if yuh get caught you'd better not mention my name," warned Meddows. "And remember: if anything goes wrong, I'm outta here and you're on your own."

"I know," answered Emerson. "Now give me a boost."

"Once you've got the apples, yuh gotta toss 'em to me then get through that fence— and fast," added Meddows. "So check things out and mark your spot soon as you're on the other side."

The two boys returned to the wall face. When Emerson placed a foot in his companion's cupped hands, he intended to count to three. But Meddows did not wait. He heaved the smaller boy into the air. Emerson gasped, flung himself forward and landed with his arms draped over the wall. In a desperate attempt to avoid slipping backwards, he threw a leg up and over and found himself sprawled atop the structure, shaking. He had thought the height intimidating when he stood on the ground looking up. Prostrate on the wall, he gazed down into a black abyss. The prospect of jumping terrified him.

"What yuh waitin' for, Jenks?" whispered Meddows.

"I can't see what's down there," replied Emerson.

"Yuh can't just stay on the wall, stupid. She'll spot you against the sky," hissed Meddows.

"It's too far down, Meddows."

"You think this side's any better, Jenks? C'mon— one side or the other but let's go."

Emerson gulped, swung his legs over the edge of the wall, hung by his fingers and dropped with a thud into the orchard. He could see nothing but the light from a window filtering through the trees. He strained his ears but heard only his own breathing. The sweet, heavy scent of rotting apples came to him on the cool night air. As far as he could tell, the layout of the orchard was exactly as Meddows had described it.

Before entering the even deeper shadow beneath the trees, Emerson crawled to the fence and located a gap through which to make a speedy get-away. From the gap in the fence, he made a beeline to the middle of the orchard. He found no fruit on the first tree he visited and just four pitifully small apples on the second. Disappointed and confused, he climbed into the tree. He was well off the ground, searching in vain for the succulent fruit Meddows had described when a dog yapped and a porch light flashed on. No forty-watt back porch bulb could produce such a light. The beam was like those used by the British Home Guard to spot enemy bombers during the London blitz. Emerson froze in place. Meddows threw himself face down on the grass.

"I see you there!" It was an old woman's voice. The dog continued its yapping.

A picture of the wicked witch of the west and Toto flashed in Emerson's mind. "Nothin' but a frail old lady," he whispered. Emerson heard a screen door slam and saw the bent crone, cane in hand, emerge from the glare. The wizened figure reached the edge of the deck, a stick-thin silhouette against the blinding light.

"I see you there!" she repeated.

Emerson considered turning himself in but, on the off chance that the old girl was bluffing, he held his position. He watched her as she veered away from his tree and approached the fence. "Ah, she's bluffing," the boy whispered in relief. Emerson's mind was processing information quickly now. "She's spotted Meddows, not me." The thought brought a smile to the boy's face. The woman hobbled along close to the fence before executing a quick turn, cutting off Emerson's escape route. The boy's smile disappeared. His mouth fell open. His eyes widened. His mind raced in an effort to revise his flight plan.

The woman made her way to the base of his tree and parked

immediately beneath him. When she pointed her cane at Emerson, the possibility of a bluff vanished completely from his mind.

"I've got you now. You stay right where you are, you little thief," the crone shouted. "The police are on their way." On hearing the word 'police' Emerson decided to vacate the premises with all possible haste. He jumped. The descent was quick but far from painless. Later, Emerson reported bouncing off every branch on his way to the ground.

Typically, when one speaks of a windfall, one speaks of a boon. The Bay Street investor boasts of windfall profits. A sweepstakes winner says he came upon a windfall. Emerson never spoke fondly of windfalls after his daring leap. For him, they represented a bane and no boon. The crab apples proved puny in size but prodigious in number. The trees had scattered their little green apples in a conspiracy to foil Emerson's escape.

The boy alit feet first, little more than a yard from the astonished woman. He pitched forward and went down hard. Before he regained his feet, the old lady set upon him with a vengeance. She straddled the fallen figure, raised her cane over her head and brought it down across the boy's back. Up went the weapon with a whistle. Down it came with a thwack. "Take that, you thief," she shrieked several times as she poked and prodded, jabbing with her walking stick the way a fencer thrusts with his *épée*.

Emerson yelped at each stroke. Meddows winced as his companion's shouts and the woman's shrieks shattered the silence. The owner of the little green apples continued beating upon Emerson's back and buttocks as he crawled and clawed his way towards the fence and freedom.

"Run," screamed Emerson on exiting the orchard. He bowled Meddows over in his headlong retreat. Emerson did not stop to see if his cohort in crime had taken the warning to heart. Meddows picked himself up, brushed himself off and began trudging back towards St. Timothy's. The old woman remained on her side of the fence and taunted the thieves, daring them to return for more of the same medicine.

In the dormitory, Emerson winced and grimaced as Meddows rubbed lotion on his back. Not until the pain abated somewhat, did Emerson speak. "Thanks, Meddows. Sorry I screwed things up so bad."

"No sweat, Jenks," replied Meddows. "Yikes!" he added as he examined the welts. "That's really gotta hurt!"

"Yeah," groaned Emerson. "Man alive, for such a scrawny old lady—"

"I know."

"But I don't care as long as we don't get kicked out," whispered Emerson.

"*Kicked out?*" echoed Meddows and laughed.

"You heard her. She called the cops," cried Emerson in near panic.

Meddows laughed so hard he had to hold his sides. He could not believe the terrified look on Emerson's face. "Ah, don't worry, Jenks. She says the same thing every year," said Meddows. "But the cops never show."

In the ensuing silence, Meddows decided that it was high time to withdraw. He backed up several steps, turned and took his leave. "Got'yuh, Jenks," he called out smugly as he stepped through the doorway and walked away.

Emerson remained on his bed, immobilized by Meddows' revelation. He reviewed the process that led to his failure, from the line-up after letter writing the previous Sunday to Meddows' recent departure. He berated himself and disparaged Meddows and Burns. Then he eased himself onto his feet, hobbled down the stairs and through the chapel to the foyer. He stood in the doorway, looking out over the school's front lawn. Through the trees, he could see the neighbour's backyard, still flooded with light. After twenty uneventful minutes, when all but sure that the police were not on their way, Emerson removed four little green apples from his pocket and tossed them far out onto the grass.

"You crossed the line, Meddows," Emerson muttered through clenched teeth. "And I'll get you for it too." As he pulled the door to, Emerson repeated the threat, "I'm going to get you but good, Meddows, if it's the last thing I ever do."

As he made his way back through the foyer, his eyes fell upon the school's crest. In the dim light, Emerson could just make out its words. They mocked him. "*Semper vigilate*," the disgusted boy mumbled.

+ − × ÷

The following Saturday afternoon, Mr. and Mrs. Jenks made their first visit back to St. Timothy's. Repeatedly, Judy Jenks tried to give Emerson a hug. Emerson evaded her every attempt. It was not that he minded hugging his mother. He just could not afford to have her discover the welts that criss-crossed his back. He had wracked his brain trying to dream up a reasonable explanation. He had come up with no even remotely plausible account.

Before leaving for lunch, Peter Jenks spoke with Mr. Fitzroy in the headmaster's office. "Emerson's written home every week," reported Mr. Jenks, "and we're surprised – but happy, mind you. He hasn't mentioned his friends – not once. We're so pleased."

Fitzroy placed his hands palms down on his desk and pushed his chair back. "Oh, I can well imagine you would be," he declared. "He's not mentioned them here either… thank goodness. Not since the day he arrived." The headmaster eyed the roll-top for a second.

Mr. Jenks wrinkled his nose and looked askance at the headmaster. With a shrug, he forced himself to dismiss recurring doubts about the man. "Well, anyways, you were right…" said Mr. Jenks, "about downplaying the whole thing, I mean. I've got to hand it to you there."

"Well, to tell the truth, I was a lot more confident in my plan than I let on," confessed Mr. Fitzroy as he stood. "I just didn't want to get your hopes up, you know. We can be thankful that all that nonsense is behind us, eh? The last thing I need 'round here," he added with a laugh, "is your son's strange friends. I'm sure you know what I mean." Fitzroy winked.

Mr. Jenks did not respond in the manner the headmaster expected. Jenks senior threw his head so far to one side that it all but bounced off his shoulder. "I… I… I don't know what to say," Jenks stammered. "His friends are fairly decent… They've never deliberately damaged… Maybe, you know, they get a bit… Well, you know…"

"No matter! It's not an issue anymore," replied Headmaster Fitzroy with a dismissive wave. He drew his watch from his waistcoat pocket and glanced at the time. "Jenks – I'm sorry, force of habit – I meant to say *Emerson* has made a number of regular type friends here. He's fit in quite nicely actually—which reminds me. We encourage boys whose parents can come… well, to invite a boy or two whose family couldn't…"

"Oh, of course," replied Mr. Jenks, still trying to comprehend what the headmaster had meant when he used the words 'regular type friends'. The thought that Mr. Fitzroy had never met Emerson's friends crossed his mind. He replied, "Judy and I'd be happy to have a couple of the fellows join us. Emerson would probably like that too. Are Meddows' parents here?"

"Oh, my, no! They won't be coming," explained Fitzroy as he escorted his guest towards the office doors. "Meddows is from Halifax you know. But it's interesting that you mentioned him, Mr. Jenks. You see, we've noticed that Meddows has seemed quite interested in…" he paused, "actually I'd say quite protective of Emerson. That's not all that common a thing for a senior boy to do. He sort of keeps an eye out for the lad, I think… keeping him out of trouble, eh?"

Mr. and Mrs. Jenks, Emerson and two friends lunched together in town that afternoon. Meddows ate in the school's half-empty refectory. At the restaurant, Emerson experienced an awkward moment. His father, in a magnanimous mood, suggested that the three boys go swimming the following day. "What do you think, Emerson? Angelo?" To Emerson's dismay, both friends were eager to swim. In fact, they were wildly enthusiastic while he, given the condition of his back, was most definitely not keen on the idea. By the end of the meal, he had managed to talk his two friends into bowling instead.

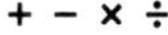

On Thanksgiving Day afternoon, on their way home, Mr. Jenks turned to his wife. "I just don't know about that headmaster," he said, shaking his head. "What strange, strange things come out of that man's mouth!"

Just You Watch This

It took Emerson days to dissuade an enraged Angelo Guardiano from delivering swift and harsh retribution to Meddows for his treachery. Although, for Emerson, those days were sheer misery, he stoically endured the physical and emotional pain. His back throbbed. He felt humiliated. He plotted his revenge.

Meddows, in contrast, enjoyed halcyon days. He told and retold his tale of triumph to as many as wanted to listen and to more than a few who did not. Like a fisherman's repeated accounts of the one that got away, the story grew out of all proportion.

Emerson told himself that if Meddows wanted war, then war it would be. He decided to play the dupe and bide his time. To Guardiano, Emerson confided, "I'll get him back myself, Ange. And, when I do everyone will know I got him."

+ − × ÷

On the first Sunday morning in November, Emerson and his schoolmates finished their letters home and lined up to drop them into the mail basket. Emerson and Guardiano dawdled before queuing up behind all but the slowest of their mates. Emerson observed Meddows, the enemy general, Burns, his lieutenant, Sergeant O'Neil and Private Matthews, the gang's newest recruit. As soon as the Meddows gang had left the corridor, Emerson and Guardiano asked their neighbours to see to the mailing of their letters and ambled down the hall, away from the crowd. They spoke in whispers.

"You remember what you have to do… right, Angelo?" Emerson asked.

"Sure I do, Em. I pull the curtains open really wide and lift that window up as high as it'll go," replied Guardiano.

"And you tell anybody who's up there—" prompted Emerson.

Guardiano did not let his friend finish. "Yeah, yeah, I know. I tell 'em I'm gonna to be real sore if they touch anything. And I remember everything else too. I ain't stupid, you know, Emerson."

"Man alive... sorry, Angelo. Really I am," replied Emerson as he dragged a hand down over his face. "I know you're not. It's just that I'm so nervous... you know."

"Don't worry, Em. I'll do just like you said." The big boy hurried up the stairs to the junior dormitory.

Emerson jogged back to the foot of the stairs to the senior dorm and dallied in the deserted classroom corridor. He ran over each step of his plan and readied himself to advance upon the foe. He strained to listen as the dormitory door opened and closed. By twos and threes, the senior students strode past the lone boy at the bottom of the stairs without paying him the slightest heed. At last, the voices Emerson had hoped to hear tumbled loud and clear down the stairwell. He took a deep breath, stepped forward and started up the steps. "Here goes. Just you watch this, guys," he muttered. When Meddows and his three cronies faced him from the landing, Emerson stopped short and conjured up the most shocked and frightened expression he could muster.

"And where duh yuh think *you're* goin', Jenks?" sneered Matthews.

Emerson ignored the newest gang member. O'Neil and Burns might not have been there for all Emerson cared. "Sorry, Meddows," he whispered and backed away. His eyes darted from one boy to another.

"If you're not sorry, you're gunna be," replied Meddows after hushing the newest member of his gang. The leader of the pack continued to nibble at the bait. Now Emerson had only seconds to wait before setting the hook.

"Oh, now I'm scared out of my wits," replied Emerson and withdrew to the foot of the stairs. As one, the four senior students closed the gap. Upon receiving a signal from Meddows, his followers stopped and grinned in anticipation.

"I told yuh that mouth of yours was gunna get yuh in trouble," snarled Meddows.

Emerson, certain that his adversary was well hooked, challenged the older boy. "Yeah, sure... four of you against one of me... that's a real fair fight." In the ensuing silence, Emerson backed all the way into the corridor.

The gang made as if to pursue but Meddows stretched his arms across the stairway and halted their advance. “Whoa!” he ordered. “You guys stay outta this. He’s mine. *I’ll* take care of *him*.” The gang stared down at Emerson and waited, like jackals determining how best to finish off their cornered prey. Shoulder to shoulder, they nudged one another and leered.

“You guys just keep an eye out for Guardiano,” ordered Meddows. “Did he leave the dorm yet?”

Burns went to check. With his attention back on Emerson, Meddows continued, “Yuh just bought yourself a heap of hurt, Jenks.” He tried to fool Emerson with a head fake, then bolted down the last four steps. His momentum carried him past his target. Emerson stepped to the side with the grace of a matador. The tall boy stumbled slightly, caught his balance and lunged for his adversary as the smaller boy dodged past him. Emerson sprinted, full-out, down the corridor past several classrooms towards the second stairwell. Meddows followed in hot pursuit, never more than three strides behind.

The older boy was a lanky fellow but not particularly well coordinated. Emerson was short and a bit on the podgy side, but agile. All-in-all, the two were evenly matched… for speed. But, having allowed Emerson a head start, Meddows had no real chance of closing the gap unless his prey tripped.

Emerson continued up the stairs towards the junior dorm. He crossed the landing, yanked the door open, entered the dormitory and slammed the door behind him.

“What’s up, Jenks?” asked one of three junior boys who leapt aside to avoid a collision.

“Meddows is after me,” shouted Emerson as he passed. The three boys, and four more who overheard the comment, scurried from the dorm to avoid finding themselves in harm’s way. Emerson made for the open window at the end of the cubicle. He opened the doors of the locker next to the window, removed a brass cylinder from behind the curtain and tossed it into the locker. With his eyes riveted on the door, he awaited his pursuer. There could be no turning back now. Emerson drew a long breath and wondered what was delaying his adversary.

When Meddows saw Emerson head for the dormitory, he slowed his pace and chuckled. It was a menacing chuckle. He saw no reason for further exertion. As soon as Emerson ran up the stairs, he sealed his doom. There would be no escape now; his prey could not get past him. Burns, O'Neil and Matthews would block the only other path to freedom. Only the headmaster's decree that seniors not enter the junior dorm stood between Emerson and his demise. Meddows scorned all such rules. He savoured the foregone conclusion of the affair: victory over his archenemy. Seven juniors gave Meddows a wide berth as they fled past him. He mocked their frightened faces as they pressed themselves against the side wall to allow him to pass. On reaching the landing, he crossed to the door, pulled it open and stepped into the dormitory. First, he glanced towards Andrews' room, then towards Willoughby-Wallows' lodgings. Finally, he turned his full attention on Emerson who slammed the locker doors, turned and stood with his back pressed against them.

"What's in your locker, Jenks?" demanded Meddows and sneered.

"Nothin'!" replied Emerson as he slid his glasses up his nose. "You'll get in trouble for coming in here, you know."

"Nothin'?" repeated Meddows, ignoring Emerson's warning.

"Nothin'!"

"If yuh got nothin' in there," Meddows suggested, "yuh won't mind me opening it up. Right?" He took several paces down the aisle between its two rows of beds. Emerson protested and continued to deny that he had anything to hide.

"Don't you open this locker, Meddows, or else!" warned Emerson. His objections fanned the flames of Meddows' curiosity. The bigger boy pushed the smaller boy to one side and reached out to open the locker doors. "I wouldn't do that if I were you, Meddows. You're asking for big trouble," Emerson warned.

"Trouble? From you? Ha! Whatcha gunna do… tell Andrews on me?" He yanked the doors open. There, in plain view, lay an old fashioned, brass-bodied spyglass. "Ah ha! Nothin', eh?" Meddows picked up the glass and pulled it out to its full length. He moved past Emerson to the open window. Emerson backed away and took up a position near the exit from where he could see up and down the dormitory corridor and hear anyone approaching on the stairs. Meddows put the spyglass to his eye and took aim across the river. "Can't see diddly-squat with this stupid thing," he complained.

"Got to focus the thing first, Meddows. Man!" Emerson spoke in a derisive tone.

"Think I'm stupid, do yuh, Jenks?" asked Meddows without taking the glass away from his eye. "Is that it? We'll see about that in a minute." Meddows lowered the telescope and examined it. His face betrayed his bewilderment.

"You have to turn the eye piece first..." explained Emerson, "to focus it, eh."

"I know that," barked Meddows. "What do yuh take me for?" He began twisting the eyepiece around. "Just wanted to take a closer look." Meddows continued the twisting and turning action.

"Put it to your eye first. Man alive, you're thick, Meddows," Emerson teased. He could no longer hide his delight. A smirk crept across his face.

Meddows raised the telescope to his eye once more and turned the eyepiece first one way and then the other. "Still can't see nothin'," complained Meddows. "What a piece of junk!"

"Give it here then," demanded Emerson and narrowed the gap between himself and his would-be tormentor. Meddows tossed the glass to Emerson who caught it and quickly backed away. The older boy, having lost interest in the spyglass, renewed his interest in teaching his tormentor a lesson.

"Someday, somebody's gotta teach yuh some respect, Jenks," stated Meddows, "about that big mouth of yours, I mean. And I figure it might as well be today and it might as well be me." Meddows fixed his eyes on Emerson, took a step forward, then hesitated as his prey backed away. The predator's gaze shifted to the door.

In that moment of indecision, Emerson gained an even greater advantage. While keeping his eyes trained on Meddows, Emerson backed up, reached behind him and, finding the knob, opened the door and stopped, half in and half out of the dorm, front leg staying, back leg going. He knew he held the high ground, that in a retreat, as in real-estate, three things are essential: location, location and location.

As the older boy contemplated his next move, Burns approached from the senior dormitory. "C'mon, Meddows. What's keeping..." he asked as he entered the cubicle. He stopped and stared at his friend. "What the heck happened to you?"

"Nothin'," snarled Meddows. "Why?"

"Nothin'?" replied Burns with a laugh. He turned and yelled down the hall. "Hey, guys, O'Neil, Matthews, yuh gotta come see this… Jenks here gave Meddows a shiner."

"A shiner?" cried Meddows. His face paled, as he tried to fathom the meaning of Burns' statement.

"Yeah, a shiner," repeated Burns. "A black eye, man… and a good one too," he added as he pointed at Meddows' face and approached for a closer look. Burns burst into loud, rollicking laughter. Meddows' other toadies hurried down from the senior dorm. Matthews guffawed. O'Neil giggled.

Meddows put one hand to his eye, drew it back and examined it. His fingers were stained black. As if to ensure that this was no hallucination, he put his other hand to the same eye. It too was blackened by the experience. Emerson judged this an opportune time to withdraw and backed completely out of the dorm. He held the door open, prepared to slam it shut and run on a second's notice.

Burns fell onto a bed, drew his knees to his chest and howled with laughter. O'Neil and Matthews pointed towards and poked fun at their boon buddy. They leaned against one another and tried to stifle their guffaws and giggles. None of the gang, not even the leader, was in any mood to continue the chase. Meddows could not react. He could barely think. The boy stared at Emerson, opened and closed his mouth, but made no sound.

"Think you're pretty smart, eh, Jenks?" snarled Meddows finally. "Just you watch this." The boy paused and looked about the cubicle. He could think of no appropriate action to follow so idle a threat. A feeling of helplessness swept over him as he imagined the indignity and ignominy that awaited him if he lost face before his greatest enemy and his three friends. The gang grew silent, watching and waiting for their leader's next move. Fearing Meddows' wrath, they tried to ignore his embarrassing predicament.

Emerson's next utterance saved Meddows further chagrin. "Just don't touch anything else in that locker… or else," he warned.

In a huff, Meddows stomped back to the locker, reached inside, withdrew a pair of white boxer shorts and wiped his face on them. The result was one very badly stained pair of shorts and one even more badly stained visage. The right side of Meddows' face, from forehead to chin, was smeared with shiny bootblack. Burns, O'Neil and Matthews who had just regained their composure, began their performance anew.

Emerson shrugged and pleaded, "Ah, c'mon, Meddows... no need for that."

"Oh, yeah?" replied Meddows. His voice rose in both volume and pitch. "Let's see how you like this? How about..." He thought for only a moment and then tossed the shorts out the window. "Ha, ha, ha!" roared Meddows. "How do yuh like that, eh?"

"Ha, ha, ha," echoed the gang members. They sounded like a Greek chorus.

"That's it, toss his whole locker," suggested O'Neil.

Emerson took one step into the dorm. He kept an eye of Meddows' three friends. "That was a really stupid thing to do, you guys," he declared. He wondered if things had already gone a bit too far. The older boy's fury was becoming a concern – but not so much so that Emerson felt like ending the game. "It was just a joke, Meddows, calm down, eh," warned Emerson, "before you get us all into trouble."

Meddows ignored the sage advice. This was, in fact, just the result Emerson desired. Meddows howled. He sputtered. Animal sounds came out of his mouth. He returned to the locker and began throwing pyjamas, shirts, towels and various other articles of clothing out the window. "That'll teach you," shouted Meddows. "How do you like that, eh? And just you watch this." He opened the drawer at the bottom of the locker and pulled out shoes and slippers. They suffered the same fate as the boxers. "You can spend all your free time pickin' your stuff up off the lawn, Jenks."

"My stuff! Who said that was my stuff?" Emerson doubled over laughing.

Meddows would have had a fifty-fifty chance of nabbing his foe had he not stopped to look at the name on the so recently rearranged locker. "Fredericks?" cried Meddows. "Fredericks!" he repeated and bolted towards Emerson. By the time he reached the exit, Emerson had retreated to the landing, slammed the door and jammed his trusty doorstop under it. As Meddows attempted to gain access to the landing, his face, half black and half a fetching scarlet, had a run-in with the door. The door won.

"Yuh missed 'im by that much, Meddows," cried O'Neil, dragging out the word 'that' so as to mimic his latest TV hero.

The leader of the gang ignored the comment. "You're... you're... you're gunna be sorry, Jenks," threatened Meddows. He pounded on the door with his fists. "I'll get yuh for this. You... you... you just wait and see." After venting his spleen on the younger boy, Meddows turned on his amused buddies who had been awed to silence by their friend's unrestrained rage. "Lotta help you guys were," howled the boy who had told them he could handle the matter by himself. "Whatcha laughin' at Burns, you stupid..." Meddows growled.

"Nothin'," replied Burns.

"Nothin'?" repeated Meddows and poked his toady on the shoulder.

"Nothin'," said Burns. He sat on a bed and massaged his newest bruise.

"Don't just stand there. Help me find Jenks' locker, you idiots," ordered Meddows.

"No way," replied Matthews, "Andrews or the super'll be up here any minute. I'm outta here."

"Get back here, Matthews," cried Meddows. "You too, Burns." Like a scolded dog, Burns had begun slinking away towards the senior dormitory, peering back, sad-eyed, over his shoulder as he tried to escape the scene. "I said help me find his locker— now!"

The toadies, reluctantly following orders, spread out through the junior dorm.

"Over here!" shouted O'Neil from the next cubicle. "I got it."

As Meddows marched towards the cubicle, Burns called out in a surprised voice. "I found it. It's right here."

"What?" cried Meddows. His face betrayed his confusion.

"Hey, wait a minute," added Burns. "Jenks has two lockers here."

"And two more over here," called Matthews from a third cubicle. Hey, guys, I think someone's comin'. I'm outta here."

If Meddows' gang had continued searching they would have found Emerson's name on twenty of the fifty lockers in the junior dormitory.

Locating all twenty however, would have availed them nothing. On his own locker, Emerson had placed a nametag that read Talbot.

Fearing discovery, all four seniors headed to their dorm. Meddows' three friends fell on their beds and feigned sleep while trying to stifle laughter. Each was busy rehearsing an alibi in case Andrews showed up. Mumbling inarticulate sounds, Meddows retired to the senior washroom, desperate to clean the black from his face and hands before the lunch bell rang.

In accordance with Emerson's instructions, when he could no longer hear voices, Guardiano tiptoed from the junior washroom to the dorm door. The doorstop remained securely in place. He hurried to the senior dormitory door and skipped down the stairs in search of his friend. As Emerson Jenks had explained to Guardiano, a prankster can never take too many precautions.

+ − × ÷

Emerson Jenks, with his Latin text in hand, took up residence outside the headmaster's rooms. His mind focussed on neither conjugations nor declensions. With an intake of air, he jerked his head around at the sound of someone approaching. He had not expected company. In fact, he was trying desperately to avoid company.

"Well, well, well! Mr. Jenks?" It was Miss Strupples. "And what might you be doing sitting here on a fine day like this?" Emerson held up his book. "Ah, a studious one, I see," the woman added. "I'd have thought you'd be out with your friends."

"It's nice and quiet here, Ma'am," explained Emerson, and turned back to his charade.

Miss Strupples smiled, marched to the headmaster's door and knocked. "You know what they say, Mr. Jenks?" added Strupples. "About all work and no play, I mean?" The headmaster's door opened. "Do you have a minute, Sir?" Strupples asked as she pushed past Fitzroy before he could answer. The man fixed his eyes on Emerson. The boy stared back and waved, then turned his attention to his textbook. When he heard the door close, he stared at it and bit his lower lip.

Five minutes passed before Miss Strupples left the headmaster's office and walked off. Emerson raised his eyes but not his head and watched her pass. A few moments later, the lunch bell rang. Emerson stood as Mr. Fitzroy stepped from his room, noting that the man walked off without locking his door.

"Sorry, Jenks…" advised the headmaster.

"Pardon, Sir?"

"You'll have to come back later then," said Fitzroy.

"Pardon?" repeated the boy.

"To see me," explained Fitzroy. "You did want to see me, did you not?"

"Oh, no, Sir," answered Emerson. "It's just that it's so nice and quiet here… for studying, I mean." He waved his Latin text back and forth.

The headmaster cast suspicious eyes upon the boy and then glanced at his watch. "Well, come along, Jenks," he added. "You don't want to be late getting to chapel."

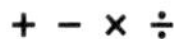

The student refectory was of simple design: a long narrow rectangle. A single door in the end wall gave access to the scullery and, from there, out across the hall to the kitchen. Tables, five chairs at each, were set in two rows, perpendicular to the side walls. The main entrance from the corridor had double doors. Centred on and pushed against the long wall, opposite the main doors, stood a lectern. Save for a simple crucifix over the scullery door, no adornments were in evidence.

This Sunday's lunch was to be very different from others. When the refectory was full, the head student prayed, but he did not signal the end of silence. Rarely at St. Timothy's, was entertainment provided at meals. That was about to change. Fitzroy, not a regular guest, entered the room, dragged the lectern away from the wall, stood behind it and let his eyes take in the scene. He said nothing. Eventually, one or two of the first year students, totally unfamiliar with this scenario, began to whisper.

"Hush!" demanded Fitzroy in a loud voice. He paused for effect before he continued. "Some unsettling news has come to my attention, Gentlemen." He paused again. "I was hoping this kind of visit might be avoided this year but I must waste our valuable time over the tomfoolery of one or two misguided individuals."

As a few sniggers reached his ears, Andrews rose, approached the headmaster from the side, stopped and scowled at the other students over the man's shoulder. The head student rocked on the balls of his feet, his head turning right and left and back again. His steady, piercing gaze quenched every flicker of frivolity.

"That's better," Fitzroy advised his audience. "You can see I mean business… can't you?" He leaned over the lectern and looked up and down the room as if to ensure that all the students could see his handsome face. "Someone has been up to hi-jinks," announced the headmaster. "Before I describe what has happened, I will, for the benefit of our new students… and Mr. Wobbally… I mean, Mr. Walloughby-Willows here, remind you of the rules concerning practical jokes." Unobserved, Mr. Willoughby-Wallows, at the invitation of the headmaster, had entered the refectory via the scullery.

For ten minutes, Fitzroy outlined the already oft repeated list of rules. In essence, he explained that pranks were discouraged but not forbidden. Participation in pranks was at the pranksters' peril. He would make every effort to bring perpetrators to justice but students were not to volunteer information and the faculty, head student and his assistant were not to ask students to inform on one another. If serious property damage or personal injury occurred, these rules would not remain in effect.

Most students were bored. But Emerson Jenks did not mind the lecture. It was good, seeing that he walked so near the line, to have the rules of engagement reconfirmed. Emerson leaned to his left. "Simple, straightforward, sensible rules, by anyone's standards," he whispered just loudly enough for Angelo Guardiano to hear. Emerson confirmed his opinion with a single, definitive nod.

With this reiteration out of the way, Fitzroy assumed the role of strict disciplinarian. "Today, not an hour ago," he reported, "Miss Strupples was out walking and heard very loud and strange sounds emanating from the junior dorm." The man did a fairly decent impersonation of Walter Cronkite. He scanned his audience. Stretching the stained boxer shorts between his hands, he raised them above his head – a thing Mr. Cronkite would almost certainly have refused to do. "Then these, yes, these… these… things, Gentlemen—" he turned to his left and right so all could see, "—fell at her feet… at Miss Strupples' feet, I say! Other articles of clothing were thrown onto the lawn as well. I am disgusted."

"Disgusted?" Emerson mumbled so softly that not even Guardiano heard him. "Why… even Mr. Willoughby-Wallows seems rather amused."

In spite of Andrews' imposing presence, a titter somewhere to Fitzroy's left set off a chorus of laughter up and down the rows of tables. "Hush!" cried the headmaster. "There is nothing to laugh about here, nothing at all." A young, innocent and unsuspecting Mr. Fredericks was about to provide the comedic element that Fitzroy deemed to be missing. When, thanks to Andrews' glare, order was restored, Fitzroy called out the boy's name. "Fredericks!" he shouted and, pinching the stained underwear between his thumb and index finger, held them out as if he were handling a dead skunk. "These, Sir, belong to you."

"Oh, no… I mean, I don't think so, Sir," replied Fredericks who blanched white before flushing bright red.

"Your name is on them, Sir," stated the headmaster.

"Oh!" mumbled Fredericks who could not have been seated further from the headmaster. The boy arose, trained his eyes on his feet and started a long, slow walk down the refectory to retrieve the black and white boxers. Fredericks' movements were those of a zombie – although a zombie moves less awkwardly than he did. Either he could not or would not allow his arms to swing back and forth in the normal manner.

There was not a sound to be heard until Badham intoned, "Night of the living dead." At this comical interjection, the students' very tentative restraint gave way. Laughter filled the room. In response, Andrews and Mr. Fitzroy's restraint gave way.

The headmaster's face turned pomegranate red. His eyes and those of Andrews bulged then narrowed and fell upon the diners, searching for the wag with so refined a sense of humour. Badham, in an attempt to blend in, transformed his rather ordinary face into that of a cherub. He only succeeded in proving that too much of anything can be as bad as not enough. The wise-cracking student escaped the headmaster's notice but his overly-innocent demeanour and the shocked faces of his tablemates caught Andrews' attention at once.

"Mr. Badham!" shouted Andrews and pointed at the boy.

"To my office… immediately after lunch, Mr. Badham," Fitzroy ordered. The man's voice changed to a falsetto as he spoke. This had a sobering effect on Badham but stimulated more snickering from the other diners.

Mr. Fitzroy pounded on the lectern. "Enough… enough I say. Mr. Willer… Sir," cried Fitzroy. "Sir!" he repeated. The Greek and Latin man had apparently choked on something. He clamped a hand over his mouth, bolted from the room and did not return. Using the confusion as cover, Fredericks sprinted to the lectern, grabbed his shorts, stuffed them into his pocket and returned in haste to his place.

"Fredericks, you may retrieve the rest of your things from the lawn after lunch, Sir," advised the headmaster. After a slow inspection of the students' faces, Fitzroy walked to the exit, turned and spoke. "And, if whoever is responsible for this disgrace does not deign to help you, Sir, I will be even more disgusted. Good day, Gentlemen."

The students remained silent, staring down at their plates. No one wanted to be the first to raise his head. Every soul in the room sat in dread of beholding Andrews' face. Before the head student reclaimed his seat, someone coughed. Someone else cleared his throat. Mr. Fitzroy returned to the room, stopping just inside the double doors.

"Meddows!" he called out and looked around the refectory. The top of Meddows' head was impossible to differentiate from the tops of so many other heads bowed over the tables. "Stand up, Meddows," ordered the headmaster and waited.

Meddows obeyed, but with the greatest reluctance. The slowness of his response spoke volumes of his desire to maintain a low profile. "Sir?" Meddows muttered.

"Meddows… look at me, Meddows," demanded the headmaster. The boy raised his head. "I can't prove it… at least not yet… but I know, Meddows, I know."

"Know what, Sir?" the boy asked in an attempt to maintain some degree of dignity before his peers.

"You know what, Meddows. We're going to dig and dig and dig. And, when we get to the bottom of this we're sure to find you there, Sir. And then, Meddows… and then." Meddows averted his gaze. "Yes, you ought to be ashamed, Meddows… yes, indeed. Miss Strupples won't swear to it but she's almost certain it was you she heard screaming. Watch your step, Meddows. Just you watch your step."

Fitzroy turned to leave once more, but paused and shot an inquisitive look back into the room. "Meddows, what in the world's happened to your face?" he asked.

"My face, Sir?" replied Meddows. He found himself on his feet once again before having actually made contact with his chair.

"Yes, Meddows... your face."

One half of Meddows' face appeared red and raw subsequent to the vicious scrubbing it had received just prior to the lunch bell. Meddows raised a hand and felt his nose, lips, eyebrows and the other facial features to which he had grown attached, as if to make sure they were still there. Once reassured that everything was present and accounted for, the boy shrugged. "Why nothing, Sir. There's nothing wrong with my face," he answered.

"Nothing?" demanded Fitzroy.

"Nothing," repeated Meddows and shrugged.

The students maintained tentative control of their mirth until they could no longer hear the echo of the headmaster's retreating footfall. The laughter they had held in with the man present began leaking, barely audibly, from the corners of their mouths. With a holler of unparalleled power – sufficient in fact to frighten himself – the head student cried, "Quiet! No one gave you permission to speak." As one, the students fell silent and began to eat.

That Sunday lunch was not at all as pleasant as those past or as most that followed. It was conducted in total silence, save for the odd chuckle and snort which Andrews quashed by uttering threats of the direst consequences. When the student waiters rolled the dessert cart into the refectory, the head student ordered it removed. "No treats today, guys," he announced in tones cold enough to send a chill through the room. "Next time Mr. Fitzroy has to come down here there will be no laughing. Do you understand? Now, everyone... to the chapel."

+ − × ÷

Immediately after prayers, Emerson stepped onto the landing and started down the stairs. He intended to get to the safety to the auditorium and cozy up to Angelo Guardiano. He had wanted to ask his friend to hang around after lunch but decided that talking during the meal, given

Andrews' mood, was imprudent in the extreme. At the sound of his name, Emerson swung around and looked back up the stairs. Burns and Meddows approached from the landing. Both wore grim frowns. Emerson sized up his perilous situation and assumed that O'Neil and Matthews were somewhere about, probably at the foot of the stairs. Without the slightest hesitation, Emerson looked past the two older boys and, with relief in his voice, greeted his friend. "Hey, Guardiano!" he cried.

Burns and Meddows stiffened and turned to face Emerson's bodyguard. There was no one behind them. They turned back to face Emerson—there was no longer anyone in front of them. The instant he had diverted their attention, Emerson had raced headlong between the two boys and escaped. Over their shoulders, Meddows and Burns caught only a glimpse of their foe's back as he bolted into the chapel. When they, with O'Neil and Matthews hot on their heels, barged into the room, Emerson was talking to Andrews. The head student turned towards the new arrivals as they tripped over each other in an effort to slow their advance.

"Got a problem, Meddows?" asked Andrews.

"Never mine, Andrews," Emerson interjected, "You're busy. I'll ask you 'bout it later."

As the head student began to interrogate Meddows and his companions, Emerson waltzed towards them. "See you guys around, eh?" he whispered and squeezed unmolested past the four seniors. At the door he stopped, turned, removed and inspected his glasses. When Meddows sneered at him, Emerson gave him a quick wink. While Meddows and his gang sweated under the head student's inquisition and Emerson Jenks sought out Guardiano's company, Badham grovelled before Mr. Fitzroy. The boy's efforts to entertain the troops resulted in one week of extra chores, loss of free-time for the next two Sundays and membership in St. Timothy's Hall of Fame… for unmitigated cheek. Fredericks found himself on the lawn at the front of the main building collecting his belongings. As the headmaster had hoped, the boy did not labour alone. Some two to three dozen fellows hung out of dormitory windows shouting down words of encouragement.

Sei Stets Pünktlich

Mr. Willoughby-Wallows stood outside the grade thirteen classroom, his shoulder against the wall, his legs crossed at the ankle, his nose buried in a book. He raised his eyes when Andrews stepped into the hall. The boy passed in front of his Greek and Latin teacher, crossed to the buzzer and stood still, gazing down the corridor. Willoughby-Wallows noticed that Andrews attend alternately to his wristwatch and to the far end of the empty hallway. Presently, Mr. von Baumgartner exited the furthest classroom. Andrews' finger moved to the buzzer. The old man closed the door and, bowing slightly, paused before removing his hand from the knob. At the instant his fingers released their grip, Andrews pressed the button and, stifling a laugh, continued to stare at the German master. Von Baumgartner threw back his shoulders, snapped his fingers, turned and walked, jauntily away. The old man stopped and waved when he noticed Willoughby-Wallows. The head student, thinking he was being hailed, paused as the old gentleman approached. Not until von Baumgartner passed him without a greeting, did Andrews realize the Greek and Latin instructor stood behind him. With downcast eyes, the boy raised a fist to his mouth, faked a cough and returned, red-faced, to his classroom.

"Ah, glad I caught you," Von Baumgartner addressed the Greek and Latin professor. "Wilf, my boy, I've been meaning to speak with you."

"Sir?" replied Willoughby-Wallows.

"How about we have lunch together today, Wilfred?" asked the old man.

"I've a moment right now if you'd like," answered Willoughby-Wallows as he slid his sleeve back and checked the time.

"Good gracious, no," replied the German master. He too consulted his watch and frowned. "No, no… can't now. Let's meet for lunch."

"Right," agreed Willoughby-Wallows. "I'd enjoy that."

The corridor hummed with activity as instructors and students changed rooms and enjoyed what remained of their five-minute break. "Very good," von Baumgartner replied. "Shall we say…" he looked at the well-worn time piece again, hemmed and hawed, and then continued, "twelve-ten?"

"Twelve-ten it is, Sir," answered Willoughby-Wallows. With his eyes, he followed the old man back down the hall to the near stairwell.

A few hours later, when Willoughby-Wallows entered the refectory, von Baumgartner waved him to his table. "Ah, here you are at last," cried the old gentleman. "Grab a bite and sit yourself down."

When Willoughby-Wallows returned, lunch tray in hand, the German master continued. "Sit down. Sit down." The young teacher took his seat and stared glumly down at his plate. "You're late. I've been waiting for over…" von Baumgartner checked the time, "—nearly five minutes, Wilf. You know what we say in German, don't you?"

"What's that, Sir?" asked Willoughby-Wallows. He raised a fork full of food halfway to his mouth and fixed his eyes upon it.

"*Sei stets Pünktlich*," answered von Baumgartner.

The younger man returned the fork to his plate and grimaced before saying, "I've no idea what that means, Sir. I mean, Rolf."

"Ah, *es macht nichts*," continued the old man.

"You'll have to excuse me," explained Willoughby-Wallows. "I don't know German."

"It doesn't matter… what I just said, I mean," replied von Baumgartner in an apologetic tone. "I just said it doesn't matter."

"I've never studied German, Rolf," Willoughby-Wallows replied. "Sorry!"

"No need to be sorry, no need at all." Von Baumgartner waved his left hand dismissively and raised his cup of tea to his lips with his right. "Me… my Latin's atrocious and I've no Greek at all… absolutely hopeless at Greek. Go ahead and eat, Wilf." Willoughby-Wallows stared at his lunch, frowned and drew back from the table. After a short pause and without explanation, von Baumgartner spoke again. "Punctuality, Sir."

Befuddled, Willoughby-Wallows looked up with knitted brow. "Punctuality?" he repeated.

"Yes, punctuality, Wilf." The old man confirmed that his friend had heard correctly. "*Pünktlichkeit*, in German but, in English we say punctuality. "*Sie stets Pünktlich*," repeated von Baumgartner, "means, never be late or always be punctual… something like that. It's been my motto… more or less, for many a long year, Sir."

"I see," replied Willoughby-Wallows, thinking back to Andrews, the bell and the doorknob incident.

"I've been meaning to ask you how relations have progressed between you and that horrible man. I was thinking about what he did to you that first day with us," announced von Baumgartner. "What a villain he is, Wilfred, my lad. Leticia's told me what happened and—"

"Warneke, Sir? Water under the bridge," said the younger teacher, with a sigh.

"I'm glad to hear you say that," replied von Baumgartner. "You'll live longer… more happily too. Never harbour grudges, Wilf. But that Warneke… my, my, my!" The old gentleman shook his head slowly and sadly from side to side. "What someone said about Oscar Wilde is true of our mutual friend, Wilf."

"Oscar Wilde!" Willoughby-Wallows arched his eyebrows and frowned.

"Oh, yes, someone once said that he, Wilde I mean, had no enemies… only friends who hated him," von Baumgartner explained and laughed at his own joke.

"Actually, Rolf—" Willoughby-Wallows looked around the room then leaned over the table and announced, in a highly confidential manner, "—I rather prefer my current roommates, Sir, if you see my meaning?" He took another quick glance around and both men chuckled.

"Yes, yes, I believe I do," replied von Baumgartner. "But we must move along. While you eat, I'll tell you something of myself."

"I'm not all that hungry all of a sudden. But, go ahead. I'm listening." Willoughby-Wallows used his fork to pick at what the cooks had labelled salmon casserole as if he was trying to determine where they had hidden the salmon.

"I was just twelve years old when I first stepped through the doors of St. Timothy's, you know," began the old man. "Spent five years here before leaving for the university. I was away five years then returned as an instructor… probationary to start… just like you. Been here ever since."

Willoughby-Wallows studied the old man's face and imagined he saw signs of sadness. "Go on, Sir," he insisted.

"Ah, how time flies..." von Baumgartner added. He slapped the table. "But it's been a good life all in all. You just go ahead and eat, Wilf." Willoughby-Wallows examined the food once more. The German master continued his story. "Let me ramble on a bit. You know, Wilf, I taught Fitzroy and Fong and our Dr. Graham too... and even Father Keegan." The old gentleman sighed. "All of them were hopeless in German... butchered the language, let me tell you. But, I'm seventy-three now... just a year after this one they'll put me out to pasture," he sighed and paused.

Willoughby-Wallows finally ventured a taste of his casserole, coughed, held his paper napkin to his mouth, coughed again and gulped down some water. "Sorry, Sir," he said. "But I just can't eat this stuff."

Von Baumgartner smiled and continued. "But no more of that! For as long as I've been here pranks, practical jokes, dirty tricks... whatever you want to call them—" he waved a hand about as if brushing away the cobwebs of time, "—they've been an unfortunate part of life at St. Timothy's. One fellow trying to outdo the other. You must keep a sharp eye, Son. We've all been victims, the students and the staff... why, even the headmasters."

"Really, Sir?" exclaimed Willoughby-Wallows. "You are right though... I guess. Warneke, as you said, put one over on me alright. I can see how he managed that... now. I won't let it happen again though."

"It may not be the last time he or someone else tries. Be on your guard. Trust no one, but especially that Warneke," advised the old man. "Beware of Greeks and all that..."

"I'll keep a sharp eye... just as you suggest, Sir," added Willoughby-Wallows. "Don't you worry about that. And I'll watch my step. But, what about you?"

"Me?" replied the old man in surprise. "Oh... they've pretty much stopped playing tricks on me. I'm too old, I suppose."

"No, not that. I meant what are you going to do when you retire?"

"When *they retire me*, you mean," von Baumgartner cried. He spat out the comment as if the words tasted as bad as the salmon casserole. The look of sadness Willoughby-Wallows observed earlier swept across the old man's face. He appeared even older. "Ah, Wilf, that's a very good question, one I can't begin to answer. I've always hoped that, with any luck, I'd keep my health and die in harness. My old father gave me a piece of advice once," continued the German master. "He told me, 'Don't ever get old, my boy.' Wilf, if we're lucky, we grow old and die healthy. Ah, but too morose... too morose." The old professor glanced at his watch. "Must be off. We'll talk again though," promised von Baumgartner. "*Sei stets*..." he added and paused, waiting for a reply.

"Sorry, Sir," Wilf apologized. "I've gone and forgotten it already."

"*Pünktlich*" instructed the old man, enunciating the word. As he spoke he removed a pen and a business card from his pocket, printed out the words and handed the card to his companion. "There you go, Wilfred... a motto to live by. Treasure it."

The Greek and Latin man read the words aloud, "Sigh-stets-Punk-lick... right, Sir. I'll try to remember that."

The German master plucked the card from Willoughby-Wallow's hand, scribbled down the phrase, phonetically, and returned it to his colleague. "Practice makes perfect, Wilf," he added as the younger man took the card and slipped it into his breast pocket. The old man took a few steps towards the exit, snapped his fingers and turned. "Oh, I know what I wanted to tell you, Wilf. Get familiar with our routines and be very suspicious of any changes," he warned. "Any variation from routine spells danger." He shook his finger at the younger man. "You'd do well to remember that."

Willoughby-Wallows had gotten to his feet at the same time as the old man. Now, he scraped what remained of his lunch into the garbage, returned his dinnerware to the scullery and left to prepare for his afternoon classes.

+ − × ÷

Exactly two weeks to the day after his lunch date with von Baumgartner, Willoughby-Wallows found himself leaning against the same wall, reading from the same book, watching the same student leave the same room in the same manner and stand by the same buzzer looking down the same corridor and checking his watch – the same watch. Willoughby-Wallows thought about routines and about how day-to-day life changed so little at St. Timothy's.

This day, there was only one small change. Andrews checked to see who, besides himself, occupied the hallway the moment he emerged from his classroom.

The head student stood by the buzzer and stared down the corridor. As the seconds ticked away, his demeanour – usually controlled and confident – grew more and more uneasy. The boy checked his watch with increasing frequency. He cast an imploring glance towards Willoughby-Wallows but received no response. Finally, in a state of agitation, he rang the bell. Instead of returning to his classroom, the boy approached the Greek and Latin teacher.

"Sir?" he whispered. "Something's very strange, Sir. Professor von Baumgartner, Sir, is… well… never late, Sir." Andrews' level of tension was always reflected in the number of times he inserted the word 'sir' into his sentences.

Apace, Willoughby-Wallows started down the corridor. Andrews tagged along. Each put an ear to the door of the grade ten classroom. On hearing the hum of many voices, Willoughby-Wallows entered the room with Andrews at his heels. The students who had been leaning out the windows and chatting snapped to attention. Rolf von Baumgartner was not in the room.

"Where's the professor?" demanded Willoughby-Wallows.

"Don't know," answered a student. "He didn't come to class today, Sir."

A very long pause ensued.

"I'll go check," announced Willoughby-Wallows. "Andrews, do your best to keep order here until I get back."

He hurried out of the room, passing dozens of enquiring faces, and raced down the stairs and along the empty corridor to the faculty wing. He pressed an ear to von Baumgartner's door and gently tapped. Upon receiving no response, he rapped louder. Still, there was no answer. Willoughby-Wallows' mouth went dry. Sweat beaded on his forehead and dampened the palms of his hands. He took a deep breath, turned the doorknob, exhaled slowly and pushed the door open. He leaned into the room. Silence greeted him. "Rolf?" he called in a whisper. No answer. The curtains had not been opened. The room was dark save for a desk lamp that bathed the ceiling in its feeble, jade green light. It had been knocked to the floor beside the professor's desk. In the gloom, Willoughby-Wallows could see no sign of the professor. He flicked on the ceiling light and spotted the old man. He was sprawled face down upon some paperwork. "Rolf?" he cried. "Rolf!" He hurried to the professor's side. A single touch convinced Willoughby-Wallows that Rolf von Baumgartner had passed on.

With a hand covering his mouth, the young teacher backed away from the body.

The headmaster, on being alerted, visited each classroom to announce the death and to cancel classes. He called the faculty and students to the chapel. There, Fitzroy reminded the students that this was not a time for high spirits and asked that their deportment demonstrate a suitable measure of solemnity and respect.

Dr. Graham, the school's physician, arrived just after two police officers. The presence of the police set St. Timothy's rumour mill a-grinding. Willoughby-Wallows, who had remained with the body, wandered aimlessly about the room trying to stay out from under of the doctor's feet. To his surprise, the police officers seemed no more comfortable in their roles than he did. Eventually, Willoughby-Wallows' eyes fell on a cream-coloured, legal-sized envelope that protruded from beneath the old man's radio. The young man stooped over the body to read the words written in von Baumgartner's spidery hand:

I imagine you'll be needing this.
S.R. von Baumgartner, M.A.

"Doctor!" whispered Willoughby-Wallows and pointed to the envelope. "Do you think we should open this, or…" he paused and then continued. "Or what?"

"No harm in it," answered Dr. Graham and glanced towards the two officers who looked at one another and shrugged. "Well, go on," added Graham and continued his examination.

Willoughby-Wallows picked up the envelope and blew away some accumulated dust. He read the short note again and then broke the seal.

"Doctor Graham, I think you should see this," announced Willoughby-Wallows as he began to read the typewritten words:

Sir:
Since you are reading this letter, I assume that a rather serious state of affairs now exists. If the good fortune, with which I have been favoured all my life, has continued... I've passed on. But, if my fortunes have changed, I have been seriously incapacitated. If the latter is the case, pray, do not let them prolong my agony – please.

I have no one left in this world. Besides my well used body, I leave precious little behind. What does remain has been bequeathed to St. Timothy's. My will can be retrieved from Hinshelwood and O'Brien's where I have left it for safekeeping.

I've but one wish – sorry, two wishes – first, I would very much like to be waked in my home – St. Timothy's. The student chapel, I think, would be nice. Second, I would prefer to have my remains cremated and the ashes spread, if it's legal etc., on the grounds – in the garden in the centre of the circle drive would be lovely but perhaps a bit too pretentious for the likes of me.

How I'd love to be there, with you... to see it all I mean, but alas...
Yours truly,

The letter was signed "S. R. V."

In the end, Dr. Graham concluded that the old man had died in the early hours of the morning, most likely from a massive stroke. The doctor flipped through a stack of unmarked assignments, turned to the police officers and Willoughby-Wallows and announced, "The old fellow once told me he wanted to die in harness. Well... he got his wish." Graham tossed the papers onto the desk, shook his head and, with a sigh, removed his surgical gloves.

When the students arrived at chapel that evening, they found the faculty already assembled. The headmaster gave a brief account of what had occurred. He told the gathering that Mr. von Baumgartner's remains had been removed but would be returned the following day when a vigil would begin. After the funeral mass, the morticians would remove the body for cremation.

Dr. Graham and the chaplain, Father Keegan, were on hand. Both were rather grim faced.

The doctor did his best to assure the students that their German instructor had died of purely natural causes and enjoyed modest success in putting to rest suspicions about murder that had been growing leaps and bounds during the afternoon. Since the arrival of the police cars, the rumour mongers' tales had grown more and more fantastic by the hour. Most of the students reacted to Dr. Graham's message with relief, a few with disappointment.

Father Keegan outlined the arrangements for the funeral mass. When telling of his long association with von Baumgartner, he launched into a sermon about being prepared to meet one's maker, but stopped short. Later, one wag suggested that, since Keegan was to give the eulogy, he did not want to upstage himself. The priest explained that, until after the funeral service, the body would rest in the chapel and that the students, in pairs, would keep a continuous vigil over the professor's remains. They would kneel and pray, in thirty-minute shifts.

That night, Emerson Jenks, in the silence of the dorm, clasped his hands behind his head and stared wide-eyed into the darkness. He knew that this unforeseen event offered wonderful possibilities for someone with his talents. Time was against him but, with classes suspended, perhaps… He needed only a plan, a little creativity and a little spunk. Before rolling onto his side and drifting off to sleep he reminded himself that planning, creativity and spunk had rarely failed him.

When Emerson awoke, it seemed to him that his mind was already dreaming up a prank. He and the other students followed the routines of the day until the usual time to attend their classes. Many of the students moped about, appearing disoriented and glum. Some went to the sports fields, others to the common rooms, a few returned to bed. Except during lunch, Emerson sat in the chapel, thinking. Early in the afternoon, Emerson's persistence began to pay dividends. From the sacristans' pew, Emerson heard the school's front doors swing open and the sound of activity in the foyer.

Directly, two gentlemen entered the chapel. They were attired in black and either one could have been mistaken for Sleepy Hollow's infamous Icabod Crane. Emerson moved closer to observe the men work. First, they assembled a chrome frame. It looked like a large TV tray but had webbed belts strung across the top where the tray should have been. The legs rested on a sheet of plywood which was held a few inches off the floor by four sturdy casters. The men fitted a heavy, black skirt completely around the frame. It hung in folds to within an inch of the floor.

"What's that thing for?" asked Emerson, nodding towards the contraption. He pushed his glasses up his nose.

"This, my fine young feller? Why this 'ere's what's called a *bier*," answered one gentleman.

"To be precise," explained the other, "it's a *funeral bier*."

"But what's it for?" asked Emerson.

"Why, to lay the deceased out on, a-course," replied the first man.

"We use it in place of a coffin," said the second, "fir 'is vigil like, see."

"Oh," exclaimed the young student.

When the two men left the room, Emerson walked to the front of the chapel and inspected the bier. He gripped the frame with both hands and gave it a good shake. The structure, with its cross bracing, proved surprisingly sturdy. The boy pushed on one end of the bier and discovered that it rolled easily on the hardwood floor. He retreated when he heard voices coming from the foyer.

To his astonishment, the morticians returned bearing Mr. von Baumgartner on a board. The old man had been dressed in his good suit – Emerson thought it not really very good at all. Over the suit, von Baumgartner wore a Kelly green cape with gold frogs down its front and at the collar: a relic from St. Timothy's past. The men deposited their burden atop the bier, made a few minor adjustments and stood back to admire their handy-work.

"Okay, Percy… be a pal and crawl under there and check them belts, eh," said the first fellow.

"Belts?" exclaimed Emerson.

While Percy did his friend's bidding, the other man turned to the boy. "Yuh see," he explained, "this 'ere gent died sittin' up, see, and the rigor mortis set in 'fore he got 'isself found."

"And?"

The man continued, "And now 'e don't lay flat-like unless—"

"—Mickey!" Percy called. "You're goin' tuh 'ave tuh press down on this feller's chest, Mickey."

Emerson watched Mickey place two hands on von Baumgartner's shoulders and apply pressure.

"That's got 'er," announced Percy, slipping out from under the bier. "Now 'e's cinched up good and proper-like."

Mickey continued young Mr. Jenks' education. "You see, Son…" he went on, "if we didn't strap 'im down that a-way, chest and knees, I mean, the rigor mortis might jus' pop 'im right back up ag'in and 'e'd end up sitting there just the way they found 'im, poor soul. We can't have that now, can we?" Emerson's mouth fell open. Mickey flashed Percy an exaggerated wink. Percy grinned and winked back. Both men wondered at the boy's keen interest. If they entertained any notion that he was contemplating a career as a mortician, they were sadly mistaken.

Percy interrupted Emerson's thoughts. "Eh there, Son, 'ow'd yuh like to fetch us the 'eadmaster? That's a good lad."

Emerson returned with Mr. Fitzroy but soon wished he had not. He sat and contemplated while the headmaster spoke to Percy and Mickey. Emerson felt a shutter run through him as, for the first time in his short life, he thought about biers, belts, bodies, rigor mortis… and death. He sniffed. There was a new odour in the chapel. It was a strange, pungent odour, an odour that seemed to come from some eerie, invisible presence. It spread through the chapel. It overpowered the now familiar smell of paste wax and incense. The boy did not like this new smell.

Emerson jumped and almost screamed when the headmaster touched him on the shoulder. "Sorry, Jenks," whispered Fitzroy. "I need you to stay here, Jenks… with him, I mean… until someone relieves you. You'll be okay, won't you?"

"Oh… yes, Sir," answered Emerson, "I think so." If the truth were told, the boy really didn't relish the task at all.

As soon as the three men vacated the chapel, Emerson hurried to the body and, after a quick survey of the room, squatted down, reached under the bier and undid the belt buckle Percy had just tightened. While watching the body carefully he loosened his grip on the strap.

He detected no change in the body, not the slightest movement, not so much as a quiver. He retightened the belt, returned to his usual place on the sacristan's bench, twisted his lower lip, stretching it left then right while staring at the body. Within a few minutes, the lip-twisting ceased. The boy clamped his eyes closed, pulled his hand away from his mouth, fingers splayed wide, and slapped his forehead. A smile transformed Emerson's face, from a grim, reflective facade to a merry, animated mask. The prankster finally had an idea.

It seemed forever before Father Keegan, accompanied by two students wearing surplices and soutanes, entered the chapel. Under the priest's watchful eye, the students arranged kneeling benches side by side, facing the funeral bier. Keegan thanked a much relieved Emerson Jenks and whispered, "The roster for the vigil has been posted outside the headmaster's office, Jenks."

Emerson bolted from the chapel and ran to check the list. He breathed a sigh of relief when he discovered that the younger boys were scheduled for the afternoon and early evening and older students throughout the night. He retired to his classroom and there, alone, began to work out the details of his plan.

After dinner, Emerson returned to the chapel, sat in the back pew and watched the flow of student vigil keepers come and go. He completed his own half hour and climbed to the dorm. Despite working and reworking a plan for what he thought would prove a dandy prank, Emerson failed to find a way to carry it out alone. He needed an accomplice: someone he could trust implicitly. Angelo Guardiano's name popped into his head but he knew Guardiano was not up to the task. The prankster was about to abandon his idea when another thought, a variation on a theme, popped into his mind.

"I have to know if I can trust you, Meddows," declared Emerson Jenks.

"You… gotta trust me? Ha!" replied Meddows in a tone midway between marvel and mockery. "What about me havin' to trust you, eh? Ever think of that?"

"Look, Meddows, you got me good with the green apple thing, okay?" admitted Emerson. "And I paid you back with the black eye and stuff. So, we're all even. But this… this, Meddows… this is big… the biggest. If we pull this off, we'll go down in history."

Meddows pondered the possibilities. "Tell me the plan first," he demanded.

"No way," cried Emerson and screwed up his face, reconsidering. "Well, okay… but you have to promise me you'll keep this to yourself. You can never tell anybody anything about this. Promise?"

"Yeah," replied Meddows.

"Yeah what?" demanded Emerson.

"Yeah, I promise. I ain't never gunna say nothin' to nobody." It took Emerson a moment to unravel and ferret out the meaning of Meddows' quadruple negative.

Emerson studied his companion's face for a moment before beginning to lay out his grand scheme. After only half a dozen words, he paused and added, "Not even Burns and—"

"—Not even them," declared Meddows. "Now whatcha got planned?"

The following morning, the day of the funeral, Meddows reported to the infirmary, complaining of stomach cramps. Emerson's plan, the boldness of which had stunned the older boy, would keep Meddows in isolation the whole of that day and, to be safe, overnight. At mid-morning, Emerson strolled down the corridor towards the infirmary. He whistled softly and pretended to study the graduation pictures of past classes that lined the walls. Since the sickroom was next to the headmaster's office, he used extra caution. He scanned the hallway before entering the room and closed the door behind him. "Brought you some comics and my copy of *The Pickwick Papers*," he said.

Meddows grunted and picked up the novel, noting its thickness. "Dickens?" he grunted in disgust and tossed the tome on the neighbouring bed. "I prefer comics if it's all the same to you."

"Anyway…" Emerson continued, "you know what you have to do, right?"

"Yeah, yeah, yeah," answered Meddows. The boredom resulting from being quarantined began to show. "I just gotta get there before anybody else—"

"—Without being seen… not even by Guardiano," added Emerson. "If you get spotted…"

"I won't get spotted. I'm no amateur. How'd Guardiano take it?"

"He'll do okay. Don't worry. He doesn't suspect a thing. He'll do what I ask him. I'm more worried about you falling asleep in here or something and missing our big chance."

"Look, you worry about you and Guardiano and let me worry about me, okay," declared Meddows. He pulled up his knees, sorted through the comics and began reading *Turok, Son of Stone*. "I'll do my part. You just make sure you see to yours."

The final pair of vigil keepers was to come on duty at 5:30 and stay throughout the funeral mass scheduled for 6:00. At 5:20, Angelo Guardiano and Emerson Jenks, appearing angelic in their surplices and soutanes, stepped into the chapel and relieved two boys who were only too happy to be on their way early. Ten minutes later, two more mourners reported for duty.

"Hey, you're not supposed to be here now," exclaimed Emerson. "We are. But, hey, if you really want to…"

The two boys did not really want to, so they shrugged and left the chapel.

Emerson began looking over his shoulder. Soon, Guardiano was doing the same. Emerson began to cough and, using mime, asked his friend for water. Without hesitation, the big fellow stood, genuflected and left the chapel. He returned a few minutes later, handed Emerson a glass of water and knelt down.

At 5:45, Burton entered the chapel and flipped on the lights. The students, teachers and a few visitors began to crowd into the pews. Two sacristans moved the candles and kneeling benches from around the bier and placed chairs for Emerson, Guardiano and three altar boys. Mass began at precisely six o'clock. More than one participant reflected that Professor von Baumgartner would have been well pleased with everyone's punctuality.

Before Father Keegan began what proved to be a sentimental and long eulogy, the three altar boys took their seats near the body, facing the mourners over the bier. Guardiano and Emerson sat opposite one another, the former at von Baumgartner's feet, the latter by his head.

When the priest finished speaking, Meddows, who during Guardiano's momentary absence, had entered the chapel and hidden himself under the bier, loosened the strap Percy had secured around von Baumgartner's chest. The professor's body did not sit upright on the bier as Emerson had promised it would. In spite of his vexation, Meddows, in an impressive display of creative problem solving, worked out a solution. He rolled up the comic book he had with him, poked it through a slot in the board until it touched the professor's back. He paused, listening for Father Keegan's voice. He heard the man reading some words in a very solemn tone.

"Wherefore he saith…" cried Keegan, "awake ye that sleepeth and arise from the dead."

Just as the priest shouted 'arise', Meddows, with all the strength he possessed, pushed the tightly-rolled comic upwards. The effort caused the boy to emit a loud groan, a groan heard throughout the chapel. Heads turned. Von Baumgartner's body rose an inch or two from its resting place. The eyes of every person in the room bulged. The old man's head rolled ever so slightly towards the assembly. As one, members of the congregation, even Emerson, inhaled. The boy imagined he felt a draught swirl around him and swore he heard it whistling past his ears. Bedlam erupted. Dozens of voices merged into one loud, lingering, high-pitched, ungodly howl. Guardiano, for lack of traction, did a particularly fine impression of an Irish step-dancer before bolting over his kneeling bench. He exited the chapel via the side doorway and continued apace through the foyer, down the stairs and out across the lawn. The departure of two of the three altar boys was slightly delayed when they became entangled in Guardiano's toppled bench and each other. The first sprawled headlong into the aisle. The second leapt over his friend, tripped and scrambled to the back of the room on hands and knees. In his desperate attempt to reach the landing by pushing against the door, precious seconds were lost. Recognizing his error, the boy yanked the door open and fled down the stairs in a frenzy. Before the door could swing shut, his companion bolted out of the chapel and headed in the opposite direction. Throughout the mayhem, Emerson remained seated, stunned. He had certainly not anticipated a scene like this.

Meddows had expected to make good his escape when Emerson,

who was to sit on the sacristans' bench next to the light switch, doused the chapel lights as soon as von Baumgartner sat up. It was the older boy who suggested that the sudden darkness would enhance the effect of the prank. Emerson failed to inform his accomplice of his minor alteration to the plan. He had decided that the prank would actually be more interesting if the lights remained on.

When the chapel remained illuminated, Meddows put his eye to a slit in the bier's skirting and peered towards the sacristan's pew. Head sacristan Burton, not Emerson, stood next to the light switch. In confusion and anxiety, Meddows searched the room for a face: Emerson Jenks' face. Emerson sat only a few feet from the bier and stared back at Meddows with a look of unfeigned shock, almost horror, on his face. The word 'trapped' flashed in Meddows' mind as he tried to conjure up an eleventh-hour getaway strategy.

"Quiet," called Headmaster Fitzroy. "Quiet, everyone, quiet please… all of you… calm down. Come now." Eventually, the man's pleas had their desired effect. The furore died a slow death as people took their seats and regained some but not all of their composure. "We'll have this looked after in a few seconds," advised Fitzroy and started down the aisle.

Atop the bier, Professor von Baumgartner remained at rest while beneath, a profusely perspiring Meddows cursed Emerson Jenks as well as his own stupidity for having trusted the younger boy. Emerson rushed to the bier before anyone else. Father Keegan, who had clutched at his heart and stumbled back several paces when the congregation screeched, recovered and arrived, second on the scene. Fitzroy was the third and final person to reach the bier. Emerson, on hands and knees, poked his head into Meddows' hiding-place-turned-prison.

"What did you do, Meddows?" he whispered. "Man alive, I didn't think he was going to move like that."

If looks could kill, Emerson Jenks would have required Percy and Mickey's services himself. Emerson grabbed the two ends of the strap and instructed Father Keegan to press down on the body. This done, he refastened the belt and rose to his feet.

"That's it, Father… Sir," he whispered to the priest and the headmaster. "I was here when those funeral home guys strapped him down,

Father," explained Emerson in a whisper. "The belt came undone, that's all."

Burton and Emerson assumed the roles of the missing altar boys. Father Keegan restarted the post-eulogy liturgy and finished mass with no further interruptions. A much relieved but much embittered Meddows awaited the funeral's finale while figuring out how to sneak back to the infirmary without being seen. "If I get caught I'm gunna have one heck of a time explainin' this get up," he muttered as he remembered that he wore only his pyjamas. "Blast him anyway!" he added.

The following day, St. Timothy's was abuzz with rumours about what had really transpired in the chapel. After breakfast, Emerson sat in the refectory among a dozen or more theorists, quietly savouring his great success. He listened but did not speak. As members of the group agreed on one point, dismissed it and then agreed on another, Headmaster Fitzroy entered the room and joined the discussion.

"Boys, there's really no great mystery here," he explained. "There was a belt holding the body down. It came loose. That's all there was to it. Right, Jenks?"

"Just came loose, hmmm?" Emerson pondered the headmaster's statement. "I suppose it must have," he replied. "What else could it be… ghosts?"

The students enjoyed their friend's little joke. Mr. Fitzroy did not. "You know exactly what happened, Jenks, so don't go putting silly ideas in these fellows' heads," cried the headmaster. "Ghosts indeed!" The look on the man's face convinced Emerson to change the subject.

"Sir, how's Meddows doing?" inquired Emerson. "Too bad he missed the funeral, isn't it, Sir?"

Meddows, not knowing if Andrews or someone else suspected a prank, had decided to dodge suspicion by prolonging his convalescence.

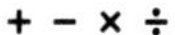

Professor von Baumgartner's wishes were carried out in precisely the manner he had requested, but for one small detail. The archbishop would not permit the scattering of the ashes. The urn holding the old

German master's mortal remains had to be buried and quickly at that. Despite Father Keenan's scrupulous search through the church calendar, he had failed to turn up any St. Rolf or even a St. Ralph. The priest was so very disappointed. He would have dearly loved to find a St. Rolf, especially if his feast day was celebrated in late November. He knew he could put together a dandy graveside message if the man's name day was near. Disappointment turned to delight when, upon viewing the plaque which was to mark the burial site, Keegan had read the professor's full name: Sylvester Rolf von Baumgartner.

Von Baumgartner had died on November 23 and was found later that morning. The vigil had begun on November 24 and ended the following evening after the funeral mass, debacle that it proved to be. Percy and Mickey removed the body to the crematorium and returned the ashes early the next day. Father Keegan, in the presence of the faculty only, officiated at the burial of the urn and supervised while old Mr. Ellis, the school's handyman, fixed the bronze plaque to the stone in the centre of the circle drive's garden. The mortal remains of the long-serving German master were laid to rest on November 26: the feast of St. Sylvester, abbot and martyr. In death, as in life, Sylvester Rolf von Baumgartner honoured his lifelong motto and so proved punctual to the very end.

After the burial ceremony, Willoughby-Wallows lagged behind his colleagues as they departed. When he reached the landing outside the main doors and everyone else had entered the building, he turned towards the garden, reached into his breast pocket and removed a small card. In his best German accent, he read the words von Baumgartner had given him: "*Sei stets Pünktlich*," he intoned.

Game On

For a month following von Baumgartner's funeral, the students and staff of St. Timothy's awoke to grey skies and greyer moods. Snow shrouded their school. Sorrow shrouded their hearts. A metronomic malaise marked their days. Despondency dampened all enthusiasm for the approaching holiday season. It was not until December 19, the day before the first of the students left for home that the spirit of Christmas finally tiptoed into St. Timothy's. On December 22, Mr. Fitzroy tiptoed out of the school, locked its doors behind him, trotted down the stairs to his car and drove off for a well deserved vacation.

On the day before the beginning of second semester, the reassembled staff and students enjoyed their last few minutes of freedom while waiting for Andrews to ring the dinner bell. Wilfred Willoughby-Wallows stepped from his lodgings and saw the head student leaving his room at the opposite end of the dorm. He watched and listened as Andrews stopped to speak to Meddows.

"Ah… it's you. Welcome back, Meddows. You'll try to behave yourself this term, I hope."

"I'll give it my best shot, Andrews," replied Meddows. "You can count on it."

"I didn't hear you talking to someone just now, did I?" asked the head student. His voice harboured an accusatory tone. Two sets of inquisitive eyes searched the cubicle.

"Now who could I possibly be talking to?" Meddows asked, all innocence. Andrews responded with an icy stare. Meddows flashed an enigmatic smile, rose and followed the head student onto the landing.

A moment later, Burns and O'Neil, no longer hearing voices, stepped out of the lockers at either side of Meddows' bed and sighed with relief. The few minutes they had been cooped up had seemed like hours. When the stowaways caught up with their friend outside the dorm they congratulated each other and joked about their lucky escape. Willoughby-Wallows, after pacing the length of the corridor, pushed the door open, stifling the boys' banter. He hustled the gang down the stairs when the call to chapel sounded.

From the cubicle closest to the dorm supervisor's lodgings, Emerson Jenks let his eyes follow Willoughby-Wallows to the senior dorm. As soon as the supervisor stepped onto the landing, Emerson hurried to the door of the man's rooms and turned the knob. Upon finding the door unlocked, he smiled and, at the sound of the bell, hurried towards the chapel. Second semester was officially underway.

+ − × ÷

"Meddows," whispered Emerson, the following Sunday morning. "We need to talk… come on."

Meddows stepped away from the younger boy and looked up and down the classroom corridor, his suspicion clearly visible to those waiting to mail their weekly letters home. "Whatcha want, Jenks?"

Emerson beckoned. Meddows exercised caution as he approached. Side by side they wandered down the hall. "Meddows…" began Emerson, in a tone conspirators might use, "tell me how you managed to soak Heffernan."

Meddows' eyes narrowed and darted from Emerson to the line-up and back. He pulled Emerson further from the crowd. "Where'd you hear about that, Jenks? Nobody's 'sposed tuh know that."

"Don't make me laugh, Meddows," replied Emerson. "You're a legend. Everybody knows that was your prank. Kids still talk about it, eh."

Meddows flashed a self-satisfied smile. "It was pretty complicated," he admitted. "You're not thinkin' 'bout trying it, are you, Jenks?"

"Why not?" asked Emerson. "That was one slick trick from what I hear. I'd like to see if I can pull it off too. But I'd need to know how you did it first. You know… so I can learn from you, eh."

Meddows looked up and down the corridor again. Emerson did the same. Only Guardiano, Burns and Matthews remained. They wore slightly puzzled expressions. Emerson slid his glasses up his nose then made a suggestion. "Let's talk about this somewhere else, Meddows? In the chapel… ten minutes. And get rid of those jokers, eh?" As he spoke, Emerson jerked a thumb towards the older boy's friends.

"Okay," agreed Meddows as he looked over his shoulder and dismissed Burns and Matthews. When he turned back, Emerson was gone.

In the silence of the chapel, Emerson waited, hunkered down, out of sight between the organ and the side wall. He had to make sure that Meddows arrived alone and was not planning a prank of his own. Ten minutes dragged on for hours. Emerson's legs began to cramp and he was sorely tempted to back out of the meeting. Just as his patience reached its limit, he heard a pew creak. He raised his head and peered over the empty benches. Meddows had entered through the side doors and was kneeling in the sacristans' bench. He appeared to be alone. Emerson stood and spoke the older boy's name.

"What's with all the cloak and dagger stuff?" whispered Meddows just loudly enough to be heard at the back of the chapel.

"C'mon," called Emerson and pointed to the rear door. "Let's go for a walk."

"Yuh got Guardiano waiting out there for me or somethin', don't yuh?" The statement was clearly accusatory.

Emerson and Meddows advanced towards the middle of the large room and lowered their voices. "Did you see Guardiano around?" demanded Emerson in a hoarse whisper. "What… don't you trust me?"

"Is the Pope an atheist?" Meddows laughed aloud. "Trust *you*? Right!"

"Keep it down, eh," warned Emerson and pressed his index finger to his lips.

"Why would I ever trust you after that stunt you pulled at the funeral?" hissed Meddows.

"Use your head, eh. How was I to know I'd have to stay up there all through mass, Meddows?" Emerson pointed towards the altar. "I didn't know rigor mortis didn't last very long. I told you, that wasn't my fault."

Meddows curled his lips and glared. "I still don't believe you, Jenks. Don't trust you neither."

"Believe whatever you like. Who cares?" Emerson replied with a shrug. "But just remember who saved your ugly butt, eh?"

Meddows looked towards the back door. "Okay, let's go… but you gotta leave first… I'll follow."

"Oh yeah. For sure," cried Emerson. "And run into your guys out there. No way! We go together… side by side." The two boys stared at each other for a moment. "How 'bout we use the side doors, Meddows?" suggested Emerson. After a moment's thought, Meddows nodded his assent.

Together, the two almost paranoid St. Timothy's students inched into the empty foyer and set off towards the locker room. Seconds after they left, Angelo Guardiano slipped out of the vestry and headed off to practice guitar. Emerson and Meddows donned winter jackets, toques and gloves, exited Disraeli Hall, walked down the main drive and crossed the highway, heading for the river. On the dock, they stood with their hands jammed into their coat pockets, rocking from foot to foot, looking out over the blanket of snow that covered the frozen river. Emerson asked the questions. Meddows gave the answers.

"Well?"

"Well, what?" answered Meddows.

"Well, how'd you do it?" replied Emerson. "How'd you get Heffernan?"

Meddows proved only too happy to satisfy the younger boy's curiosity. "I finish my shower, see," he began "and here comes Heffernan wanderin' in… late like usual. He tosses his PJs on the bench and goes in the showers, right?"

"Yeah…" said Emerson, "and?"

"And when he's showerin', I take 'em and stuff 'em in someone else's locker… his PJs, I mean." Meddows could not help laughing as he reconstructed the scene. Emerson laughed along with the older boy by way of encouragement.

"Well? Come on," demanded the younger boy.

"Take it easy," hissed Meddows as he booted a chunk of snow off the dock. "Don't rush me, okay?" The older boy shook his head to convey his annoyance and drew a long breath. "Anyways, I takes 'em, the PJs, eh, and then I stuff 'em in a locker, see? And I take off." Meddows chuckled again. "So… I'm back on the dorm landing and I've got this glass of water, see… a real big one, right… and cold as I can run it."

Meddows paused a moment, savouring the memory before proceeding. "Lights go out and I'm waitin' in the dark. Then I hear Heffernan comin' up the stairs… only I don't know for sure it's Heffernan 'til later, right?" added Meddows, getting into a rhythm with the telling. "He's real slow, right? He's tryin' to be quiet so he don't get caught. When he gets near the top, I let him have it… yeah, right smack in the kisser! Whoosh! Well he starts in a-yellin' and I run back inside and hop into bed. Everybody's hootin' and hollerin' and the super ain't back 'til everything's back to normal and… and… well, that's it."

Emerson hesitated, looking straight into Meddows' sparkling eyes. "Awesome!" the younger boy cried and slapped the storyteller on the shoulder. "That was brilliant, Meddows… dog-gone brilliant."

Emerson cupped his hands over his mouth and blew warm air through his fingers. Meddows ground the toe of his boot into the crusty snow as he absorbed his companion's adulation. He had always thought that his pranks deserved more admiration than they had received. Now, he resented others for not having exhibited the kind of appreciation Emerson had just expressed. He began to like the younger boy a little. He thought that he could even forgive the upstart for the black eye incident. The thought vaporized when alarm bells and sirens went off in Meddows' head.

"Too bad," groaned Emerson.

"Whatcha mean?" asked Meddows. His eyes narrowed to mere slits.

"I don't think I want to try it… way too dangerous… too many things to go wrong." Emerson frowned. "If anyone came along… well… I'd be in a heck of a mess. Man alive, I'd have to be some kind of fast-talker… like you, I mean… to get myself out of a jam like that." Meddows remained silent. "And I'd never find anybody dumb enough to fall for that one again," continued Emerson.

"Want'uh bet?" demanded Meddows. "I'll betcha."

"I don't know, Meddows. Maybe you're right… maybe not," replied Emerson. "I sure don't want to try it though. But… well… I was just thinking how great it would be to see you do it again."

"Oh, no, Jenks," cried Meddows as if to say, I know what you're up to. He continued, "I ain't stupid, you know."

"You're right. You'd probably get caught, eh?"

"No way," replied Meddows. "I ain't never been caught." Memories of *The Chapel Landing Incident*, *The Black Eye Episode* and *The Funeral Fiasco* seemed to have faded from the boy's memory. Meddows gazed off over the river with a dreamy smile gracing his face.

Emerson observed Meddows with the eyes of a hawk, imagining that his companion was reliving the prank. "C'mon, Meddows… do it again," urged the younger boy. "You're the best."

As Meddows stared at Emerson, a self-satisfied smile appeared on his face. Then, more quickly than it had formed, the smile vanished. Meddows studied the younger boy, frowning, squinting, pondering. Wariness hung like a veil upon his face. Emerson realized that something was wrong. He wondered whether he had pushed too hard or if his timing had been off. Emerson knew he had to refocus Meddows' thoughts.

"Man alive! Are you ever paranoid, Meddows!"

"I'm what, Jenks?"

"Paranoid… you know… suspicious."

"Oh!" said Meddows. "I knew that. But I got good reason tuh be pairin… perran... suspicious, Jenks." The boy shrugged and looked past Emerson to the far shore. His eyes seemed to glaze over. After a few moments, his face lit up. For a mere second, an evil sneer replaced a frown. The change did not escape Emerson's eye.

"Hey, Jenks," Meddows announced, "I got a great idea. You can do it but I'll help yuh. Yuh know, walk yuh through it, eh?" Emerson did not respond. "Help yuh get somebody just like I got Heffernan," continued an excited Meddows. "C'mon… it'll be fun."

Emerson could not have missed the sudden change in the older boy if he had tried. He ploughed snow over the edge of the dock with his foot and said nothing. The word 'caution' flashed bright orange in his head. He found Meddows' eagerness to help problematic but intriguing. Emerson felt ill at ease, unsure if the meeting was progressing as well as he had hoped or not. He thought for a full minute then looked at his grinning companion, weighing the situation in his mind. He was positive that Meddows had dreamt up a prank. He was not at all sure he could figure out some way to turn it back on the older boy. "You're positive?" he asked hesitantly. "I wouldn't want to get caught or anything, eh."

"Don't be such a chicken, Jenks," chided Meddows. "Let's go."

Instantaneously, the exact same thought crossed each boy's mind: game on!

Fifteen minutes later, the two boys stood together on the landing outside the junior dormitory, leaning over the railing and talking. Meddows explained the intricacies of the plan. "Listen, Jenks..." he instructed by way of a review, "I'll find some way to keep a couple of guys from gettin' back from the showers on time." In silence, Emerson stared at his companion. Meddows seemed spurred on by what he took for admiration. "We'll come back here, I'll get yuh some real cold water and then you're on your own."

"Okay, Meddows," replied Emerson and started for the stairs.

Meddows turned and grabbed the younger boy by the shoulder as he passed. "Be in the shower room by 9:15 at the latest. I'll take care of the rest."

Emerson nodded again and left Meddows alone on the landing. "And don't be late, Jenks," ordered Meddows as he leaned over the railing again and watched his intended victim depart.

Emerson stared back and repositioned his glasses. "Shower room... 9:15," he replied.

After chapel that evening, as the other students scampered up the stairs to the dormitory, Emerson scampered down the stairs to the showers. He had already stowed his towel, soap and shampoo in his gym locker to save precious minutes. He needed to check the area for signs of any pranks Meddows and his crew might have in store for him. The shower room was actually two rooms. A larger area held banks of army green metal lockers and candy apple red wooden benches. The smaller room was divided into three dozen individual stalls. Emerson found no one hiding in the showers or the gymnasium. He considered checking inside the lockers but realized that a person hiding in a metal locker would make too much noise to surprise anyone. Next, he blocked the door leading to the auditorium stage with a bench. Anyone opening that door would set off his makeshift alarm. If a threat did exist, it would have to come at him head on.

Students entered the new building and proceeded – non-threateningly Emerson judged – towards him. The showering routine unfolded with no perceptible deviation from the norm, except that Meddows was late. He arrived just as Emerson, draped in his towel, was about to enter the showers. As his accomplice approached, Emerson felt the needle on his internal threat indicator jump. Something about his collaborator's behaviour, some subliminal signal, set off alarms. Meddows nodded as he passed.

Ten minutes later, the two pranksters sat side by side. Like a boy obsessed, Emerson dried between his toes.

Willoughby-Wallows glanced at the two boys in passing, checked the time, stuck his head into the steam-filled shower room and told the slowpokes to speed it up. The dormitory supervisor continued to pace the locker room. "Would you two get a move on," he grumbled. "You're taking an awfully long time there, Mr. Jenks." Again, he pushed the door to the showers ajar. "Come on," he called. "Speed it up in there." Two more students, then a third emerged from the steam and dried themselves. Water continued to run.

Emerson slid closer to Meddows and whispered, "Who's left?"

Meddows put a finger to his lips, "Badham, for sure. I seen him... and Albertson, I think."

Emerson grunted. He had kept close tabs on those who came and went so realized that his companion spoke the truth.

Willoughby-Wallows paced by once more. The boys ignored his suspicious glances.

When he could no longer hear the dorm supervisor's footsteps, Meddows leaned close to Emerson. "The water's still running so somebody's gotta be in there. Now, listen," ordered Meddows, "you gotta get going before the super catches on."

"You fellows better not be talking over there?" threatened Willoughby-Wallows from the back of the locker room.

"Better get goin'," whispered Meddows as Emerson uttered a loud denial. "I'll be right behind you."

As Badham stepped from the showers, Emerson gathered up his belongings, gave Meddows a wink and joined three others as they hurried off towards the dormitory. When he reached the landing, he waited, one hand on the doorknob, ready to advance or retreat should his plan begin to unravel. To pass the time, he practiced excuses he could use if Andrews or Willoughby-Wallows discovered him there.

Emerson's heart leapt when Meddows pushed the door open and stepped from the dorm onto the landing. Under a towel, the older boy carried a two quart, open-topped, plastic container filled with water. "Here," he said. "It's really cold too… been out on the windowsill for hours… in the snow, eh. Now… all you have to do is wait 'til lights-out," instructed Meddows. "Andrews just left to ring the bell. You gunna be okay?"

Emerson did not answer immediately. Meddows was being far too helpful for comfort. "Yeah," replied Emerson eventually, while looking into his companion's eyes. "Everything's cool." He worried that somehow he had overlooked some all important detail. He watched Meddows' every move, listened to his every word, evaluated his every gesture and facial expression. Meddows' efforts to help were either genuine – which Emerson found hard to believe – or, the older boy was working a very well crafted prank.

Just ten seconds later the lights went out, leaving the two conspirators in complete darkness. The landing was so dark the boys could not see one another. Meddows whispered, "Good luck, Jenks… see you in the morning. Yuh gotta tell me all about it, eh." He opened the door and re-entered the dormitory.

"Okay," muttered Emerson to himself. "Here goes." He took a deep breath and exhaled gently to slow his heart rate. He moved to the door, used his free hand to locate the knob and turned to face the stairs. He could see nothing but the faint glow cast onto the lower landing by a shaded nightlight. With nothing to do but wait, Emerson asked himself what he would have planned for Meddows had their roles been reversed. A troubling thought flashed in Emerson's mind. He reached back and clutched the doorknob. It turned easily and he felt the catch draw back and release. Reassured, he exhaled and nodded. Meddows had not locked the door on him so he could still make good his escape. Emerson's heart raced once more when he remembered his own use of doorstops. "False alarm," he whispered when he recalled that the dormitory doors opened onto the landing. In case someone directed Andrews to climb the stairs to the junior dormitory for once, Emerson set the water on the floor to avoid any possible delay in abandoning his post.

Emerson tried to remember the last time he had so many misgivings about a prank. "High risk... high return," muttered the boy who waited all alone in the darkness. To calm his jangling nerves, he began reviewing Meddows' behaviour in the classroom corridor that morning, in the chapel, on the dock at the river, on the landing earlier in the day, in the shower room and again just a few minutes earlier. He could not stop thinking that the fellow had been up to something. But try as he might, Emerson could not discover what it could be.

Momentarily, a barely audible noise – had he heard something or only though he had – caused Emerson to empty his mind of everything not directly related to his present circumstances. He became extraordinarily alert. His skin tingled. He raised a cupped hand to his ear and cocked it towards the sound. He heard the unmistakable, tentative shuffle of a person's feet. The noise, he was sure, was not made by Andrews. Emerson felt an unexpected calm pass through his body. He checked his breathing to ensure it would not alert his mark. He bent down, picked up the container of cold water and moved to the head of the stairs.

After Meddows left for the dorm, Willoughby-Wallows chased Badham and Albertson from the locker room. The two boys had dallied as long as they dared. Now, they ran full-out through the main building towards the dorm and, halfway up the far stairs, passed Andrews on his way to ring the last bell of the day. Meddows' threats had persuaded them to avoid the stairs to the junior dorm.

After Badham and Albertson hurried off, the Greek and Latin teacher listened to the running water and ordered the stragglers to hurry up. When his words were ignored, Willoughby-Wallows entered the showers and found the room empty. In the stalls furthest from the door, the taps had been left running. Willoughby-Wallows grumbled about wasting hot water, turned off the faucets, snapped the light switch to off and headed to the dorm. On his way, he checked the gymnasium. The lights had been left on – more grumbling about the price of electricity. He checked the common rooms and found them in darkness.

Willoughby-Wallows had just entered the main building and walked halfway across the broad expanse of the ping-pong room when Andrews threw the main switch and the lights went out. The dorm supervisor stopped dead in his tracks, pointed his flashlight ahead of him and slid the thumb-switch forward. Nothing happened. He tapped the light against the palm of his hand, shook it violently and tried again… still nothing. He banged the flashlight against his hip and slid the switch back and forth in vain. When he raised it to his face to determine the cause of the problem, he laughed a loud sardonic laugh and shook his head in disbelief.

Prudence dictated that he wait until his eyes grew accustomed to the dark before proceeding. Creaks and cracks he had never heard before sounded all around him. He breathed in odours that he had never smelled before. As the moments passed, the noises and smells grew in intensity. Willoughby-Wallows became aware of how cool and draughty the old building was. He waited for what seemed like an hour, alone in the inky blackness. The wait proved fruitless. The man could still see nothing. He squinted as he passed his hand in front of his face – nothing.

Willoughby-Wallows felt his heart knock hard against his ribs. He spoke to himself in an effort to calm his rattled nerves. "Just relax, Wilf," he whispered. "Take a few deep breaths."

He held his arms out at shoulder height and inched forward. Groping about like a blind man, he pawed his way forward in the dark. He felt himself growing increasingly desperate as he searched for the room's side wall. He wondered how far away it could be. It was then that he heard, or imagined he heard, a scurrying sound. He gasped and froze in place with one foot wavering in midair. At the thought of mice, or worse, rats, his groping quickly turned to windmill-like flailing, as if he had determined to navigate by dumb luck. It took Willoughby-Wallows five seconds to travel ten feet.

"At this rate they'll find me here in the morning… rat-bitten," he muttered." He sighed. "Oh… don't think about rats, Wilf."

The panic driven approach having failed, Willoughby-Wallows changed gears, inhaled deeply and adopted a more methodical approach. He slid his left foot forward and stopped then brought his right foot up beside his left and stopped again. He repeated the process with greater confidence and managed to move a bit more quickly. Things were going well until a stray cobweb brushed his face. He jumped and thrashed about in a frenzy. Although its volume did not fully register with him, a howl escaped his lips and echoed down the hallway. The wide-eyed dormitory supervisor stifled his scream by clasping both hands over his mouth.

In the far stairwell leading to the senior dorm, Andrews stopped, cocked his head to one side, clamped his eyes closed and strained his hearing. Had he or had he not heard someone shout? No further sound reached him. He considered investigating. He even took two downward steps, but stopped, shrugged and, as was his habit, climbed the stairs to his room.

When almost fully recovered from his fright, Willoughby-Wallows patted his chest and made huffing, puffing sounds. He was thankful that no one could see him. That thought led to a good-natured laugh at his own expense. He imagined himself an actor in a B-movie trying to portray a ghoul or a mummy back from the grave. "Now don't go thinking about ghouls, Wilf," he whispered. Willoughby-Wallows' left foot slid forward once more and he made slow but steady progress. Upon reaching the wall, he regained his bearings – and some of his composure – and passed through the corridor with relative ease. He arrived unscathed at the bottom of the stairs which would take him past the chapel to the junior dorm. He tried his flashlight again... still no luck.

He slid his foot along the floor until it touched the riser, lifted the other foot and set it down on the first step. His success allowed him to risk a self-satisfied smile. "One," he whispered with pride. By the time he reached the bottom of the last set of stairs he was making exceptionally good time, considering the pitch darkness. "Left hand on railing, twenty steps to the landing, a 180-degree turn to the right, twenty more steps and I'm at the top," he mumbled in an effort to reassure himself.

Willoughby-Wallows had just made the last turn when he heard, or imagined he heard, movement on the landing above. In the velvety blackness, he froze and strained his eyes, desperately wishing his flashlight would work. He could see nothing. He listened but heard nothing. Dismissing his concerns, he made sure of his starting point and began to climb the final twenty steps.

"One... two..." he counted in a low mutter. "Five... six..." he added before a pause. "Nine, ten... halfway there," he whispered. Willoughby-

Wallows felt no real relief but he felt he was at least on the cusp of relief.

On hearing approaching footsteps, Emerson moved almost noiselessly to the head of the stairs, stopped and listened. He thought he could discern mumbling. Yes… his victim was drawing within firing range. Emerson could hear the footsteps halt on the lower landing. The boy breathed again only when his mark began counting off the steps. He's making this way too easy, thought Emerson. He could now discern the sound of heavy breathing. His victim's count reached twelve and then thirteen. Emerson raised the container and tried to calculate the distance to the fifteenth step. When his target's count reached fourteen, Emerson brought his arm back and then forward in the motion used by lob-ball pitchers.

Willoughby-Wallows stepped forward, whispering the word 'fifteen', just as the cold water struck him square on the chest. The loud splash, a gasp and guttural, not-quite-human noises informed Emerson that he had hit his mark.

The dorm supervisor shrieked and made shocked, sputtering sounds. Emerson had never heard the like. It was the intensity of the commotion that caused the boy to remain frozen on the landing, not the fact that his victim was the school's Greek and Latin professor. Emerson had never intended to waste such a great prank on the likes of a Badham or an Albertson. He had marked Willoughby-Wallows long before he entered the man's lodgings to disable his flashlight. This prank was intended for none other than Wilfred Willoughby-Wallows and Emerson supposed that it had come off very well indeed.

Emerson had made only one minor change to his original plan. When he had arranged the scheming session at the river, he had wanted Meddows to throw the water, believing the super's flashlight was disabled when it most definitely was not. Well at least now, Emerson figured, Meddows will have to admit that he is no longer St. Timothy's best prankster.

Amusement, not good judgement, kept Emerson at the scene of the crime longer than usual. He basked in his own success until Willoughby-Wallows began to regain his composure. At this juncture, the boy decided it was prudent to quit the landing. He grabbed and twisted the doorknob in one flowing motion, yanking it outwards. Emerson heard a clink followed by a clank from within the dorm. The knob in his hand moved effortlessly – indeed too effortlessly – towards him; the door did not. He stood on the pitch dark landing caught between a sopping wet dormitory supervisor and a door he could not open. In his hand he held a totally useless doorknob.

A loud banging began on the opposite side of the door. Someone – some-many given the commotion – tried to gain access to the landing. Emerson heard complaints about the missing door handle. Before he had time to properly assess his predicament, he heard Willoughby-Wallows' voice.

"Who's there?" demanded the dorm supervisor. Emerson made no reply. "You, I say… you on the landing… who's there? You can't get past me, Sir," cried the dormitory supervisor. "Speak up… answer me."

Emerson remained silent, his mind working frantically. He could see nothing. He did not need to see in order to tell that the perpetually calm, cool, collected Greek and Latin instructor was working himself into a lather.

"Okay… I'm fed up with this nonsense. I'll ask you just one last time…" continued Willoughby-Wallows. "And you'd better speak up." The man's determination was perfectly obvious. "What is your name, Sir?" Willoughby-Wallows waited for a reply.

Under such adverse conditions, a less resourceful prankster would strike colours, but not Emerson Jenks. The boy had escaped from many a tight spot before. He was not one to concede defeat before doing so was unavoidable. He took a deep breath and wracked his brain, trying to make the best of a bad situation. A thought, a daring thought, a desperate thought struck him. Emerson decided he had but one chance to escape, albeit a long-shot, and a dangerous long-shot too. He braced himself, hoped for the best while fearing the worst and rolled the dice.

Willoughby-Wallows advanced a step and spoke again. "I will count to three, Sir… one… two…"

In a voice only slightly louder than a whisper, Emerson – a tiny twinge of conscience notwithstanding – replied. "It's me, Sir… Meddows."

"*Meddows!* I see, Meddows. What do you think you are doing, Sir? Are you completely out of your mind?" After a pause, the dormitory supervisor spoke again. "You get this mess cleaned up and right now... no, wait... first thing in the morning, Meddows, before the fellows have to come down these stairs," shouted Willoughby-Wallows.

"Sir," whispered Emerson.

The dorm supervisor continued, "I shall have to report this to the headmaster, you know."

"Sir," whispered Emerson again.

"Now, get to bed, Meddows. What on earth were you thinking? You must be mad." As if he had only then heard the racket coming from the dorm, Willoughby-Wallows shouted, "Quiet in there. Get to bed... all of you." As the dorm supervisor gained the landing, Emerson started down the stairs.

"Where do you think you're going, Meddows?" demanded the man.

"Door's broke," whispered Emerson.

Willoughby-Wallows turned his attention to the din emanating from the dorm. Emerson tossed the doorknob back onto the landing and hurried off. The prankster knew he was not yet safe. He would breathe normally again only when under the cover of darkness in the company of his mates. He made his way to the senior dormitory and slipped undetected into the flow of traffic shuffling towards the far end of the floor. Students were still huddled around the door in the dark when he arrived on the scene of confusion. Emerson melted into the throng.

Willoughby-Wallows worked on his side of the door. Andrews, with flashlight blazing, helped on the other side. Together, they managed to get the door open.

"To bed now... all of you," ordered the dormitory supervisor. "I think we've had just about enough excitement for one night."

"Quiet!" shouted the head student and flashed his light from face to face. "Get to bed... NOW." Andrews' bellow finally restored order.

Emerson jumped into bed, pulled the covers up under his chin and sucked in a great gulp of air. His breath escaped in a prolonged, silent sigh. "You are one very lucky boy, Emerson Jenks," he said just loud enough so no one could hear. An uncontrollable shudder swept up his spine and raised the hair on the back of his neck.

Poltergeist

The effects of the evening's events proved more disturbing than Willoughby-Wallows could have imagined. In horrid dreams he was spirited off to dark places… gloomy, ghastly places inhabited by ghosts, goblins, ghouls and horrifying wraiths. He tossed and turned throughout the long night and arose even earlier than usual in the morning gloom. Bathed in the glow from his desk lamp, he sat, staring at a blank form, pondering Meddows' fate. An inner voice told him to let the matter rest. Willoughby-Wallows asked himself what real harm had been done. Another voice insisted that he had to follow through with discipline or risk having every boy in the place up to mischief. The young man ran his fingers through his hair, scowled and made his decision.

"Mr. Meddows… you'll just have to pay the piper," he declared aloud. "I'm sorry, but I can't help it." The dormitory supervisor took up his pen and began to write.

When finished, thoughtfully pursing his lips, he slipped the report into a manila envelope, tapped it against his palm several times and then tossed it across his desk. He gathered up a towel, toiletries and his flashlight and started for the door. He tried the flashlight again – he really did not expect it to work; it didn't.

"Well… off you go," muttered Willoughby-Wallows as he stepped out of his lodgings.

The dormitory was cloaked in darkness. Only the rhythmic breathing of the sleeping students could be heard. With his right hand dragging along the wall he made his way to the far end of the corridor where he knocked on the head student's door. It took Andrews only a minute to answer. He stepped from his room with his flashlight tucked under his chin. The beam of light danced about the dorm as he fumbled with the belt on his housecoat.

"Who's there? What's the matter?" he asked.

"It's me," answered Willoughby-Wallows.

"Sir?" replied Andrews. His voice conveyed confusion bordering on alarm.

"It's alright, Andrews… relax. You know where Mr. Meddows sleeps, right?"

"Of course I do, Sir… why?"

"Would you please get him up and have him clean up that mess he made last night? The water on the stairs, I mean."

"Oh! Yes, Sir. Glad to. I'll supervise myself, Sir!" replied Andrews.

Willoughby-Wallows, whistling softly, started off for the staff shower room.

Andrews located Meddows' bed and, aided by the wooden-handled mop he had acquired on his way, rousted the boy from between his sheets.

"What?" demanded Meddows after raising himself on an elbow and squinting into the beam from Andrews' flashlight. "Who's that?"

"Do you really need to ask?" answered Andrews. "Come with me, Meddows."

"Hold on, Andrews," complained Meddows. "What'd I do? I ain't done nothin'… honest." He flopped back onto his bed.

Andrews focussed the light on the boy's face. Meddows blinked and tried to shield his eyes while protesting his innocence. Andrews shook his head in disbelief. Meddows massaged the sleep from his eyes and dragged his fingers across his face before sliding out of bed and stepping into his slippers. He padded along behind Andrews unsure of where he was being led. Not until they reached the landing outside the junior dormitory did the head student speak again.

"Now you listen, Meddows and I'll talk… okay? You're going to go get a scrub bucket and use this—" he held out the mop, "—to clean up this mess. Got it?" Meddows was too shocked to protest. "I'm going to stand here and give you enough light to see by," Andrews added. Meddows opened his mouth to speak. "I don't want to hear it, Meddows. Now, more work and less talk, okay? Oh yeah… and fix the door when you're done."

"But, Andrews…" Meddows whined.

"You're pathetic!" declared Andrews, cutting the boy off. "Absolutely pathetic!" He pointed to the wet floor and hissed, "Just do it. I'll be right here watching."

On his return, Willoughby-Wallows found the head student alone, sitting on the top step. Andrews shone his flashlight back and forth over the stairs and landing.

"Is that good enough, Sir?" asked Andrews. "If not…"

Willoughby-Wallows nodded his appreciation before Andrews finished speaking. "Well done, Andrews. Thank you."

Andrews drew Willoughby-Wallows' attention to the doorknob. "It's back in working order, Sir."

"Fine work, Andrews…" replied the dormitory supervisor, "the way you handled the situation, I mean." He returned to his room, dressed and left to ring the morning bell.

At 5:45, a familiar loud clanging filled the dormitory. Minutes later, upon entering the dorm, Willoughby-Wallows shouted, "*Laudate fideles*… up and at 'em, boys." His cheerful voice echoed down the corridor and through the cubicles. Boys scurried to the washrooms, returned to their lockers, dressed and dragged themselves off to morning mass.

At the end of the service, Andrews did not signal permission to proceed to breakfast. Heads turned to discover that Mr. Fitzroy had entered the chapel. His baritone voice filled the room. "Mr. Meddows," he called. After a dramatic pause he added, "My office… now, Sir." He nodded to Andrews who sounded the dismissal.

The boys left their pews with downcast eyes and in better order than usual. They filed down the stairs into the refectory. The topic of discussion at breakfast was Mr. Meddows' likely fate.

Meddows reported to the headmaster's office, knocked and, on receiving no response, took a seat in the corridor. He placed his elbows on his knees and buried his face in his hands. But he could not remain seated. He fretted, pacing and sighing, sighing and pacing, until Fitzroy arrived fifteen minutes later.

"Come," ordered the headmaster and entered his office. He carried a full cup of steaming coffee and what remained of a toast in his hands.

"Yes, Sir?" inquired Meddows.

Fitzroy walked to his desk while instructing Meddows to close the door behind him. The man sat and, after adjusting his glasses, tipped his head forward and peered over them. Silently, he studied the pasty-faced boy in front of him. Meddows stood before the headmaster, his lower lip clamped between his teeth, shifting his weight from foot to foot and saying nothing.

"I'm waiting, Sir," barked the headmaster and counted silently to five before adding. "I'm simply dying to hear your explanation."

"Pardon, Sir?" Meddows screwed up his face and cocked his head to the side.

"Pardon!" demanded Fitzroy. "What do you mean, pardon?"

Meddows looked around, frowning and scratching the back of his neck. He avoided eye contact with his inquisitor. Fitzroy watched the boy's performance and waited.

"My explanation a… a… about what, Sir?" asked Meddows.

"So that's how it's going to be?" replied the headmaster. "More games is it, Meddows?" He stood, removed his glasses and began to polish the lenses as he walked around behind the squirming boy, looking at him askance in passing. "I've got you this time, Meddows. I told you I would… sooner or later." Meddows cringed but dared not turn around. "Figure you can wriggle out of this one too, eh," suggested Fitzroy. "I thought as much."

"But… but… what did I do, Sir?" gasped the befuddled boy as he wracked his brain trying to determine which of his many petty crimes and misdemeanours had brought him to the office. The thought that Emerson had squealed entered his head but was dismissed. Meddows believed Emerson Jenks was a jerk but he knew the younger boy was not a snitch. The boy's mind raced. A question flashed in Meddows' mind. If Jenks had squealed, why wasn't he being called to account too?

"Well?" demanded Fitzroy, interrupting the boy's rapid flow of thoughts.

Meddows was not about to confess before he knew of what he was accused. "What's this all about, Sir?" he asked.

"Sit," ordered Fitzroy. The boy sat. The headmaster gave him a minute to reflect then marched to the office door, opened it and peered outside. "Come in, Sir, come in," he said. Mr. Willoughby-Wallows entered the office and followed the headmaster across the room. "Young Mr. Meddows here has suffered a memory lapse. He seems to have forgotten all about his little escapade last night," advised Fitzroy. Turning to the boy, he added, "That's right, is it not, Sir?"

Meddows' hands grasped his temples as his brain grasped for answers. He stared at the floor. Mr. Fitzroy took a manila folder from his desk and handed it to Willoughby-Wallows. "Would you be so kind as to refresh this gentleman's memory, Sir?" he asked.

Willoughby-Wallows removed the report from the folder, cleared his throat and read. The highlight of the account, Meddows' admission of guilt on the landing, came as quite a shock to the boy. He came out of his chair as if he had been pinched. "But… but… but, Sir…" Meddows stammered before he was silenced. His mind remained mired in mystification and misery. Every thought but one fled far away. In his head, like the message on a theatre marquee, flashed the word 'doomed'.

The written report ended with a recommendation for leniency due to the boy's forthrightness upon being caught. Adlibbing, Willoughby-Wallows reported how Meddows had already done a commendable job of cleaning up the mess. The headmaster stared at the boy with a self-satisfied smirk on his face. "Well now, young man, what have you to say for yourself now, eh? You'll not weasel out of this one. Ha!"

"It wasn't me, Sir. I…" began Meddows.

"It wasn't you?" replied the headmaster and threw his hands into the air in astonishment bordering on hysteria. "You confessed, Sir." He gathered himself and, with a chuckle added, "He confessed, Mr. Walloughby-Willows. Did he not confess, Sir?"

The supervisor nodded and gave the boy a pitying look.

"But, Sir, I didn't… really I…" muttered Meddows. He clamped both hands on his head and tried to speak, but his tongue failed him.

The headmaster stared at Meddows, or rather through him, with an unblinking gaze. "If you didn't do it… if you didn't confess… why on earth would you go and clean up the mess this morning? Answer me that," demanded Fitzroy. He returned to his chair and sat down like TV's Perry Mason after presenting an open-and-shut case to the judge and jury.

Meddows' mouth fell open. He looked to Willoughby-Wallows with eyes that pleaded for deliverance. Meddows was rarely at a loss for words but he found himself dumb before his accusers.

"Come, come, Meddows," admonished Fitzroy and groaned. "Let's not prolong this. Mr. Wallo… sorry, I meant Willerly… or rather…"

"Willoughby-Wallows, Sir."

"Yes, of course, Mr. Willoughby-Wallows here clearly identified you as the culprit who soaked him to the skin." In triumph, Fitzroy turned to his Greek and Latin man in anticipation of even more damning testimony.

"Well, Sir…" began Willoughby Wallows. The dorm supervisor raised and lowered one hand in front of him, palm down, while carefully studying Meddows' height.

"Well what?" demanded Fitzroy. "Well what, I say."

"I believe, Sir…" added Willoughby-Wallows, hesitating, "that this young man… Meddows, I should say… may be the victim of a… a… of a nasty trick, Sir."

"Pardon me!" demanded Fitzroy and fixed his bulging eyes on the dormitory supervisor.

"Well, Sir… now that I think about it, I believe that the person I encountered on the stairs…" He studied Meddows' frame once more and continued. "He was… well, Sir… somewhat shorter than this gentleman, Sir… I think. And the voice, Sir… I just can't be sure—"

"—But you must have gotten a look at him, man? Surely…" cried Fitzroy, interrupting.

"But it was pitch black, Sir. The lights *were* off, you know," replied a defensive Willoughby-Wallows. As the two men exchanged comments, a bug-eyed Meddows skulked away backwards into the shadows.

"But you had your flashlight," the headmaster stated. "You did, didn't you? You did remember to use it, I hope."

The headmaster's sarcastic tone seemed not to register with Willoughby-Wallows. "I did, Sir… have it, that is, but it… it wasn't working, Sir."

"Wasn't working!" repeated Fitzroy in near horror. "What do you mean, it wasn't working?"

"That *was* odd, Sir," continued Willoughby-Wallows as he scratched his head. "When I checked the batteries just now… they were in backwards, Sir. I can't imagine how I could have made such a silly mistake. For the life of me…"

Fitzroy looked at Willoughby-Wallows with disgust and at Meddows with disappointment. "Once again Mr. Meddows… I know you're involved in this disgrace… up to your eyeballs too… and I'll prove it."

"Yes, Sir… I… I… I mean, no, Sir," stuttered Meddows, unsure of exactly what he meant.

"Just go, Meddows!" ordered the headmaster and pointed to the exit. In haste, Meddows backed to the door and turned to leave.

"Meddows!" called the headmaster. "You watch your step, Meddows. You tread too near the line, Sir."

"Sir," replied the boy and stepped from the office. Three times before rounding the corner in the corridor, he glanced back over his shoulder to see if he would be recalled.

"Wilfred!" Fitzroy shouted the name. "I suggest, Sir, that you be more careful in future." The headmaster paused and looked at the younger gentleman. "And might I suggest you begin locking your door when out of your lodgings. To do otherwise is to invite disasters like this." Willoughby-Wallows made no reply as he handed the report back to the headmaster. "And…" Fitzroy continued and paused, "from now on, please check your flashlight… *before* you head out in the evening."

"Yes, Sir. Will that be all, Sir?" The headmaster turned away. Willoughby-Wallows broke for the door, forgetting to close it when he stepped into the hall. Fitzroy dropped the useless report into the wastebasket and sighed. Before it landed in the trash, the dorm supervisor was hurrying down the corridor, his mind preoccupied with his flashlight's mysterious failure. "What a strange coincidence… that I'd put the batteries in wrong like that," he muttered. "And just when I needed it most… how very peculiar?" In his dazed state, he failed to notice Emerson Jenks as they passed.

After the Greek and Latin professor left him, Fitzroy raised his coffee cup to his lips. On tasting the tepid liquid, he set it down and then sat forward with his hands pressed palms down on his desk. He shook his head in frustration when he heard a light tap on his door. "Come," he muttered, barely loud enough to be heard through the open doorway. The man's voice was the voice of the utterly vanquished.

Emerson poked his head into the office. "Sir… do you have a minute, Sir?" he asked. Upon being beckoned forward, Emerson continued,

"You told me to let you know if those gho… I mean, my friends came back, Sir… remember?"

Fitzroy fell back in his chair, pressed his fists to his forehead and gazed at the boy. "Yes, of course," he moaned, sitting up again. "Go ahead, Jenks."

"Well, Sir… they're back… and I think they mean to stay, Sir," announced Emerson as he advanced.

Fitzroy set his glasses on the end of his nose and squinted at Emerson over them. He stood and folded his arms across his chest. The fingers of his right hand beat a tattoo on the bicep of his left arm. "Continue, Jenks."

"They didn't say anything else," answered the boy. "They just popped in and told me they liked the place and that they've come to stay. That's all, Sir."

A long, uncomfortable pause delayed the exchange. "Popped in?" Fitzroy asked after a prolonged, probing stare into the boy's unblinking eyes. For several seconds, Emerson stood stock still, a study in serenity. "This wouldn't have anything to do with last night's disturbance would it, Jenks? I mean… that didn't get you upset or anything did it?" inquired Fitzroy.

"Oh, no, Sir," answered Emerson. "I only ran into the… to my friends that is, Sir, on the landing… just now, Sir."

"I see, Jenks… is there anything else?"

"No, Sir."

"Well then," continued Fitzroy as he glanced first at the roll-top desk then at his pocket watch, "I suppose you should get yourself off to class." Emerson adjusted his glasses as he backed haltingly away and, upon reaching the door, opened his mouth as if to speak. "Was there anything else, Jenks?" asked the headmaster.

Emerson's eyes darted to the door of the headmaster's sleeping room before he spoke. Fitzroy's eyes followed the boy's glance. "Uh… I guess not, Sir."

"Off you go then." The headmaster's eyes remained fixed on his bedroom door.

Emerson stepped into the hallway, pulled the door to and pressed his back against it. He smiled a satisfied smile and skipped away, whistling softly to himself. He arrived in his classroom early, positioned himself out of sight behind the open door and waited for the bell. The last people he wanted to run into were Meddows and his gang.

Fitzroy sat down and buried his face in his hands for a moment before punching the intercom button. "Mrs. Woods… get me Mr. and Mrs. Je—… never mind… uh… Dr. Graham. No wait! Ah… Dr. Graham, I mean…" As he waited for his secretary to place the call, he stared at the roll-top desk, then let his eyes wander across to his sleeping room door.

As Willoughby-Wallows was about to leave his room for his morning class, he noticed the confiscated penlight Andrews had given him. It stood upright on his bookshelf exactly where he had left it. Upon opening it, he discovered that the batteries were inserted incorrectly. He stared long and hard at his door, removed his key from a wall hook, tossed it in the air, caught it and deposited it in his jacket pocket. The dormitory supervisor, sadder but wiser for the experience on the landing, exited the room and, after locking the door, hurried to the classroom corridor.

Fitzroy tidied his desk and prepared for the upcoming directors' meeting. He found it extremely difficult to concentrate on budgets and fund raising with concerns about Emerson Jenks and seeds of doubt about spectral visitations swirling in his mind. His eyes strayed from the rows and columns on the balance sheet and darted about the room in response to every sound. He scoffed at himself each time he thought his staunch disbelief in ghosts might be flagging.

Meddows ate a late breakfast with his three closest friends gathered around him. They failed to determine precisely how Meddows' prank had gone so badly wrong and plotted their revenge. For days Meddows' miraculous escape provided grist for the school's rumour mill. Despite a hundred different theories, no one could fathom how someone – only Meddows and his gang knew who – had managed to turn the tables on the older boy.

Emerson did his best to steer clear of Meddows and stay close to his best friend whose guitar playing received more than the usual amount of attention.

+ − × ÷

After night prayers the following Friday, Mr. Fitzroy walked to the front of the chapel. "Gentlemen," he announced, "I'll be leaving early tomorrow and will not return until late Sunday night. In my absence, Mr. Willoughby-Wallows, and, if he is not available, Miss Strupples, will be in charge. I do hope you will not take advantage of their inexperience during my absence." He continued, saying, "Also, I have very good reason to believe that one or more of you has been entering the faculty wing to perpetrate silly pranks on my staff. Several upsetting events have been reported. They all point to mischief by someone in this room. Beware Gentlemen… serious consequences await anyone caught in the east wing. Am I understood?"

Emerson and Meddows cringed and exchanged glances. Neither could determine if the other's gaze signified implicit guilt or jealous admiration.

Fitzroy scanned his audience in vain, looking for someone in a crisis of conscience. "And, finally…" he paused then added, "immediately following dismissal, I need to see you in my office, Mr. Jenks." A dull thump was heard and the students, except for Emerson, Meddows and Andrews, stood to leave. Frozen in place, Emerson stared straight ahead. The chapel was almost empty before the hair on the back of his neck settled down. The mention of his name, after the news of students in Gladstone Hall, had given him a start. Meddows knelt with his elbows on the back of a pew, feigning a level of piety of which few would have believed him capable. With his chin resting on his clasped hands, he watched Emerson react. From the back row, Andrews watched Meddows' every move… indeed every nuance of his every move. Emerson, when he stood and turned to go, noted Meddows' mocking sneer and the perverse pleasure lurking behind it.

Minutes later, a nervous Emerson Jenks met the headmaster outside his office. "I've spoken to Dr. Graham about… well, about your friends, Jenks," the man advised. Emerson looked into the headmaster's face but did not speak. "He wants to see you on Monday," the headmaster continued, "for a little chat."

"A chat, Sir?" asked Emerson.

"That's what he said… Dr. Graham, that is," replied Fitzroy. "First thing Monday morning."

"I see, Sir. But what about class?"

"I'll see to that," answered Fitzroy. "You go straight to the infirmary after breakfast on Monday, okay?"

"Yes, Sir. Is that all, Sir?"

+ − × ÷

Emerson watched Fitzroy drive away on Saturday morning then meandered along the corridor towards the double oak doors, whistling and glancing up at the dusty graduation pictures. Upon reaching Fitzroy's office and finding the coast clear, he pressed down on one of the latches. When he heard a faint click, Emerson opened the door an inch or two then drew it closed. As he ambled back down the corridor, he wore a menacing smile.

Over the weekend, preparing to meet Dr. Graham proved daunting. Emerson had to dream up a story the doctor might buy. As his mother had assured the headmaster, he had a very active imagination. His creative powers were being put to the test. He was burdened further by having to design and, if possible execute, a prank on the headmaster.

An hour before dinner on Sunday afternoon, Emerson revisited Mr. Fitzroy's office. He stepped inside and closed the door behind him. "Ah, to work!" he whispered. Expertly, he darted from desk lamp to floor lamp. He walked to the window behind the desk and peeked through the drapes. There was no one in sight. "Well… that makes things easier," he muttered. He placed a piece of tape across the crack between the window and its frame before breaking it and raising the window as high as it would go. He then inched the main door open, made sure no one was about and left the room. He hurried around the corner into the infirmary and, finding it empty, removed a paper bag from a cupboard and dumped its contents onto the bed – an old tennis ball, string, some thumbtacks and other odds and ends. He inched back the curtain and peered outside. Sixteen feet away, in the wall opposite, the headmaster's open window gaped back at him. Emerson tossed the tennis ball in the air and caught it. "Bingo," the boy muttered. "Bing… go!"

Emerson completed his preparations and, with the paper bag under his arm, returned to the headmaster's rooms where he attended to several essential details. The prankster double-checked his work and mentally scratched off the steps he had taken. He smiled, tucked the bag of leftover supplies under his arm and moved to the doors. As his hand touched the latch, he remembered the open window and cringed. Emerson returned the window to its original position and removed the tape. He let his eyes run over the scene a final time and, when fully satisfied that all was well, left the room, closing the doors behind him. It was only then that he realized he lacked one key piece of information… information upon which the success of his prank hinged. The acquisition of that knowledge would have to wait for lights-out. He crossed his fingers. "Now, if only Fitzroy doesn't get back too early," he whispered as he crept down the hall.

After dinner, two study halls and night prayers, Emerson skulked around the grounds keeping to the shadows. He kept his eyes and ears open for Andrews. He checked to ensure that Fitzroy's car had not returned and to see if the headmaster's rooms remained in darkness. When he returned to the dorm, he changed into his pyjamas and stared out over the front lawns until the head student doused the lights. From his bed, Emerson watched for the telltale flicker of headlights on the dorm ceiling. He listened to the breathing of his dorm-mates. Twenty minutes later, as far as he could tell, they were all fast asleep.

Emerson eased himself out of bed at what he guessed was eleven o'clock, tiptoed out of the dorm, inched his way down the stairs and entered Fitzroy's office. He located the light switch and flicked it up and down. "Lucky me," he whispered in relief when the room remained in darkness. He hurried out of the office, trotted around the corner and entered the infirmary. Everything was as he had left it.

It was after midnight when Emerson finally heard what had to be Fitzroy's car tires rolling over the snow-packed gravel in the drive. In the infirmary, the boy slipped behind the curtains, raised the window a few inches and waited. After what seemed hours, he heard footsteps approaching along the hall. Emerson cocked his head to one side and listened for Fitzroy to pass. Without warning, the infirmary door flew open and someone with a flashlight entered the room. Emerson froze and held his breath. In horror, he realized that his legs, from knees to toes, were exposed to view below the curtain's hem.

"Where are you hiding?" cried Headmaster Fitzroy as he rummaged around somewhere on the far side of the room.

Emerson clamped a hand to his mouth to stop himself from blurting out the answer to Fitzroy's shocking question. The boy, during the next few moments, learned what people mean when they say their hearts stopped and their blood ran cold. He could barely hear the man's words, so loud was the drumming in his ears. Sweat beaded on the boy's brow and upper lip. His heart pounded, hammer-like, in his chest.

"Now… why stick the aspirin way back there?" complained Fitzroy. Just moments later, the headmaster opened the door and stepped into the hall.

Until the door was drawn closed, Emerson clenched his teeth, grimaced and clamped his left eye closed as the drapes fluttered and flapped in the seemingly hurricane force draught that flowed past him into the room. Emerson was still struggling to control his breathing and heart rate when a dim flicker appeared in the headmaster's window. Soon, Emerson saw a brighter, steadier light illuminate the man's bedroom. He waited for darkness to return. When it did, he started to count. "One one thousand, two one thousand…" he said aloud, until two minutes had passed.

Mr. Fitzroy had not enjoyed interviewing for a new German instructor. He returned frustrated and weary, happy to escape the hustle and bustle of the city. He had a pounding headache. He needed a good night's sleep. The bitter taste of the aspirin lingered in his mouth. They had not gone down well without water. Just one more irritant to end two irritating days. It was a worn out man who fluffed his pillow before falling back in bed and arranging his covers. He flicked off his bedside lamp and took several long, deep breaths.

Fitzroy proved surprisingly agile as he reacted to an exceedingly discomfiting crash and clatter in his office. Within seconds, he stood in the open doorway staring into the room. The beam from his flashlight swept from corner to corner, resting momentarily on each object in its path. "I know you're there," he cried in a forceful voice. "Step into the light." When no one replied, the headmaster paced briskly to his desk intending to turn on the lamp – nothing. "Drat!" he shouted. He had no better luck with the floor lamps, so retrieved a more powerful flashlight from his bedside table. Still, he could find no one in the room. What he did discover, however, flabbergasted him. Between his desk and his window, a drawer which had spilled its contents over the carpet, lay upside down on the floor.

The headmaster began a more thorough search for the intruder. He spoke as he rummaged about. “The longer this takes, the worse it will be for you, Sir,” he announced. “If that’s you, Meddows…” There was a self-questioning quaver and a hint of indecision in his voice. With a growing sense of foreboding he poked and peered into every nook and cranny capable of hiding even the smallest human body. By the end of his fruitless search, it dawned on Fitzroy that what he was looking for might not be a human body.

He wracked his brain in a vain effort to explain the eerie phenomenon. The headmaster opened his door and flashed a beam of light down the corridor – empty, with not a sound to be heard. The man tried to banish all thoughts of ghosts from his mind. “And don’t you dare come back,” he shouted into the darkness in a voice that betrayed his desperation. He closed the door and inspected the mess on the floor, more carefully this time. It was a frightened man who picked up a set of bear-bells. These he hung from a door handle. He stood for several moments staring at the bells, gave his head a definitive nod and headed for his bed. Before he closed his bedroom door, he turned and focussed the flashlight’s beam on the antique roll-top.

From the infirmary window, Emerson stared across at Mr. Fitzroy’s rooms. When darkness returned to the headmaster’s lodgings, Emerson gave the man two minutes in which to ponder his predicament, to give Fitzroy’s imagination a chance to set to work. Only then did the boy execute phase two of his prank.

At the sound of rattling chains, Mr. Fitzroy lurched for his flashlight while leaping from his bed. He flew into his office. Light flooded the room only slightly faster than adrenalin had flooded his body. The headmaster’s eyes darted about. Nothing was out of place. The bells hung unmolested upon the door handle. Nothing had been touched since his search had ended. Of this Fitzroy was convinced. The headmaster frowned. He pinched his lower lip into an elongated ‘V’. Stupefied, he scratched his head, massaged the back of his neck and paced. Try as he might, he could think of no rational explanation for the eerie events.

Recollections of Emerson Jenks and his ghostly friends – *fiends* they seemed now – repeatedly entered his mind and, with ever-increasing difficulty, were dismissed. The light from the flashlight danced across the floor and walls.

From the infirmary window, Emerson saw the light sweeping back and forth in Fitzroy's office. When he imagined what thoughts must be running through the headmaster's mind he had to stifle his laughter. For what seemed an extraordinarily long time the flashlight remained on, pointed here and there about the room. Emerson debated with himself, shrugged and initiated the final step of his prank.

Fitzroy slipped behind his desk. He rifled through the mess on the floor and found his cigarettes and lighter. After inhaling, he began to cough. He stared at the cigarette in disbelief, alarmed by its wretched taste and acrid, sulphur-like smell. His face registered disgust as he stamped it out. He walked to his favourite armchair, sat down and covered his face with his hands.

Without warning, a book flew off its shelf. Fitzroy's head jerked up and his eyes bulged out of his head. The man froze in place, not breathing. Light reflected off the plastic dustcover as the volume somersaulted through the air and landed on the carpet. He watched it skitter to within a few feet of his desk. The man blinked several times. He could not fathom the events playing out before him. Several seconds passed before he could gather his senses and react.

He leapt to his feet, raced to the double doors, pulled them open and charged headlong out of the room and down the corridor. His self-control, which had been on the wane, abandoned him altogether. His first bloodcurdling scream filled the darkened corridor. A second terrified shriek leapt from deep within him as he fled down the stairs, knees pumping. A final screech, sharp and shrill, echoed down the hallway of the faculty wing, waking staff members on both floors.

As Fitzroy tore past the infirmary door, Emerson Jenks was cramming his implements of terror into the paper bag. He stuffed the bag into its hiding place and hurried from the room. He reached the door to the dormitory having neither seen nor heard a soul. He cracked the door open and listened – nothing. Emerson crept into his cubicle and crawled into bed. He could not help but smile to himself. All in all, he thought, things had gone exceptionally well. "One of your best yet, Jenks," he mumbled as he tucked the bedcovers under his chin. "Yeah, that was definitely one of your best."

+ − × ÷

Leticia Strupples found St. Timothy's headmaster cowering at the end of the corridor furthest from the faculty wing's main entrance. She flashed the beam of her penlight over the quaking figure. As she cautiously approached in the darkness, Strupples heard an unfamiliar, quavering voice.

"Stay back. Stay back, I say," cried Mr. Fitzroy as he cowered in the corner and drew his knees up into a foetal position.

Not until the full light of day did the headmaster dare to return to his lodgings. Several members of his staff followed him at a distance. Strupples, Willoughby-Wallows and Warneke accompanied the distraught headmaster to the threshold of his office. The troupe found both doors ajar. Fitzroy stretched out his arm and gingerly pushed the oak doors fully open. He jumped back and clutched at his throat at the jangle of the bear-bells. Crammed together in the doorway, he and the three teachers peered cautiously into the office. Strupples was the first to step inside. She turned in a circle, inspecting the room.

Warneke followed her lead. The English master picked up the book from the floor, closed it and glanced at its binding. "At least your ghost reads the classics," he stated and held the volume out to Fitzroy. "Charles Dickens… A *Christmas Carol*," Warneke explained. "This prankster has a good sense of humour, too, I guess." He slid the book back into its place. "Humph, a great little prank, my friends," he added as he examined the bookshelf. He walked to the window, threw open the drapes and peered outside. "Beats me how he pulled it off though," he added. Warneke sat down in Fitzroy's favourite chair, crossed his legs and lit a thin, black, and what proved to be a very smelly cigar.

"That window's ajar, Sir," reported Strupples. "Could someone have—"

"—You've got it, Leticia!" shouted Warneke. "Now, if we can just find the thirty-foot-tall intruder. See any tracks outside, Sherlock?" The big man already knew the answer.

Willoughby-Wallows joined Miss Strupples at the window. They stared down on an undisturbed blanket of snow. "But whoever it was just had to get in through the window," insisted the Greek and Latin teacher. "Your door was locked when you left, wasn't..." He decided not to finish his sentence when he noticed Fitzroy's scowl. "Oh!" muttered the young teacher and turned away.

Even with the assistance of his three associates, Fitzroy could find no earthly explanation for the events of the previous night. His companions stared at him in amazement. His already pale face had turned chalky white. He still wore his pyjamas and dressing gown. He held one hand over his mouth and ran the other through his uncombed hair. He moved about the room in a hesitant, jerky fashion.

"A poltergeist!" he cried aloud, hardly able to believe his own words.

As Strupples, Warneke and Willoughby-Wallows left for their morning classes, Fitzroy left his office and wandered to the infirmary. While waiting for Dr. Graham to arrive, he worried that he was headed for a breakdown.

"My, my! You don't look at all well, Scotty," the doctor commented upon entering the room. "Let's have a look at you. Have you not been feeling well?" Fitzroy related a sketchy record of events. Dr. Graham listened and tried to reassure the headmaster that his experiences were due to stress: a combination of Jenks' tales, his own overactive imagination and fatigue from overwork. "That long drive on the weekend capped it all off," explained Graham. Fitzroy was not convinced. The bell rang, calling students to class. The distraught man stood to go. "Scotty," added Dr. Graham, "I want you to take some time off. Go away for a week... immediately. Rest... relax. You'll see all this in a different light when you get back." Fitzroy nodded in a half-hearted fashion. As he left the infirmary he stopped short. Emerson Jenks sat in the hall. The headmaster turned and trudged back towards his rooms without a word. He needed to think.

Dr. Graham, with one hand in his pants pocket, leaned against the doorpost watching Emerson watch Fitzroy. "You're Jenks, right?" he asked.

"Yes, Sir," replied Emerson as he approached the doctor. "Pleased to meet you, Sir."

The doctor did not so much as flinch. "I just bet you are," he replied.

Emerson sidled past Dr. Graham, looked around the room and asked, "Where should I sit, Sir… I mean Doctor, Sir?"

Graham closed the door, crossed the room, pulled a chair to the centre of the floor, pointed to it and observed Emerson take his seat. The doctor picked up a file folder, leaned against the wall, held a pair of glasses as if they were a magnifying glass and began to read. Emerson could barely see the doctor out of the corner of his eye. For some unknown reason he was afraid to turn his head and look at the man. Every twenty seconds or so, Graham looked up from the chart and stared at his newest patient. Emerson noticed. The doctor noticed that Emerson noticed. As the boy rehearsed his story, panic set in. He now doubted that the doctor would buy his explanation.

Dr. Graham smiled as he observed Emerson drying the palms of his hands on his pants. Still, the doctor delayed asking his first question. He saw the skin on the boy's forehead wrinkle each time he strained to look sideways without turning his head. The beads of sweat forming on the boy's brow did not escape his notice. A full five minutes passed in silence before Dr. Graham walked to his desk, dropped the file, turned to Emerson and spoke. "Okay, Jenks, no more of your nonsense… understand? You're no fool and neither am I, so please don't treat me like one."

"Pardon, Sir?"

"Don't stall for time with your 'Pardon, Sir' routine, Jenks. You know darn well… and I know too. You don't see ghosts… let alone talk to them. You're a clever boy… but not clever enough to fool me." The doctor paused, waiting for Emerson to respond. "You certainly have the headmaster on the go though… no doubt about that. But you're not putting a thing past me." The doctor peeked at the name on the file tab. "Emerson, my lad, let's be honest with each other… okay?"

"Yes, Sir," was all Emerson managed to say.

"Yes, Sir, what?" demanded Graham.

"Yes, Sir... I'll be honest with you, Sir," replied Emerson. After a moment of silent consideration, he continued, "I didn't mean any harm, Sir... really I didn't."

Dr. Graham shook his head, pulled out his own chair, spun it around backwards and sat opposite the boy. "I have no idea how you make books fly—" he glanced at the name on the file again, "—Emerson, but it's got to stop. You gave Scotty... sorry... Mr. Fitzroy a real start last night."

"I guess I did, Sir. I didn't think—"

"That's precisely the problem with pranks, Sir. People don't think. Now, here's what I'm going to do," explained Dr. Graham. "I'm going to send your headmaster off on a week's holiday. He can use the rest anyway. I'm going to tell him that you and I have had a chat and I have no concerns about you... unless of course, you continue to have these... these ghostly experiences of yours." Graham's piercing stare gave Emerson goose bumps. "Do you understand, Emerson?"

"Yes, Sir."

"Yes, Sir, what?" asked the doctor.

"Yes, Sir... no more ghost pranks, Sir," answered Emerson.

"Good boy, Jenks. I knew you were clever. We have a deal then, do we?"

"It's a deal, Sir," replied Emerson and stuck out his hand.

Dr. Graham reopened the file and scratched a few notes, leaving Emerson's hand wavering like a windsock in a light breeze. Emerson stuffed his hands in his pants pockets, hunched up his shoulders and stared at the floor. Graham spoke without looking at his patient. "Now... I'll not tell Scotty that you were behind all this... this prank, okay? But, that's not to say someone else won't put two and two together and come up with four. Perhaps your headmaster will figure things out while he's away."

"Thank you," said Emerson. "You won't tell anybody else about... about me, eh, Sir?"

"Not a word..." Graham replied then paused before continuing, "unless of course..."

"No more ghosts, Sir," Emerson promised while using his thumb to draw an 'X' on his chest.

"Jenks... your heart's on the other side," advised the doctor.

"May I go now, Sir?" Dr. Graham waved his arm in the general direction of the door without looking up from the file. Emerson stood and walked slowly away, head down. He pulled the door open and was about to step into the hall when the doctor called his name.

"Emerson!" the doctor said. "You know I used to be a student here, don't you?" Surprise registered on the boy's face. "Well, I was. I saw a lot of pranks pulled in my time, Son. But I have to admit… yours, Emerson, was one nifty piece of work."

"Thank you, Sir," replied Emerson in a near whisper.

"But no more ghosts, my boy," Graham reminded the departing student.

"No more ghosts, Sir." Before completely closing the door, just as the doctor turned his attention back to his work, Emerson poked his head into the room. "Thanks again, Dr. Graham," he said. "That really was one great little prank though, wasn't it, Sir?"

April Fools

If a boy at St. Timothy's were asked to name his favourite day of the year, he would most likely say Christmas. Visions of family, friends and fine food – and gifts of course – would flood his mind.

A few students might cite the school's patron saint's name day. On the eve of that feast, St. Timothy's Day itself and the day following, the boys enjoyed sleep-ins and freedom from chores and classes. The cooks doled out generous portions of the best their larders offered: sausage, eggs, turkey and that universal favourite, pie with ice cream. Students and staff enjoyed three days without an apple in sight. Students competed in euchre, cribbage and ping-pong tournaments. At evening *soirées*, they entertained with skits and music. For the sports-minded, the hockey rinks beckoned from dawn to well after dusk. The most avid players came to meals wearing most of their equipment, knowing that Andrews would pretend not to notice. Yes, the feast of St. Timothy was a great favourite.

A single student, Emerson Jenks by name, preferred April Fool's Day. What St. Patrick's Day is to the Irish or St-Jean-Baptiste Day is to French Canadians, April Fool's Day was to Emerson.

Early in March, though neither Emerson nor the English master realized the fact, Professor Warneke set the scene for what was to be a memorable April first.

"Now boys…" announced the English master at the beginning of his grade nine class. He initiated a hand washing motion and continued, "We're about to have the grandest time together." Anticipation graced the faces of the naïve. The less credulous gawked at their peers with amused grins. The professor continued. "We're going to study *poetry*. Now, what do you think of that?" The students groaned. "I knew you would be pleased," added Warneke. "So I've saved the best for last. You, my fine fellows, will not only get to read the great bards, you'll get to write your own poems… join their ranks in some small way. Ha, ha!"

The groans grew louder. In glee, Warneke twisted the ends of his moustache and waited for the moaning to die down. "Quiet now, quiet! Try to restrain your enthusiasm, please. We start today with the ballad. You'll hand in your work each Friday at the end of class." Warneke's charges sat and stared at him in dismay. "Ah… whatever's wrong?" he asked.

In full expectation of peer support, Talbot gazed from one face to another as his hand rose slowly into the air and wavered there.

"Mr. Talbot… some detail escapes that exquisitely keen mind of yours, I see."

"Well, Sir," said the boy as he peered over his shoulder. Loud snorts from Callaghan and his bosom buddy, Kelly, distracted him. "It… it… it's just seems like… well… an awful lot of work, Sir." Since his arrival at St. Timothy's, Talbot had earned a reputation for being slow on the uptake and a master of the understatement. *The 100 Years War lasted a long time*, Talbot declared in the opening sentence of a history essay.

Mumbling, Warneke shook his head. "Now then, we're off… page 136, please… the ballad." Boys scrambled to find the correct page in their texts. Talbot's glassy-eyed stare remained fixed on the professor. "A lot of work, you say, Talbot?" Warneke smirked. "But that's the whole point, don't you see?" A look of despair crossed the boy's face. "Hark, what have we here?" asked Warneke. "It's the Knight of the Woeful Countenance. Now… page 136, quick march."

At the end of class, Warneke snapped his book closed, slipped it under his arm and addressed the students. "Your ballads will be at least twenty-four lines long," he shouted over a chorus of boos. "Quiet… quiet, I say! In past years, students have ventured to submit poems they'd begged, borrowed and stolen. Don't even think about it. The penalties are severe."

"How severe, Sir?" inquired Talbot to the chagrin of his classmates.

"At the end of the year, good little boys leave early; bad little boys stay 'til the bitter end," explained the professor. "Is that clear, fellows?" Even Talbot understood. Warneke left the room but returned a few seconds later, interrupting the classroom banter with an announcement. "I forgot to tell you… if you run into any difficulties… any snags… you may help one another… but just don't come pestering me." Warneke's gruff laughter echoed in the corridor as he strolled to his next class.

That evening, Emerson and his classmates straggled into first study hall and Andrews' assistant, who supervised the junior session, closed the door behind them. Several times, Emerson was distracted by the sound of Talbot tearing up sheet after sheet of paper in frustration. By the break, foolscap littered the floor. Emerson retrieved a sample of Talbot's work. He had to agree with its author, the ballads belonged in the trash. Between study halls, Emerson watched Callaghan and Kelly engage in a *tête-à-tête* with Talbot. The master prankster stroked his chin as he watched Talbot return to his desk wearing a relieved smile.

The following morning, after breakfast, Emerson caught up to Talbot on the stairs near the chapel. "Hey, Talbot!" he called. "Wait up, will you?"

"What for?" snapped the boy.

"Last night… Callaghan offered to help with your poem, right?" said Emerson.

Talbot's eyes narrowed. "What's it to yuh?"

"Nothin'," replied Jenks. "But it might be something to you. Better be real careful, Talbot."

"I can take care of myself, Jenks."

"Okay… but you might want to ask yourself why Callaghan would want to help you. Think about it, eh." Emerson shook his head as Talbot climbed on up the stairs.

+ − × ÷

On the following Friday, Warneke entered the classroom wringing his hands like a starving man seated before a juicy porterhouse. "The day of which I've long dreamed has arrived. So… who's willing to read for us, eh?" The professor's eyes darted about seeking out the most hesitant student. He spotted Talbot. The boy sat with his elbows on his desk, his hands clasped to his head, eyes downcast. "Mr. Talbot… you look eager to oblige," cried Warneke. Callaghan and Kelly had to cover their mouths to keep from laughing aloud. "Stand up there, my lad." Warneke plucked the reluctant boy up by his ear. Talbot cast a pleading look at the man. Warneke pretended not to notice. "Your title, Sir?" he asked as he cupped a hand behind his ear.

"Ti… ti… title?" stuttered Talbot as he flipped through his binder as if the omitted title might have materialize out of thin air. "I… I… I don't have a title, Sir," he stammered.

"Gentlemen… no giggling!" announced Warneke. "We have for your enjoyment, for your edification, nay I say, for your enlightenment… an untitled ballad by young Master Talbot. Go ahead, Sir… read on."

The boy cast a last pleading look at his professor and began. "*Have… have… have you… gazed…*" read Talbot in a near whisper.

"Louder, please," demanded Warneke. "We can't hear you, Sir."

"*Have you gazed on…* ahem… *naked grandeur… where there's nothing else to gaze on,*" Talbot was reading only a bit louder. Emerson, hands in lap, leaned forward until his forehead rested on his desktop. A few of Talbot's mates groaned. Callaghan chuckled. Kelly chortled. Many looked about with a quizzical, questioning expressions. Talbot looked up from his binder. Professor Warneke, who had leaned against the blackboard with his arms crossed over his chest, continued to stare down at the floor.

"Go on, Mr. Talbot. I pray thee, go on," he urged.

Talbot cleared his throat and continued. "*Set pieces and drop-curtain scenes galore…*" On hearing Callaghan's sardonic snigger, Talbot looked up again.

"Oh, bravo!" shouted Warneke. "Bravo, Talbot… drop-curtain scenes! What inspired imagery! I can almost see them hanging before me. But, go on, Sir. You must go on."

Talbot could not go on. "I… I… I can't, Sir," pleaded the boy.

"Tongue-tied, are we?" asked the English master. "Need some help, do we, Talbot?" Cackles of laughter erupted throughout the room. Warneke roared and order was restored. Talbot and his mates held their breath, anticipating fireworks, thunder and lightning, sparks, smoke and fire. Instead, the English master's tone turned mellow, almost Shakespearean. "*Big mountains heaved to heaven…*" Warneke quoted the line and raised a hand to his brow in a theatrical gesture before going on. "*Which the blinding sunsets blazon… black canyons where the rapids rip and roar.*"

As Warneke spoke, Talbot stared slack-jawed into his binder and read those very words. He turned fierce, fiery eyes upon Kelly. "But how… how…" the boy muttered.

"A five point bonus for anyone who knows Talbot's next line," cried

Warneke. "Anyone?" With his head still resting on his desk, Emerson raised a hand. Warneke called on him. Emerson looked up, squinted with his left eye, muttered the first lines under his breath and continued, "*Have you swept the visioned valley...*"

"Follow along, Mr. Talbot. Follow along, my amazed little friend." Warneke almost sang the words. "Sorry, Jenks. Please continue. Astonish this talented poet of ours."

Emerson continued, "*Have you swept the visioned valley... with the green stream streaking through it... searched the vastness for something you have lost?*"

"Together now, Mr. Jenks," said Warneke.

"*Have you strung your soul to silence?*" Student and instructor recited the words in unison. "*Then for God's sake go and do it; Hear the challenge, learn the lesson, pay the cost.*"

Warneke directed a surprised but approving nod towards Emerson. "Well done, Jenks." Turning his attention back to Talbot he continued, "How appropriate a line, Mr. Talbot. You'll learn a lesson alright, Sir, and you'll definitely pay the cost. Sit down. We'll have a nice long chat after you find your tongue."

When class ended, everyone except Emerson and Talbot fled to the corridor to enjoy the break.

"I told you, Talbot, you donkey," muttered Emerson, softly so the boy would not hear. To Talbot, who had not moved from his desk since Warneke left the room, he said, "That was a dirty, rotten trick they pulled on you. I'm really sorry."

Talbot refused to speak. Emerson noticed tears welling up in the boy's eyes so walked away. He glowered at his classmates in the corridor as they enjoyed a laugh at Talbot's expense. "Cheap shot, but you'll pay for it, Callaghan. I'll see to it personally," he muttered. "And you too, Kelly."

When the day's lessons ended everyone except Talbot bolted from the classroom. Most headed to the dorm to change clothes or to the chapel landing to check their weekly job postings. Talbot was in no mood to do either. Emerson was in no hurry. He dallied in the corridor until it was empty before he headed back to talk to Talbot.

"That was Callaghan's doing, wasn't it, Talbot?" asked Emerson.

"Nah," answered Talbot. "It was that stupid Kelly."

"Kelly, eh? Same thing. He's Callaghan's toady, that's all." Talbot did not respond. "Look, Talbot, there's nothing you can do to change what's happened." Talbot glared at Emerson in disgust. "If you help me though, I promise they'll regret what they've done." Talbot looked into Emerson's face but said nothing.

The two boys left the classroom together. Talbot stopped at a window and gazed blankly out towards the deserted sports fields. Emerson stood beside him. Neither spoke as they watched several students jump over the last traces of the winter's snow and race towards the powerhouse and the student barber shop. After a few minutes, Talbot turned towards Emerson. "Okay, Jenks, what do I have to do?"

"Nothin', Talbot," replied Emerson, "at least not yet. First, I need to know how they got you into this mess."

"Callaghan told me he would help. Kelly said he'd write two poems and I could have one of 'em," explained Talbot. "So I said sure."

"So you copied it out and handed it in, right?" asked Emerson.

"Right," replied Talbot. Emerson shook his head as Talbot continued, "But what I can't figure is how you and Warneke figured it out."

"Man alive, Talbot! Don't be so thick. Kelly didn't write that. Robert Service did."

"Who?" demanded Talbot after screwing up his face. He appeared completely mystified.

"Robert Service! He's one of the best... oh, never mind, Talbot. Give me a few days. I'll figure something out. Just don't go and make a big scene, okay? And keep blaming Kelly, not Callaghan... got it?" Talbot nodded. "And don't let on to Callaghan whatever you do," Emerson continued. "Oh! We can't let anybody see us talking like this. So be careful or you'll tip them off." Emerson turned, checked to make sure they had not been observed and headed towards the stairwell. From the foot of the steps, he called down the corridor. "Hey, Talbot, where's that poem Kelly gave you?"

"In the garbage," answered Talbot. "I tore it up and threw it in the garbage." Emerson shrugged, gave Talbot a quick wave and began mulling over what Talbot had told him as he set off to do his chores.

+ − × ÷

On Saturday evening, Emerson found himself in the sacristy setting out vestments for Sunday mass. For him, another week of chapel duty had arrived. His stay was longer than usual. Burton, the head sacristan, had told him to replace the altar candles. He had no idea exactly how the candles worked, but he soon learned that what most people thought were candles were actually white, steel cylinders with candles inside. Emerson examined the spring mechanisms and the brass heads through which the candles were forced upwards as the wax melted away. Upon realizing how the candles worked, a grin spread across his face.

On Sunday morning, after letter writing, Emerson returned to the sacristy to perform his official duties. He departed with a handful of wooden matches and walked to the school's garage. When he was sure no one was looking, he entered the building and filled an old tin can with gasoline. Once he reached the orchard and made sure he was alone and hidden from view, he stood back several feet from the fuel and tossed a lighted match towards the can. It missed. He tried again… and again he failed. On about the twentieth attempt, from just half the original distance, a lit match dropped into the can. Emerson leapt back waiting for an explosion; nothing happened. Cautiously, he approached and saw the dead match floating atop the gasoline. It was a very confused boy who stood in the apple orchard scratching his head. The results of his experiment defied all the information he had ever been given about gasoline and lit matches. In frustration, Emerson kicked the can over. The fuel spread rapidly through the long spikes of dry grass and formed a puddle on the hard ground.

Emerson heard an inner voice telling him he had one match left and that he should try one last time. After striking the match on a stone, he held it between his thumb and index finger and stretched his arm out as far as it would go. He leaned towards the gasoline. Six inches from the puddle of fuel, the feeble flame flashed into a fireball and a mighty whoosh sucked the air out of the boy's ears and nose. An intense heat wave raced up Emerson's arm and struck him full in the face. The boy tumbled backwards to the ground.

"Wow!" he exclaimed and picked up his glasses. "That was a close one." He sniffed the air and turned up his nose at a sharp, acrid smell. Before replacing his glasses, he ran a hand over his face which felt hotter than it should. Bits of grey ash stuck to his fingers. He jumped up, and after stamping out the flames, peered through the branches of an apple tree to see if the explosion had drawn anyone's attention. Before leaving the orchard, he inspected his body with hand and eye to make sure no vital parts were missing.

Upon looking into a mirror in the dormitory washroom, Emerson declared his experiment a woeful failure. He needed a less volatile accelerant. Rather than appear red-faced at table, Emerson stretched out on his bed with a damp cloth pressed to his face. Throughout the afternoon, Angelo Guardiano and a few dorm-mates stopped by to ask if he was alright. By the time he answered the dinner bell, most of the redness had vanished – as had the boy's eyebrows, eyelashes and most of his forelock. As Emerson exited the chapel, on his way to the refectory, the head student pulled him from the procession. While St. Timothy frowned down like a judge from his bench, the younger student fabricated a tall tale about an exploding box of matches in the sacristy.

Andrews did not believe a word of the boy's yarn but neither did he press the matter. "Watch your step, Jenks," he warned. "I've got my eye on you."

Before first study hall, Emerson entered the library to peruse St. Timothy's meagre collection of reference material. In vain, he searched the shelves. After careful consideration, he ordered a book from the public library. To do so, he had to complete a form, give his name and the title of the book he needed. He ordered a book about early photography or antique cameras and how they worked. A detailed book, please, he added in block letters.

For the next two weeks, Emerson was a busy boy. Secretly, he helped Talbot with Warneke's assignments. First, they worked on the haiku and then on free verse. Talbot badmouthed Kelly to everyone who would listen, especially to an overly sympathetic Callaghan. Emerson had to use every available minute of free time to collect and cache items he would need to execute his April Fool's Day pranks.

In time, Emerson received not one but several books from the city library and they proved more valuable than he had dreamed possible. He returned them with a note of thanks after he had copied out the list of ingredients he would need. Emerson knew where those ingredients could be found. His dilemma was how to get his hands on them without getting caught. Miss Strupples guarded her lab supplies with the tenacity of a prison-camp guard dog.

Emerson realized that he needed a helper: someone naïve. Talbot's face materialized, phantom-like, before Emerson's mind's eye.

Two days later, ten minutes into Miss Strupples' class, the grade nine students heard a loud popping sound and gasped as an orange and blue flame leapt from Talbot's desk and spread out along the ceiling. The boy's lab partner shrieked and dove for cover. Strupples rushed across the room to investigate. She interrogated Talbot then lectured him on the safe use of a Bunsen burner. While her back was turned and all eyes were on Talbot, Emerson deftly removed the chemicals he had previously located among Strupples' supplies. As the class progressed, he scooped powders into empty matchboxes he had stolen from the sacristy. When he finished, he cleared his throat, drawing the attention of several classmates. All eyes were redirected to Talbot after the boy nudged a glass beaker onto the floor. While Talbot received his second tongue lashing of the day and his classmates searched for the smallest shards, Emerson replaced the borrowed jars.

"Why'd I have to do that?" Talbot asked Emerson after class. "You coulda got me into a lot of trouble, yuh know."

Emerson answered Talbot's question with two of his own. "But I didn't, did I?" he demanded. "Do you want to get even with Kelly and Callaghan or not?"

Talbot answered with a shrug followed by a nod.

+ − × ÷

On the Monday of the last week of March, Warneke announced the topic for the coming week. "We arrive now at the very apex of poetry. We come to the perfection of the form… the jewel of English literature. Ah, the *sonnet*," he announced with a rapturous smile gracing his face.

"Those I-tal-yuns may have invented it but we English made it an art form, Gentlemen."

After dinner that evening, Emerson followed close on Talbot's heels as he walked towards the common rooms. Before Talbot could turn and climb the stairs, Emerson grabbed him by the shoulders and shoved him bodily down the hall to the locker room, shushing him the entire way. Once satisfied that they were alone, Emerson whispered, "Talbot, here's what you have to do. Now listen carefully..."

Talbot ran off looking for Callaghan and, upon finding him, begged for help with his sonnet. "I got the haiku thing okay and the free verse... well, any fool could do that... but the sonnet... I just don't get it," he whined.

Callaghan could not help but smile. It occurred to him that Talbot was a bigger chump than he had thought. To Talbot he said, "Why sure, Talbot. I'd be glad to help. I can dash off a sonnet for you in a snap." Talbot was no scholar but he demonstrated potential for method acting when he thanked Callaghan for saving his life.

Callaghan passed Talbot a handwritten copy of a sonnet on Wednesday night. On Thursday morning, Talbot passed it to Emerson Jenks. That afternoon, Emerson spent half an hour of his free time in the library, sitting at the ancient Underwood, hunting and pecking his way towards the completion of a very special poem.

St. Timothy's English master did not merely walk into class the next Friday afternoon... he waltzed in. He was in high spirits indeed. "I can't wait to hear someone read his sonnet for me. Anyone?" he asked. "Come, come, where's your volunteer spirit?" Emerson, to draw attention away from the others in general and from Talbot, Callaghan and Kelly in particular, leaned to one side and pretended to hide behind his neighbour.

"Mr. Jenks... you're not waving your hand in my face as usual, Sir. Ah! You didn't forget about the assignment now, did you? Tell me it ain't so."

"Ah... why no, Sir," answered Emerson with just a hint of nervous hesitation. He pushed his glasses into place. "I'd be very happy to read mine for you. I think it's pretty good, Sir."

The thought that Emerson was bluffing crossed Warneke's mind. He took a moment to evaluate the situation, stroking his moustache thoughtfully. "Well then… there's no need to be shy, is there, Mr. Jenks?" He smiled at the boy and laughed to himself. "We're all your friends here, you know. Come on up here, won't you? Come… come!"

Emerson stood before the class and read his well-crafted sonnet with flair. Anyone looking at Warneke's face while Emerson read would have seen the man's expression change from surprise, to disappointment, to a look of deep, deep thought: consternation in fact. "It's not Shakespeare, but it's pretty good," admitted Warneke as the boy took his seat. "Yes, indeed!" Emerson noted a hint of suspicion in the compliment.

At the end of the lesson, the students queued up to hand in their work. Emerson dawdled, gabbing with Callaghan and Kelly, so they would be last in line. He ended up last, standing behind Kelly. Kelly had lined up immediately behind Callaghan. He heard the two boys snigger and saw them poke one another when Talbot placed his binder on Warneke's desk and flashed Callaghan a thumbs-up before heading out the door. Finally, Callaghan and Kelly deposited their work on the stack.

Emerson did not follow his classmates into the corridor for the break. He waited in front of Warneke's desk, his binder in hand, and fiddled with the stack of assignments. A few papers fluttered from the top of the pile to the floor. Emerson bent down, picked them up and set them back on the desk. "Sorry, Sir," he said and placed his work atop the pile.

"Why, thank you, Jenks," replied the professor who had been waiting and watching with great interest, wondering why the boy was deliberately stalling.

"You're welcome, Sir." Emerson glanced around to make sure they were alone. "Did you really like my sonnet?" he whispered.

Warneke still wondered what the boy was up to. "Why, of course I liked it, Jenks," he replied. "I wouldn't have said I did if I didn't."

"Oh, I appreciate that… coming from you and all, Sir. But, I really should be going, Sir… the other guys… well, you know."

Warneke's eyes followed Emerson Jenks as the boy left the room and disappeared into the hallway crowd.

\+ − × ÷

During an hour of free time on Sunday afternoon, Emerson slipped out the back door of the shower room. He crossed the field, keeping to the trees as much as possible, and entered the school's old barn. He removed a brown paper bag from a rusted milk can and emptied the contents onto a workbench. The boy began to replace the items one by one, checking off each against his handwritten list. "White shoe polish, check. Coloured felt pens, check. Paint brush and spoon, check. Preparation-H, check. Duct tape and Scotch tape, check, check," muttered the boy. When he had accounted for all but one of the items he would need, Emerson lifted an old, rusty coffee can from a shelf and removed a matchbox which held a gingerly prepared concoction of Potassium perchlorate, German aluminum powder and minute amounts of three other chemicals. "All set," Emerson said. He dropped the matchbox into the bag, stuffed the bag under his arm and returned to the dorm.

On Sunday evening, when the students arrived at chapel, Headmaster Fitzroy was standing at the lectern. "Tomorrow is April the first, Gentlemen," he announced. "I'm here to warn anyone who thinks he'll get away with silly tricks that he's sadly mistaken. The staff, your head student, his assistant and I will be on the prowl… and we mean business."

Emerson's eyes bugged out. He gulped. He saw his plans drifting beyond his reach, like corks on an ebb tide.

"If it were up to me," continued Fitzroy, "I would ban pranks and not just on the first of April. But a school must have its traditions, I suppose. I am here to warn you that if some—" he almost used the word 'idiot' "—some… I mean, if you get caught pulling the fire alarm or ringing the buzzer or anything, you'll be going home on the first train out of here. I repeat, on the first train home." The faces of misguided individuals from bygone days flashed before his eyes. "Am I quite understood?" the headmaster asked. He signalled Andrews to begin evening prayer. Emerson averted his eyes as Fitzroy passed his pew.

When the lights went out that evening, Emerson continued staring into the darkness, thinking. He heard Andrews enter the dorm at the junior end rather than the senior end as was his custom. He saw the beam from the head student's flashlight jump from bed to bed. Andrews performed a more thorough check than usual, then headed to his dorm room. Emerson rolled onto his side and listened as, one by one, his dormmates dropped off to sleep. He heard the odd whisper or giggle but soon, only the sound of snoring reached his ear. Without warning, Andrews' light flickered over the beds again. Emerson did not budge. The light moved along the corridor towards the far end of the junior dorm. On his way back to his room, the head student performed yet another tour of each cubicle.

Emerson debated whether or not to proceed with his plans. He realized the stakes had risen to a dangerously uncomfortable level as a result of Mr. Fitzroy's recent announcement and Andrews' increased dedication to duty. At the thought of abandoning his pranks, he lamented the loss of so much time and effort. He particularly regretted the pleasure he would sacrifice if he made the more prudent decision. When he thought about following through with his plans, he was plagued with visions of returning home in disgrace and having to face his parents. His mind wandered and he found himself somehow thinking about mice. He came to a better understanding of how a mouse must feel as it sniffs about a trap. The morsel of cheese, so very enticing, attracts while the ominous metal bar, so very disconcerting, repels.

It was not until well after midnight, on April Fool's Day morning, that Emerson finally made up his mind. He rolled from his bed onto his knees and stuffed miscellaneous and sundry articles of clothing under the covers. He donned a pair of black pants, a black sweater and black socks. He tiptoed through the darkened dormitory to the trunk storage area where he had hidden his supplies. He continued on to the senior washroom where he removed several articles from his bag before prowling about in the dark dormitory. He paid brief visits to the lockers of Meddows, the boy's three toadies and three others. When finished, Emerson spent twenty minutes in the junior dorm's washroom. Finally, leaving his paper bag sitting on the top of a radiator beside the junior dormitory's door, he crawled on hands and knees to Kelly's bed, felt along the floor until he located a pair of shoes, stood and carried them away with him. Emerson was halfway to the door when he heard it open. He dropped, rolled between two beds and lay on his back looking up at the light flickering on the ceiling. His heart pounded. The light swept over the sleeping students.

"You idiot, Jenks!" Emerson muttered through clenched teeth. "The bag!"

Whoever wielded the flashlight inched down the cubicle between the two rows of beds. The light rested briefly on each body before being extinguished. Emerson held his breath until he heard footsteps moving off towards Willoughby-Wallows' rooms. He sighed in relief only when he heard a door open and close. Commando-style, the prankster shimmied to the corridor and stared along the floor at the thin line of light under the dormitory supervisor's door. Only when the light disappeared did he proceed. A person with owl-eyes, but no one else, could have seen the boy make his way out of the dormitory and down the stairs.

The sacristy reached, Emerson closed the door and used an old towel to prevent light from a single candle from escaping the room. Forty minutes later, he returned to his bed, stopping to replace Kelly's shoes on the way. Emerson slipped under the covers, his work done for the night. He was too wound up to sleep.

The sun was just about to peek over the horizon on the first day of the new month when the bell summoned students from their beds. Meadows' chief toady, Burns, followed immediately by O'Neil and Matthews, hooted loudly as did three of Jenks' other victims. To insure mass confusion, Emerson had deployed his weapons in all four corners of the senior dorm. Upon opening locker doors, large paper cups filled with water tipped forward on duct tape hinges and rained down on six heads. Meddows escaped a double soaking only because he was a late riser. Chaos erupted. Andrews knocked wildly on a locker in a vain attempt to restore order. As loud as the noise was in the senior dorm, it could not surmount the Babel of squeals and shrieks emanating from the junior washroom. Andrews ran to see what was happening at the far end of the floor.

Several students who shared the ill-advised habit of leaving personal hygiene supplies by the sinks overnight were coughing and looking about in wild-eyed wonder. They had just had their first taste of haemorrhoid treatment. Emerson had spent a good deal of time jamming Preparation-H down the nozzle of each victim's toothpaste tube. As his dorm mates gagged and spat, Emerson joined in the show, pretending to be a casualty himself. It was not the boys' taste buds that told them what they had ingested. They discovered the secret on the back of the washroom door where Emerson had pinned the half-empty tube of cream under a sign that read:

PUCKER UP, BOYS.

Willoughby-Wallows' arrival re-established order. His demands for silence ended threats of anarchy. "Hurry up, you fellows," he called out as he moved between dorms, "you'll be late for chapel."

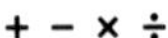

Emerson Jenks, sacristan, assisted Father Keegan in the vestry while, across the foyer, Kelly slipped into his surplice and soutane. Over one hundred students in various stages of consciousness sat waiting for morning mass to begin. Burton lit a long, thin taper and approached the altar. As he had done hundreds of times for almost five years, he raised the taper to the first candle. A loud whoosh and a flash of lightening-bright luminescence filled the chapel and brought every student to a state of confused alertness. Burton staggered back in shock. A surprisingly small amount of acrid smoke rose into the air, thinning out and disappearing as it reached the ceiling. Students sniffed the air and turned up their noses at the sharp, invisible stench spreading through the chapel. Three or four inches of Burton's taper had been vaporized in the blast. Trembling, he returned to the sacristy for a replacement.

At the chapel door, Emerson and Kelly stood at Father Keenan's side. The priest's eyes asked what had happened. The head sacristan shrugged as he passed, as if to say he had no idea whatsoever.

Quite a bang, thought Emerson, surveying the result of his prank. He watched those sitting in the pews as they questioned their neighbours trying to determine exactly what had happened. Father Keegan ushered the two boys back to finish preparations for mass.

Burton returned with a new taper and attempted to light the first candle once more – with greater caution this time. It would not light. He went on to the second candle using the same degree of care. The wick caught fire and blazed into life. So did the third and fourth. Burton had regained his confidence by the time his taper touched down on the fifth candle. Another flash lit up the chapel. Almost everyone witnessed the second explosion. Some spoke to their neighbours. Some smiled and laughed. Andrews banged on his pew. Burton looked around as if expecting someone to explain what had happened. He did not try to light the sixth candle.

As Andrews followed Burton out of the chapel, intent upon interrogating him, Father Keegan entered the room behind Kelly. The altar boy knelt and responded to Keenan's *Dominus vobiscum*. A course of giggles rippled through the room. Boys nudged their neighbours and nodded their heads towards the altar. Heads tilted to the right and left in an effort to see. Students whispered the words 'his shoes' to one another. As Kelly knelt with his back to the congregation, his black loafers stuck out from under his black soutane. Emerson had painted the soles white, added a big black eye on each heel and a large, bright red nose and lips, half on the right sole and half on the left. The folds of the soutane, like long tresses, adorned the clown's face. The effect was stunning, a face one might see on a Barnum and Bailey poster.

Ripples of laughter became waves of laughter and were followed by billows of laughter. The students' efforts to stifle themselves and each other proved futile. Each time Kelly moved his feet, the clown smiled or frowned, setting off a new round of sniggers and snorts. Both Father Keegan and the boy peered over their shoulders towards the congregation, trying to determine just what was so funny.

The unusual noises coming from the chapel drew Andrews back from the sacristy. His arrival proved a failsafe remedy for the giggling epidemic. A few boys directed the head student's attention towards Kelly and mouthed the word 'shoes'. Andrews' eyed flared. In disgust, he stomped to the front of the chapel and spoke to Kelly. The boy removed his shoes, looked at the clown face and turned the soles towards the confused priest. Keenan's face registered the deepest displeasure. He turned and continued mass. Andrews cast threatening glances at the students as he carried Kelly's shoes to his pew. His eyes fixed on the altar boy's back. Kelly was the head student's prime suspect now. Andrews had long since learned to focus first on those with the best alibis.

Mr. Fitzroy entered a perfectly quiet refectory in the middle of breakfast. He was in a state of high dudgeon. "I warned you. I pleaded with you," he cried, "and this is the result. Shame on you… shame, shame, shame. Enough! No more! And when I get to the bottom of this, some people here are going to regret their actions. I swear. There is a gang of you behind all these disgraceful, despicable shenanigans and I will tear this place apart until I know who you are." His eyes searched for and found Meddows. The headmaster wagged a finger towards his own favourite suspect and declared, "If you think I'm fooling just you try me." He stomped out of the room and down the corridor. Andrews was not alone in thinking that Fitzroy was losing his grip.

For the first time in his short life, Emerson thought he just might have gone a prank too far.

+ − × ÷

A little over an hour later, Professor Warneke arrived for class and began handing out the sonnets. "Fredericks, good work: B-plus. Jenks, an A. Talbot… will surprises never cease? A-minus."

Emerson watched Callaghan and Kelly's faces when Talbot's mark was announced. The two stared at each other and, in unison, shrugged and raised their eyebrows. Warneke continued passing out the papers. Callaghan and Kelly continued to wait. They were still waiting when the professor stopped calling names. "Now… Mr. Callaghan and Mr. Kelly… no, I better take you one at a time. Callaghan, come up here… come on… right up to the front." Callaghan came out of his chair at the speed at which a rubber boot comes out of deep, miry clay. Snail-paced, he inched forward. He looked about, seeking help. No one had help to offer. Alone, at the front of the room, he turned and faced his peers.

The English master shook his head and looked at Callaghan. The man appeared dumbfounded. "I've seen some pretty stupid attempts at cheating in my day," he cried. "Earlier this month, I actually though Mr. Talbot here had set an unassailable mark to which others could, but in their wildest dreams, aspire. But this…" The man shook his head. "Mr. Davies knew boys alright." Warneke scowled. "*Every mother thinks her son a genius, yet the world lacks not for cabbages*," quoted the English master. "Oh, how right he was. And now, Mr. Cabbage… I mean, Mr. Callaghan…" Warneke handed the boy a single sheet of paper. "I believe that's your handwriting, Mr. Callaghan… or am I mistaken, Sir?"

The boy looked at the paper. His arms stiffened and shot straight out before him as if he feared the words written upon the page. His eyes widened. In disbelief, his head shot forward like the head of a heron when it is fishing. "It… it… it's my writing but… but…"

"That's all I need to know, Sir. You see, you forgot to sign it and I wanted to be sure it was yours before we proceed. Would you read it for me, please, Sir?"

"But Sir, I didn't hand this in."

"You didn't? Well then, please explain how I came by it," demanded Warneke.

"I… I… I don't know, Sir," stammered the student.

"You don't know? Then tell me… how did you come to write that… that… You did write it, didn't you?" With growing impatience, Warneke gestured towards the paper that Callaghan held in his trembling hands.

"I don't know, Sir," whined the boy. Students' heads swung left and right, following the action as if a tennis match was in progress. "This isn't the poem I handed in though, Sir," added Callaghan.

"And where, may I ask, is the poem you handed in, Mr. Callaghan?"

"I don't know, Sir."

"I don't know, Sir," mimicked Warneke. "Well, never mind that now, Callaghan. I think we are going to have plenty of time before the end of your school year to discuss this. Read on, Sir. I pray, read on."

Callaghan took a deep breath and began to read slowly and softly. The room was as quiet as death and the boy's every word could be heard. "*Shall I compare thee to a summer's day?*" he read and stopped – not a sound. "*Thou art more lively and more temperate*," he continued.

"I believe William Shakespeare used the word 'lovely' there, Mr. Callaghan… *lovely* and more temperate, but perhaps he was enamoured of a different young lady?" Callaghan's classmates – all but Kelly who had awakened to the fact that his doom now winked at him over the horizon – could no longer restrain their mirth. The classroom reverberated with laughter. Talbot roared longer and louder than anyone. "You may sit down, Sir," declared Warneke and pointed to the room's only empty desk. Callaghan wasted no time in regaining his seat. He glared at Talbot and drew a finger across his throat.

"Now, Mr. Kelly, please step forward. It's your turn, Sir." With a graceful sweep of his hand, the English master invited Kelly forward.

Kelly dragged his quaking body to the front of the room and held out a trembling hand, anticipating that he would now have to read his sonnet.

"Oh, no. Mr. Kelly. This poem shall not be read… ever. I have never seen such garbage… never in all my life. It took me some time to figure out just what you had done but at last it came to me. Shall I explain to the class, Sir?" asked Warneke. With no idea what the English master was talking about, Kelly remained dumb. "Gentlemen… Mr. Kelly thinks me a fool. You see… he took sixteen of Mr. Shakespeare's lesser known sonnets… am I right so far, Mr. Kelly? And then he used a line from each and, with only half a dozen spelling errors, cobbled together this piece of junk. This garbage, Mr. Kelly, is unfit for human consumption. It's hardly recognizable as English let alone as a sonnet. You've learned nothing in this class, Sir. Have you…"

As Warneke raved, Kelly turned several shades of red. His classmates roared. Warneke, apparently oblivious of the noise, continued his rant with ever increasing vigour. He threw himself into an uninterrupted harangue, blasting Callaghan and Kelly and every teacher the two boys ever had. Warneke finished by saying, "Why anyone in his right mind would spend time writing this twaddle, let alone wasting paper and expensive ribbon typing it out, is beyond my powers of comprehension. It boggles the mind, Sir. You get a zero, Mr. Kelly… a big, fat, worthless zero." The man had to pause for breath but continued, "Nothing, zip, a goose egg, *nada*." Warneke tore the typewritten page into tiny pieces, threw them into the air and watched them float to the floor. He stomped on them, kicked them about, turned and marched to the door. There he stopped, turned and let his eyes sweep over his charges. Quoting his beloved Bard of Avon, Warneke roared, "*You blocks, you stones, you worse than senseless things*," then retired.

Science Fair: Part One

An all-out effort to bring St. Timothy's pranksters to justice began before first class on that first day of April. Mr. Fitzroy roused his staff to action at breakfast, going so far as to offer enticing rewards. For several days, students, noting their teachers' suspicious glances and odd comments, adopted the most innocent demeanours. Andrews, feeling that the culprits had shown him up, that he had been weighed and found wanting, was bound and determined to lay hold of the conspirators. He watched those he believed to be capable of perpetrating such pranks even more carefully than usual. Students gave the head student and his assistant an even wider berth than usual. Father Keegan and the sacristans declared the chapel pranks sacrilegious and pledged to bring the miscreants to justice. Like a posse, they mounted up and galloped off in hot pursuit of their prey. Emerson decided that mounting up and riding with them was his only available option. Meddows and his embittered band knew the who but not the how of the pranks almost before his toadies had dried off. They vowed vengeance. Emerson, from a safe distance, kept a close eye on the gang. He spent more time at Angelo Guardiano's side: his usual place of refuge when caught in a tight spot.

After lights-out on April Fool's Night, with no one any closer to solving the puzzle, Meddows, in bed, plotted payback while, two floors below, Burton considered possible suspects. In his room, Andrews tapped his pencil next to the name at the top of his shortlist: Meddows' name. He thought the boy's lucky escape from a drenching was all too suspicious. The head student sneered with malice, contemplating the punishments he would mete out for such impudence. Emerson Jenks was tucked in bed, too worried to sleep. He was befuddled by how personally people seemed to be taking his harmless activities.

At the same time, in the staff refectory, Fitzroy quizzed his staff, hoping for leads. Unfortunately, no one seemed to have the slightest idea who could be responsible. He told the gathering how determined he was to track down the culprits.

"Mr. Fitzroy, you couldn't detect your way out of a wet paper bag," Strupples commented. She spoke so softly she could not be heard except by the dorm supervisor who sat next to her. She noticed the young man's silent disapproval. Willoughby-Wallows suggested that perhaps Meddows was guilty. Hope flickered in the headmaster's eyes. The light faded when the dormitory supervisor produced not a shred of hard evidence to support his supposition. When Warneke, who knew Fitzroy was no Mr. Bucket, suggested that any prankster capable of such fine work would surely have covered his tracks, Strupples leaned towards Willoughby-Wallows and said, "It takes one to know one." Instantly, a plan formed in her mind. As soon as the meeting ended, she started her investigation. I'll make him pay, she thought as she walked back to her room.

Emerson had to stand behind the tall, portly, sloppily dressed conductor until the train stopped. Only then could he squeeze by and step down onto the platform. His eyes met those of his parents. His mother leaned on his father's arm. She held a damp hanky to her nose. Mr. Jenks appeared more haggard and gaunt than he had when Emerson had last seen him. Glenda was there, her head bowed in shame. Even their neighbour, Mr. Wilson, waited in the station house, peeking out from behind the curtains. Meddows and Callaghan along with several other faceless St. Timothy students gawked through the train windows, pointing and jeering.

"Whoa up… your ticket, please," bellowed the conductor. Emerson stopped and searched his pockets but could not find the stub. In panic, he turned to explain and found himself looking into the smirking face of Conductor Warneke.

Emerson screamed as he sat up in bed. He found himself breathing hard and covered in perspiration.

"You okay over there, Jenks?" whispered his neighbour.

"Yeah… sorry," panted Emerson. "Bad dream." The boy in the next bed rolled over and went back to sleep. Emerson remained wide awake.

He was more worried than he had ever been. He chided himself for so grossly underestimating the lengths to which people would go to unmask the perpetrator of the April Fool's Day mayhem. In the anxiety of the moment, Emerson swore off pranks… forever. He waited at least an hour before conducting a clandestine cleanup of his dorm locker, his shower room locker and his suitcases. He even risked a trip to the incinerator, stopping into the infirmary for a few items on the way. He was retracing his steps in total darkness when, halfway up the stairs, he heard Mr. Willoughby-Wallows' loud whistle. He retreated and slipped into the chapel until the danger passed.

After breakfast the next morning, Andrews collared Emerson in the sacristy and escorted him to the dorm. The youngster found Fitzroy and Willoughby-Wallows waiting by his bed. "I wanted you here to see Mr. Andrews turn out your locker," explained the headmaster as he eyed the young boy, "unless of course you have some objection, Jenks." Emerson noted the sly gleam in Fitzroy's eye. The boy assured the headmaster he had no objection whatsoever. In an attempt to drive his point home, Emerson stepped past Fitzroy, pulled out the locker's sliding drawer and threw wide its double doors. On finding nothing incriminating the search party was at a loss.

"Want to check under my mattress too, Andrews?" Emerson asked. Andrews studied the younger boy's face. This was high-stakes poker without cards. Andrews flipped the mattress on edge and scanned the area beneath… extra carefully. "Satisfied?" asked Emerson. "Or maybe you'd like to check my gym locker or my luggage? What are you looking for, anyway?"

"Okay, Jenks!" Mr. Fitzroy interrupted, scratched his head and shrugged. "Someone—" his eyes darted towards Willoughby-Wallows, "—just remembered that he heard somebody prowling around in this cubicle the other night. We have to check… right?" Emerson did not answer. "Sorry, Jenks, you're free to go." The two men moved to a bed on the opposite side of the cubicle. The headmaster looked at Andrews and said, "Better go get Kelly."

When the headmaster was alone with the dorm supervisor, he admitted, "I really didn't think Jenks did this… or Kelly either. They're only grade niners and Jenks there is a loner. This, Sir, is the work of a gang. Mark my words. My money's on Meddows and his bunch."

Enthusiasm for the hunt soon died down. The investigation lost momentum and was eventually given up altogether though the pranks would be remembered for years to come. Emerson reconsidered then forsook his oath and began plotting his next campaign.

+ − × ÷

Early in April, a beaming Miss Strupples told each of her classes that the annual Science Fair was approaching. She rested her chin on the fingertips of her clasped hands and poked out her boney elbows while making the announcement to Emerson and his mates. She looked like a little girl waiting for permission to blow out her birthday candles.

"The competition takes place on the second Saturday and Sunday in June, less than eight weeks from now," she announced. The boys shrugged, stretched, scratched and stared at one another. Some doodled on the covers of their notebooks. They did everything but raise their hands. If Strupples could have collected all the students' enthusiasm and poured it into just one body, still she would not have had a single volunteer. "I expected more exuberance," she announced with her hands now resting on her hips – or, to be more precise, on what for Miss Strupples passed for hips. "Not one of you interested in representing your school…" she admonished. "Well then… why don't we just think about it for the rest of the day?"

"Right!" mumbled Emerson to his lab partner. "And while I'm at it, I'll think about sticking my tongue in a live light socket." To Miss Strupples he said nothing.

"There'll be a meeting in my lodgings tonight for anyone interested." Given the prospect of Strupples' chocolate milk and bakery-bought cookies, interest flared. "But don't come unless you're seriously considering a project," she added. She might as well have turned on a fire hose. The flames of enthusiasm fizzled and died.

At 8:05 that evening the bell sounded to end the break between first and second study halls. The students dragged themselves back to their desks. Doors closed. Boys flung themselves down and shuffled through their books and papers. Emerson noticed that three of the grade nine seats were empty. He checked off students against a mental list of names. Callaghan and Kelly were missing. So was Fredericks. Emerson slid his feet forward until his head rested on the back of his chair. The prankster splayed his legs wide, thrusting them into the aisles and gazed up at the ceiling. Part of him figured that enough was enough, that he should take a break for the rest of the year. Another part of the boy argued that he would never be caught and that he should get back to planning his next masterpiece.

Miss Strupples collared Emerson as he exited the refectory the next morning. "You didn't come to the meeting last night," she said. "I was disappointed. You could do really well, you know."

"If I didn't want to go home so badly…" Emerson lied. "I can probably leave early, see." Strupples stared, saying nothing. "I may not have to write any finals, Ma'am."

"Ah… now I understand," Strupples replied. "Full recommendations, is it?" The woman nodded her head and pursed her lips. "I guess that idea just when up in smoke," she added. She was not sure, but she thought the boy flinched. She turned away, swung back and asked, "Would you at least consider helping Callaghan, Fredericks and Kelly? They will need all the help they can get."

Emerson did not want to say yes. In fact, the words 'not a chance, Ma'am' had formed in his mind. But he could not bring himself to refuse. Instead, Emerson did not reply at all.

"At least, may I tell them they can ask you for assistance if they need it?" asked Strupples. Teacher and student stood gazing at one another. The boy had to avert his eyes.

"Sure," he replied finally, "I can do that much, Ma'am… I guess."

"Thank you, Jenks," replied Strupples. "Oh, and please, don't let them blow themselves up or anything, eh," she added as she walked past him.

Emerson followed Strupples with his eyes and wondered what she could have meant. He had learned not to write off such occurrences as mere coincidence. He turned and started for the stairs in a pensive mood. He was considering Strupples' use of the words 'up in smoke' when he heard his name spoken.

"Jenks!" the Science teacher called after him. "I hope you've not been too homesick. Just remember… you'll be home quick as a flash."

Emerson bounded up the stairs two at a time convinced that Miss Strupples knew more than he wanted her to know. How much more, he wondered.

+ − × ÷

During Science class on the following Friday, while others reviewed their lessons, Fredericks approached Miss Strupples. The teacher cleared her throat. "Ahem!" She directed a steady gaze at Emerson. He raised his head, took a quick look around, turned back to the teacher, placed a finger on his chest and mouthed the word 'me'. Miss Strupples nodded and beckoned him forward. When he arrived at her desk, she whispered, "Fredericks here has been hunting around for a Science Fair project." She looked at Fredericks. So did Emerson. Fredericks flushed. "I'd appreciate it if you could sit down with him and maybe give him a few ideas," the teacher added.

Emerson nodded. "Right after dinner tonight," he told Fredericks. "Meet me in our classroom." Unlike Strupples, neither Emerson Jenks nor Fredericks appeared well pleased.

Emerson was at his desk when Fredericks arrived. "What's eating you, Fredericks?" Emerson asked.

"I really don't want to do this stupid project thing, Jenks," answered the boy.

"What?" demanded Emerson. "Then why the heck did you say you did?"

"I need to get my grades up, eh?" answered Fredericks. "I figured this might help." Emerson snorted and shook his head. "I've got time, see," added Fredericks. "I gotta stay 'til the very end anyway. I'll be writing everything… 'cept Math… maybe."

Emerson studied the boy for a moment then shrugged. "Well… what do you want to do, then?" he asked as he tossed his *Popular Mechanics* magazine on the desk.

Fredericks turned a chair around and sat with his chin on the top of the backrest. "You got any ideas?" he replied.

"You could just tell Strupples you've changed your mind," answered Emerson. "Or..."

"I can't quit," cried Fredericks, sitting up straight. "I meant do you have any good ideas for a project I can do?"

"Oh!" said Emerson. "Okay! Let's see." He tossed Fredericks one of the magazines. "Look through that and see if there's anything interesting."

Ten minutes passed in silence. "I got it!" announced Fredericks with a sudden shout.

Emerson jumped at the unexpected outburst. "What?" he asked.

"Look," replied his companion. He slid the magazine across the desk.

Emerson studied the picture Fredericks pointed out to him. "A rocket ship?" Emerson laughed aloud. He stared at his companion in wide-eyed amazement and shook his head. "I don't think so. What the heck do you know about rocket ships, Fredericks?"

"Nothin'," admitted the boy. "At least not yet."

"Nothin'! That's what I thought." Emerson shook his head. "You have to know something about your topic. Man alive!" The two boys continued leafing through the magazines. "Ant farm?" suggested Emerson.

"Nah," whined Fredericks and grimaced. "Dirty little beggars... ants."

The boys' efforts continued for nearly forty minutes. Fredericks paraded wildly impractical concepts past Emerson who rained on each and every idea. Emerson showed a marked preference for something simple and straight forward. His suggestions failed to enthral Fredericks. As his efforts were approaching the sixty-minute mark, the last lingering trace of empathy for Fredericks walked out of Emerson's heart and slammed the door.

Minutes later, as Emerson's frustration approached its absolute limits, Fredericks gave a loud hoot. "Wow, look at this, Jenks," he shouted, standing and coming around the desk. He flopped open a *Popular Science* in front of his helper and tapped his finger on a drawing of a telephone with a large flashing light above the dial. Emerson stared.

"It's a telephone for deaf people," announced Fredericks before

Emerson could ask the question. He pulled away the magazine and added, "I can do that."

"You can?" replied Emerson and frowned. "How?"

"Well… I gotta read it all and think about it first, eh?" Fredericks' tone declared Emerson a complete idiot. Emerson sat back, smiled and watched the look on Fredericks' face grow more and more intense as he studied the article. Two minutes later, Fredericks closed the magazine, turned to his colleague and declared, "I'm going to do it." His face glowed with pride and relief. "I probably won't even need your help, Jenks. It's that simple. Old Olive Oyl's gonna love it."

"Well, there you go, Fredericks. Good for you," replied Emerson with a definitive nod. "Mind if I check in on you once in a while?"

"Sure, Jenks, sure," answered Fredericks. His infatuation with the topic was written in bold letters across his face. "But, only if you don't help," he added. "I want all the credit for this for myself."

"Absolutely," promised Emerson as he began stacking the magazines. "You won't catch me interfering." With paper, pencil and protractor, Fredericks hunched over his work, busier than Emerson had ever seen him. He shook his head as he walked down the classroom corridor. "I'll never have to prank Fredericks," he said. "Fredericks'll probably prank himself."

+ − × ÷

On Sunday, Emerson approached Callaghan and Kelly with a question. "Hey, did Strupples tell you guys I'd help if you wanted?"

"Yeah!" snapped Callaghan. "But we'll manage on our own."

"What are you going to do?"

"Spiders," replied Kelly in great excitement. Callaghan gave his buddy a fierce look. Kelly failed to notice.

"Spiders?" repeated Emerson. "What can you to do with spiders?"

"C'mon. We're heading for the barn," explained Kelly. "We'll show yuh." Callaghan poked his toady in the ribs. "Ouch! What the heck was that for?" demanded Kelly, lifting his T-shirt and inspecting his side.

"Yeah, what was that for?" Emerson asked. "Think I'm going to steal your idea or something, Callaghan?"

"Get lost, Jenks," cried Callaghan. "We don't need any help... not from you."

"Ah, who cares?" Emerson replied. "Suit yourselves." Dismissively, he walked away but his curiosity had been aroused.

The barn had been abandoned when the health department banned the students' consumption of unpasteurized milk. Now the building was chock-a-block with old desks, decrepit farm equipment and assorted junk. Rarely did anyone enter the barn. Emerson refused to go anywhere near the building for fear of alerting his two classmates to the fact that they had become targets for his next prank. He had paid the two boys back for their cruelty to Talbot. The principal amount was settled but not the interest.

It took a week for Emerson to persuade Callaghan to let him visit. The boys showed him a crude display case. It stood five feet high, nearly three feet wide and one foot deep. An old, six-paned storm window served as a front cover. Inside were three spindly spider webs. In the centre of each web was a pathetic looking spider. Emerson's classmates gazed at their visitor and smiled when he nodded his approval.

"You think it's okay then, Jenks?" inquired Callaghan.

Emerson nodded and said, "Okay? I'll say. What's your plan?"

"Well," answered Callaghan, "we're going to study 'em and see how they hunt and kill prey and stuff... not just how they build a web and flies get stuck you know, but the design of the web, how strong it is, how the spider knows when a bug gets stuck... well, everything."

"How long it takes to build the web in the first place," added Kelly as he took down a clipboard from a nail and began jotting down data. "Well, Jenks?" the boy added. "Neat idea or what?"

Kelly and Callaghan's answers had taken Emerson by surprise. He had no idea his classmates had the smarts to develop such a sophisticated experiment. "Clever," admitted Emerson. "I mean really clever. Does Strupples know?"

"She ain't been out here yet, but she's looked at our drawings and stuff," answered Callaghan.

"She likes it," added Kelly.

"Me too," Emerson agreed. "It's pretty cool, guys. How's it going so far?"

"So far, so good," declared Callaghan.

"'Cept for getting the things to eat," added Kelly. For this, he received another withering stare from his Science Fair partner.

"Kelly!" grunted Callaghan.

"What?" asked Kelly and shrugged.

"Yeah, what?" demanded Emerson, gazing from one face to the other. Callaghan did not want to speak. Kelly was afraid to. "They won't eat, eh?" asked Emerson as he stared into the box while massaging the back of his head.

When Callaghan saw that Emerson was genuinely interested, he hunkered down like a baseball back catcher in front of the spider case. Emerson squatted beside him. Kelly squeezed between his two companions and, placing his hands on his knees, leaned forward with his face close to the glass. "Nah!" admitted Callaghan. "They won't eat and we can't figure out why."

"We drop flies in," explained Kelly. "Watch, I'll show you." Kelly removed a dead fly from a matchbox and dropped it on a spider's web. The spider sprang to life and scurried about for a few seconds, stopped abruptly and then returned to the centre of its web.

Emerson stared at several desiccated flies hanging motionless in the webs. "And the spiders won't eat them?" he asked while rubbing his chin.

"Eat them?" answered Callaghan. "They won't even go near them."

"We've lost two sets of spiders already," Kelly added. "Soon as they go in the box they stop eating." He glanced at his buddy, hoping he had not gotten carried away with his explanation.

Emerson stood, rubbed his chin with one hand and scratched the back of his neck with the other. "Hmmm..." he said. "I wonder. Do you think they might need live food?"

"What?" exclaimed Callaghan and Kelly in unison.

"Well..." Emerson continued as he rubbed the top of his head. "Outside the box they'd eat live flies, right? Maybe they don't like dead ones or something. Here, watch."

Emerson walked to a dirty window where several flies buzzed and bumped against the glass. He returned with a sacrificial victim. "Open the top," he ordered. Kelly obeyed. Callaghan stood back and observed.

"Watch now," Emerson instructed as he dropped the fly into the spiders' den. The fly did not land in a web but took flight. Like a helicopter with a broken tail rotor, it conducted a haphazard tour of the box. It bumped against the glass several times. As the winged captive sought its freedom, it flew too near one of the sticky strands and touched it with a wing. The insect proceeded to hopelessly entangle itself. Its wings fluttered and buzzed, stopped and started again… all to no avail. The boys watched intently, their eyes fixed upon the struggling fly.

"Look!" shouted Kelly. "The spider!" Three pairs of eyes opened wide and stared as a spider nimbly approached the captured fly. "Wow!" shouted Kelly as the spider pounced.

"Hungry little critter," exclaimed Callaghan. "You were right, Jenks… thanks." Emerson was not listening. He was thinking about how much the ways of spiders resembled those of pranksters. "Jenks?" cried Callaghan, trying to get the boy's attention. "Jenks!"

"Oh… sorry. Just like Shelob, eh?" said Emerson.

"Like who?" asked Callaghan.

"Like whom," mumbled Emerson absentmindedly. His two mates seemed not to hear. "Never mind. I guess that's how they know they've trapped something," suggested Emerson. "They must feel the vibration through the web or something. Gee… Neat!" Callaghan and Kelly had to agree. They raced to the windows. It took a considerable time for them to catch even a few flies. The spiders' appetites seemed insatiable. Their victims came to a bad end. "You're going to have to figure out a better way of catching flies," called Emerson from the door. "They're eating the things up as fast as you catch them."

The following morning Emerson loitered outside the Science room until Miss Strupples arrived.

"Morning, Mr. Jenks," the Science master called as she approached. She inserted her key into the lock and added, "What can I do for you this morning?"

"Callaghan and Kelly need help with their Science Fair project," answered Emerson. "Something to catch live flies," he advised. "I have a drawing here."

Miss Strupples blocked the doorway of her lab while she examined the design. She nodded approvingly. "Nicely done, Jenks," she admitted.

"Go ahead. Whoa! One second… glass parts might break. Why not use plastic?" She pushed the laboratory door open. "I've some odds and ends over there." She pointed to her junk box.

"When?" asked Emerson.

"When, what?" replied the Science professor.

"When can I come work on it… without disturbing you, I mean, Ma'am?" asked Emerson as he tried unsuccessfully to slip by Strupples.

"Ah, yes… well, let me see." Strupples glanced over her shoulder. "No… I think not, Mr. Jenks. But why not work on it this morning during my class?" she suggested. "You don't really need today's review anyway, do you? You're getting full recommends and leaving us early, right?" She returned the drawing.

At the end of Science class, Emerson grabbed Callaghan by the arm and led him across the corridor. Kelly followed. "Look at this," bragged Emerson. He held up a coil of flexible, red rubber hose and bits and pieces of clear plastic.

"What the heck you got there?" asked Callaghan.

"Flycatchers," replied Emerson. "What did you think they were?"

"Looks like a weird slingshot or something," replied Kelly with a laugh.

"How do they work?" asked Callaghan.

"I'll show you… c'mon." The boys crossed the corridor and Emerson pushed the washroom door open. Dozens of flies, buzzing and humming against the panes of glass, warmed themselves in the spring sunshine. Emerson uncoiled the two contraptions. The first he kept for himself. The second, he handed to Callaghan. "This funnel sticks into this long rubber tube… here. You trap a fly against the glass, under the funnel like this." He demonstrated. "Now, when you suck on the other end of the tube—" Emerson sucked hard, "—the fly gets pulled through the hose into this bulb. See!" The bulb, located between two lengths of hose, held a large fly, lethargic but still very much alive.

"Gross!" grunted Kelly.

"Yeah," added Callaghan. "Grrr… oss!"

"I put a little bead with a hole in it right here," Emerson pointed at the bead. "That keeps the fly from getting in your mouth. See." He stretched out the flycatcher between his two hands. "Funnel, tube, bulb, bead and more tube, that's all there is to it. See?"

"Here let me try," demanded Kelly as he grabbed the flytrap. Callaghan held his apparatus out towards Emerson. "Show me how this one works, Jenks," he ordered.

"What? Don't you trust me?" Emerson asked. Undaunted, he caught a few more flies and then let Callaghan try.

The two Science Fair competitors managed to trap well over a dozen live flies before the bell sounded for their next class. The three boys scurried from the bathroom just as a frowning Mr. Fong was closing their classroom door.

Emerson maintained close surveillance on the spider boys, as they were being called. Callaghan and Kelly skipped down the front steps and walked to the barn together every day after lunch. Emerson nodded approvingly – not because they were so dedicated, but because they were so predictable. On occasion, Callaghan and Kelly invited Emerson to accompany them. He did so at every opportunity, taking time to familiarize himself with the barn. He kept his ears open too. One day Kelly let slip that Callaghan had installed a secret security system.

+ − × ÷

On the next to last Sunday in May, the students were granted a rare sleep-in. Mass was delayed to accommodate the local Archbishop's annual visit. Emerson Jenks was up early. After nine months of routine, his internal clock rang as loudly as the bell. Kelly and Callaghan slept late. Emerson decided he would never get a better opportunity to visit the barn alone. Before entering the old structure, he examined the door but could find no tape, no elastics, no thread, no tacks. When he discovered two pennies on the top edge of the door he noted their location and configuration. The first was tails up, the second tails down. He pocketed the coins and entered the building. Moments later he stepped outside and replaced the pennies exactly as he had found them.

The spider boys were still asleep when he returned to the dorm. Emerson donned his pyjamas and crawled into bed, determined to feign sleep until either Callaghan or Kelly passed by. When Kelly shuffled into the washroom, Emerson arose and followed him. He faked a yawn, stretched and rolled his head about. He was doubly pleased when, halfway through his routine, Callaghan entered the room. "Just perfect," said Emerson to himself as the warning bell for chapel rang.

After the Archbishop and Father Keegan finished mass, a sumptuous brunch was served. The moment the meal ended, Emerson slipped out of the refectory. Angelo Guardiano took his friend's dishes to the scullery. Emerson wanted to stay clear of the spider boys. From a classroom window he gazed down at the front stairs expecting to see Callaghan and Kelly at any moment. Neither of them appeared. No one else left the building either. Emerson waited for ten minutes, rubbing the back of his neck and wondering where the boys could be. He climbed to the dorm and found it empty. Puzzled, he headed for the common rooms. As he approached the chapel he discovered where everyone had gone.

Voices, praying the rosary, floated into the stairwell. Emerson decided he had better try to slip into the chapel unnoticed. He hurried to the room's side entrance and slid into the sacristan's pew. After reciting three Hail Marys, he turned his head to the left, just far enough to get a clear view of the head student. Andrews glowered back and indicated that Emerson should come kneel beside him.

When the service ended, Andrews took Emerson aside. "You just made my life a whole lot easier, Jenks," he stated. "Change into your work clothes, then go help Reynolds clean the headmaster's car. It's gotta be spotless. Mr. Fitzroy's driving the Archbishop to the train right after dinner." Emerson, knowing better than to argue, hurried off. "Jenks!" called Andrews. "Come find me when you're done. I need to check things over before I let you go."

The outside of the car was clean in thirty minutes. The interior took the boys over an hour. While Reynolds saw to a few finishing touches, Emerson located Andrews in the senior common room. Being a junior and unable to enter the room, he had to call to the head student from the door. "Can you come and look at the car, Andrews?" he called.

Andrews raised his hand, signalling Emerson to wait. He counted the little green houses on Park Place. When he finished he said, "Plans have changed. The Archbishop had to leave already… with Father Keegan." To the player on his right he said, "Rotten luck, Osterholt." To the banker he added, "So what's he owe me?" Turning back to Emerson he continued, "I'll trust you guys this time, Jenks. Beat it."

As Emerson hurried past the door to the junior common room, someone yelled, "Hey, Jenks. Callaghan and Kelly were looking for you. Fredericks came by too." Another voice called out, "You better have Guardiano with you when you run into Callaghan." Raucous laughter echoed out of the room and chased Emerson down the hall and out through the double doors.

He walked past the barn, whistling. Finding the door swinging on its hinges, he peered inside. He found one flycatcher on the floor, smashed. The other was more or less intact but tossed carelessly on the workbench. Kelly's clipboard was bent almost in half and had been left upside down on the floor, a footprint on its back, its pages strewn about like autumn leaves. Emerson chuckled and rolled two plastic beads in his hand as he imagined the shock the two spider boys must have had. He figured he had introduced at least one and possibly both of them to the taste of live fly. It was time to find Angelo Guardiano.

As Emerson entered the dorm he found the spider boys waiting for him. "You went in the barn, didn't yuh, Jenks?" demanded Kelly.

"Yeah!" added Callaghan, scowling.

Emerson was taken aback. All recollection of his hastily prepared alibi abandoned him. He could admit going into the barn and think up some excuse for having done so. Alternatively, he could flatly deny being anywhere near the place and hope there were no eye witnesses to contradict him. Rather than choose, he stalled for time. "What are you two talking about?" he asked dismissively.

"No use denying it, Jenks. Who else would trash the place?" Callaghan replied. There was a challenge in his voice.

"Trash the place?" cried Emerson. "You mean someone trashed the place?"

"It was you," accused Kelly. "We know it. Who else would do it?"

"Who else?" replied Emerson with a snigger. "Anybody else… that's who. Look… I was out washing Fitzroy's stupid car all afternoon. Go ask Andrews. Ask Reynolds. They'll tell you. I just finished… honest."

Kelly looked to Callaghan, seeking guidance.

Callaghan paused to reconsider. "I'll just do that," he replied, squinting and glaring at Emerson, who stared back. Kelly took turns looking first at Callaghan and then at Emerson. "But I know it was you, Jenks," Callaghan cried.

"It wasn't," responded Emerson.

"Was too, Jenks."

"Was not."

"Was too."

As the stalemate persisted – no one knew quite how to end it – the door opened and Albertson's head appeared. "Strupples' got us lookin' all over the place for you guys. Where the heck yuh bin? C'mon. She said she'd wait in the lab." Callaghan and Kelly started for the stairs. Emerson strolled towards his locker. "You too, Jenks," added Albertson. "She wants all three of yuh."

The trio entered Miss Strupples' laboratory. Kelly led the way. Emerson followed. Callaghan, not about to let Emerson out of his sight, brought up the rear. Before any of them could say a word, Miss Strupples leapt from her chair, slapped her hands to her cheeks and began to speak. A torrent of barely decipherable words poured forth. "It's my fault… all my fault. I'm so sorry, boys," she wailed.

"Sorry?" replied Emerson. The last thing he expected from the Science professor was an apology. "About what, Ma'am?"

"About the spider project, of course. I hope I didn't do any serious damage," she added. "Oh, it's all my fault. I should never have gone out there… not without permission… not without you. I'm so sorry, boys."

"You trashed… I mean, you were the one who went in the barn?" asked Callaghan.

"Let me explain, please. Oh, I can't tell you how badly I feel. You see, I mentioned the spiders and people were asking for details and I didn't know… I mean… I felt I should know… and I couldn't very well say I didn't after bragging the way I did. Oh, my! So I said yes and walked out to look at your spiders and…"

"You didn't try to catch a fly, did you?" asked Emerson without thinking of the implications of his question.

"No, no, no…" answered Strupples. The woman hesitated. "And that's when everything went so very wrong. One of your flycatchers fell on the floor and got stepped on. The flip chart got knocked over and the pages flew up into the air. I'm so, so sorry. Oh, I didn't mean to… I didn't know what to do. The spider box started to go over and I just managed to steady it in time. Oh, the coughing and choking… and the spitting! And, that's when they ran out of the barn."

The three boys, one as confused as the other, blinked in their efforts to understand. Kelly found his tongue first. "Who, Ma'am? Who ran out?"

"Why, Father Keegan and the Archbishop, of course…" cried Miss Strupples. "Haven't you heard?"

Revenge So Sweet

The students liked Miss Strupples. Many loved her. But this stopped few from calling her Olive Oyl. Most male teachers empathized with students; Strupples sought out the upset and lonely. Each year she invited every student to tea. Like the animals summoned to Noah's Ark, they arrived at her door in pairs. She had a soft heart which was sometimes mistaken for a soft head. But Strupples was no fool.

"Ah, Mr. Jenks," declared Leticia Strupples when she opened her door and found Emerson standing in the hall. "Come in. Please sit down."

After the April Fool's Day pranks, Miss Strupples interrogated Burton and Andrews for first hand information about the flashes they had witnessed in the chapel. She concluded that there was something chemical in their accounts. The Science teacher conducted a thorough inventory of her supplies and a wider investigation. This resulted in Emerson's second appearance in her lodgings – alone on this occasion.

The boy crammed himself into a corner of Strupples' loveseat with his hands clamped between his knees. His eyes darted about the room. Emerson knew this visit was not for tea. He sat and tried to imagine why he had been summoned.

"I'm not quite sure how to proceed," Strupples began. She paced about her room, stopped, scrutinized her visitor then paced some more. Emerson studied her every movement. She held her hands, palm against palm, in an attitude of prayer. Her chin rested on her fingertips. "I must ask you something before we start," the Science teacher announced and stared into Emerson's eyes. "I need the absolute truth. A simple yes or no will do."

"Yes, Ma'am."

"No matter what you answer – yes or no – I'll take no action against you," added Strupples. Emerson winced. She turned her back to the boy. "Do you understand?" He was not at all sure that he understood so made no answer. The Science instructor waited and then repeated, "A simple yes or a no is enough, Mr. Jenks."

The memory of his teacher's comment about being home in a flash took residence in the back of Emerson's mind and stirred his guilty conscience. "Yes, Ma'am," he replied.

"Good! Now, Mr. Jenks… did you sneak into my room last evening?" asked Strupples as she swung around to face her guest.

The boy scrambled to his feet, blushing. "No, Sir— Ma'am!" declared Emerson in a most emphatic tone. "Absolutely not! I'd nev—"

Strupples waved her arms dismissively. "Hush, hush." She spoke in a soothing tone. "Just a yes or no." She rested a hand on the boy's shoulder. "It's as I suspected, but I had to ask."

"Yes, Ma'am."

"Now, let's sit over here and talk," suggested the woman. Miss Strupples led Emerson to a round oak table, pulled out two chairs and took a seat. Emerson joined her, eying her cautiously.

"Now we can begin," she continued. "I believe I can trust you." Miss Strupples evaluated her guest for a moment. "I *can* trust you, Jenks… can't I?"

"Of course you can, Ma'am," replied Emerson.

"May I call you by your first name?"

"Yes, Ma'am… if you like." Emerson grew more and more suspicious with each question.

"This is a… shall we say… a delicate matter, Emerson. You see… I need your help."

"My *help*, Ma'am?" His surprise was obvious. He drew his first relaxed breath in hours. Relieved, he expected her to ask him to help Fredericks again. "If I can, I mean, and if I have the time, Ma'am."

"I'll explain," Miss Strupples continued. "Last evening, I left my room… to have tea with Professors Darling and Fong… in the staff refectory. When I returned, I discovered that someone had been in my room."

"In your room?" Emerson showed even more surprise. "How'd you know that?" he inquired as he placed his elbows on the table, leaned forward and rested his chin on his fists. Jekyll-and-Hyde-like, the boy's alter ego was emerging unbidden.

"Well, when I came back, the tape was off," explained Miss Strupples.

Emerson's eyes narrowed and he tensed.

"The tape, Emerson… that I'd stuck on my door," explained Strupples.

The boy had been surprised the woman knew someone had been in her room. Learning how she knew gave him an entirely new appreciation of the woman. "You taped *your door*?" Emerson asked as he slid his glasses up his nose.

"I always tape my door," replied Strupples as casually as she would have said 'I always brush my teeth.'

"Really?" declared Emerson.

"Really," replied his host. "You would too if you had to live over here… with him."

Emerson scratched his head with one hand and rubbed his chin with the other. "Oh?" he answered. "Why not just lock it, Ma'am?"

"Lock my door? In my own home?" Strupples was clearly distressed at the thought. "Never!" She stood and paced the room before she continued. "It took me over twenty minutes to find that dead fish stuck behind the radiator," explained Strupples. "If I hadn't found it, this place would have stunk and probably been full of wasps or something when I returned from class today."

"Nothing else had been touched or anything?" asked Emerson.

"Not that I noticed," answered Strupples. "He didn't look in any of my drawers, I know that much." The student narrowed his eyes and tilted his head a little to one side. "Oh! I put tape there too," explained the Science professor. "I've started to get really paranoid, you see."

Emerson laughed. "You know what they say, Ma'am… just 'cause you're paranoid doesn't mean someone's not out to get you."

Strupples eyed the boy, evaluating him while he re-evaluated her. She returned to her seat. "And…" continued Emerson, "how can I help?"

"Have you ever heard of a hit man?" asked Strupples.

"Like in the mafia, Ma'am?" inquired Emerson.

"Exactly!" replied Strupples. "Just like in the mafia. Emerson, you can do two things for me... I think. Help me figure out who did it and get him back for me."

Emerson scratched behind his ear. A grim smile formed on his lips. He studied Miss Strupples' calm, unaffected face. "I really want to get him..." the woman added, "to make him pay." Emerson made no reply. "You're a very cautious little fellow," suggested the woman. "I can see why you never get caught."

"Pardon, Ma'am?" cried Emerson in a most indignant tone.

"Oh, Emerson!" Strupples laughed a hearty laugh. "Come, come. Let me ask you..." She walked to a counter and stood with her back to her guest. Emerson heard water running. "If you were stumped with a problem... in Latin say," she asked over her shoulder, "to whom would you go?"

"Mr. Willoughby-Wallows, I suppose, Ma'am," answered Emerson. He wished he knew where the question was leading.

"And if the problem was, say... in Math?"

"Mr. Darling, Ma'am."

"You will take tea, Emerson?"

"Yes, Ma'am, please," answered the boy. He anxiously awaited the next question.

"Now, let's say the problem was Chemistry?" continued Strupples.

"Oh, I'd come to you, of course, Ma'am," replied Emerson. "Why?"

"But you didn't, did you?" continued Strupples. She turned and moved towards a very shocked Emerson Jenks. "You looked it up... right?"

"Looked what up, Ma'am?" Emerson coughed into his fist.

"We'll come back to that, Emerson." The woman continued her interrogation by saying, "When one needs professional help, one turns to a pro. And, Emerson, I know that you are the consummate pro when it comes to pranks." An amused smile danced across Strupples' face. She watched and waited for the boy's reply.

Emerson stared back, his face a blank page. But he felt a churning inside, as if his stomach was doing a load of wash.

"Oh my! You are very good at your game," his teacher added. "Very good indeed! How can you just sit there like that... so calm... so innocent... not so much as a blink? But I know exactly who I'm dealing with, young man. Do you know what they said about boys like you a few hundred years ago, Emerson?"

"Boys like me, Ma'am?"

"Boys like you, Emerson. *Born, bound for Botany Bay*, Sir," she said and wagged her finger.

"I think you've made a mistake, Ma'am," suggested the boy.

"Oh, no, Emerson," replied the woman. "You, Sir, made the mistake." Emerson stared past the woman and tried to think of what he could have overlooked.

"Fingerprints, Emerson... *your* fingerprints on your binders, all over *my* Potassium perchlorate and my German aluminum powder and on the—" declared the woman.

Emerson could no longer resist Strupple's skilled interrogation. "—Oh, the kettle, Ma'am," he shouted and redirected his gaze. Miss Strupples continued to stare into the boy's eyes. The kettle's whistling grew anxious and then angry. The corners of Emerson's mouth began to turn upwards. Strupples laughed again and attended to the boiling water.

Emerson had to laugh too. "I guess you got me, Ma'am," he admitted.

"Emerson..." Strupples continued as she made tea, "this is not just about last night. Someone over here has been playing dirty tricks for a long, long time... for years, in fact. It's high time someone paid him back."

"But, Ma'am..." exclaimed Emerson, "since you figured me out, you must be able to figure—"

"—But, Emerson, I didn't figure you out. Oh my, no! Not for sure that is... until just now anyway," replied Strupples. "I know nothing at all about fingerprints, you see."

"Then how—" inquired Emerson.

"Well... when I got a good description of what happened in the chapel, that candle thing – that was clever – dangerous, of course, but clever, too." Miss Strupples prepared to pour. "You did say you'd have tea?" she asked. "I know you were careful, Emerson. Otherwise you'd have blown your fingers off." Emerson inspected his hands. "Anyhow, I figured someone must have gotten their hands on some flash powder.

Well... I asked myself where in the world someone could get his hands on flash powder. You don't just buy it in a store. But then you knew that, right?" Emerson's eyes grew wider and wider. "So, I figured someone must have made it. And, Emerson, when I checked and found out you'd sent for those photography books... well?"

"Oh?" replied Emerson. "I was afraid of that."

"I wasn't absolutely sure, just sure enough to ask you to come here this evening," continued Strupples. "And I'm not absolutely sure who I'm after or how to find out either. I can't very well invite *him* here."

"Ma'am, you can't always know for absolutely sure," explained Emerson. "You might never get enough evidence on a really good prankster. You just have to go on what you do know. If we had a decent library... sorry... except for those books, you'd never have caught me. I'd like to help you, Ma'am." He paused then continued, "But I'd need to know all about whoever you figure it is." The boy noticed Strupples balk at the idea but ignored her misgivings. "Ma'am, you have to ask, when the pranks started... like this year or last, who gets picked on, who has the skill to do the pranks... that kind of thing. You weed people out and see who's left."

"I'm pretty sure it's Professor Warneke," declared Strupples. "Professor von Baumgartner used to say the pranks really got out of hand when—" The woman stopped in mid-sentence.

"When what, Ma'am?"

"Well... when Warneke arrived," she answered. "And," she continued, her eyes flashing, "almost everyone has been a victim... especially me... and Mr. Fong. Oh, and this year, Mr. Willoughby-Wallows. Warneke went to the junior dormitory and somehow or other doused that poor young man—"

"—Ahem!" Emerson cleared his throat. Strupples stopped and stared. "You can't blame that one on Professor Warneke, Ma'am," he said.

"Oh?" exclaimed Strupples in her innocence. Emerson flashed a sheepish grin. "Oh my, Emerson... you?"

"So, what kind of things has he been doing?" asked Emerson. "Mr. Warneke, that is." He was more than happy to redirect the conversation.

"Well..." answered Strupples, "someone locked—"

"—Ma'am?" interjected Emerson. "Think Warneke, not someone. Warneke locked..."

"Oh, okay," replied the woman. She poured more tea.

"Well, I know he... Warneke, that is, fixed the draw to decide who had to go to Stroud Island. I don't know exactly how he, I mean, Warneke did it, but he did it alright. I think he was the one who tied— oops!"

"*Warneke* was the one who tied..." corrected Emerson.

"But, Emerson, I get so mad every time I say his— Warneke's — name," cried Strupples.

"That's why I want you to keep saying it, Ma'am," explained Emerson. "Motivation, Ma'am."

The statement gave the woman pause. "As I was saying, Warneke tied Mr. Fitzroy's doors closed that same night. Unless..." Strupples looked hard at Emerson.

"No, no, that wasn't me, Ma'am," declared the boy. "Honest!"

Strupples continued, "Warneke locked Fong in his room and he taped my door closed. Oh, when I think of it, I could just scream. Emerson, he's the only person it could be," she added. "And this might be important. He's the only one who hasn't been picked on."

"Ah, now, that's really important to know," exclaimed the boy. "That can be a dead giveaway after a while."

"You're right, Emerson. I suppose I've always known it. And, when I really think about it, only Warneke could be behind all this nonsense," she declared.

"Oh, Ma'am..." replied Emerson with a sharp intake of breath, "pranks aren't nonsense. Pranks are very serious business, Ma'am... if you're going to do them right."

"Business then... or pleasure, maybe?" suggested Strupples with a laugh.

"So you want to hire me as your hit man?" asked Emerson. "Hit men get paid, right, Ma'am?"

"I see," replied Miss Strupples. "So this is business after all? Have you ever heard about the alligator with the bone stuck in his throat, Emerson?"

"Ma'am?"

"The alligator offered a heron a reward for removing the bone," explained Strupples. "The bird stuck its neck down the alligator's throat and pulled it out… the bone, I mean. When he asked for his reward the alligator said, he'd already got it… he didn't get his head bit off."

"Ma'am?"

"I'm the alligator, Emerson… You're the heron."

"Ah… I see," the boy muttered. "So, I guess we better start tailor-making that prank for the professor then, Ma'am."

Strupples shook her head and laughed. "I was right, Emerson. You're a pro alright."

"Just one thing, Ma'am. Why don't you do it… yourself, I mean? It should be your prank – if you want to get full satisfaction out of the thing."

Strupples said nothing. She stared at the student with a puzzled frown.

"And to be yours, it has to come from what you know."

"Do you think I could… *really*?" asked Strupples.

"I'd help. You know – just so everything goes smooth – smoothly, I mean."

"Do it myself… Hmmm!" The woman considered the suggestion.

Emerson added, "Think Science… you know Biology and Physics and Chemistry, Ma'am. I'll help… but you should do this yourself. It can be very…"

"—Stimulating?" interjected the teacher.

"That too," replied Emerson. "But I was going to say *gratifying*."

After a few moments, the Science teacher's face lit up. "I'll do it," declared Miss Strupples. "I'll do it myself… with your help, of course. Yes, I will!"

"To begin with, Ma'am, start writing down all the pranks Professor Warneke has pulled so we can study them. That will tell us a lot about him… maybe even about some of his weaknesses. And we'll need all the information you can get… things you've seen and heard. But you can't go asking a lot of questions or spying on him and stuff like that, Ma'am. That's way too obvious. Besides, the more people involved, the more likely you'll fail," he explained. "And if you're not careful, someone will make you the target. You know… turn the tables on you. You need to look for patterns and predictability."

"You're very good at this, Jenks," admitted Leticia Strupples. "I place myself in your capable hands."

"I'll have to think about it some more, Ma'am. Are you in a rush?" He stood up, walked to the door and stood with his hand on the knob.

Strupples approached. "No, there's no hurry, Emerson," she replied. "But, can we do it before the end of school?" Emerson screwed up his face and rocked his head from side to side. Strupples continued, "I don't want to wait 'til next year."

"No hurry, eh?" grunted Emerson. "That only gives us a few weeks, Ma'am. But… I think we might just manage it," he added with a laugh.

"We've a deal then, Mr. Jenks." Strupples spat on the palm of her hand and offered it to the boy. Emerson smiled, nonplussed, at the childlike gesture, then spat on his palm and sealed the deal with a long handshake.

"Before exams are over, Ma'am," he replied. "Guaranteed."

The Science instructor's first class in advanced pranksterism ended.

+ − × ÷

Just two days later, Emerson received a note from Miss Strupples. It contained the information she had been able to gather. At the bottom of the memo she asked when they could meet again. Another two days passed before Emerson asked Strupples for help with a Physics experiment. Strupples provide a slip which allowed him to go to the lab instead of first study hall that evening. When teacher and student met, Emerson asked questions. Strupples supplied answers. The subject matter was Science, but not in the strictly academic sense. Emerson directed the woman's attention to an item under the heading, *THINGS I'VE HEARD.*

"What's this about?" he asked.

"Well, Emerson, they say he— Warneke, I mean —has a key to the kitchen and he sneaks food."

Emerson shook his head in disbelief. "That's a possibility. And this, Ma'am?"

"Several teachers have told me they think Professor Warneke steals their shampoo if they forget it in the showers," explained the Science instructor. “Oh, and Wilf—Mr. Willoughby-Wallows that is—once told me Warneke’s got a collection of stolen stuff in his lodgings.”

“Unbelievable,” muttered Emerson. “What about this drawing of names thing?” The conversation continued moving down the long list of items. “All this gives me a lot of ideas for pranks but nothing…”

With a smile, Miss Strupples finished Emerson’s though for him, “Elegant enough?”

Emerson nodded and massaged his lower lip as he continued to study the list. “I think I have it, Miss Strupples,” he announced at last. “I’m pretty sure we can work this one somehow. But I’ll need some more information.” An interrogation ensued.

“Do you have a pen and some paper, Ma’am?” Emerson asked when he had finished. Strupples produced the needed items and made ready to take notes. Emerson thought aloud while Leticia Strupples scribbled on her paper. “Now, one,” he touched his right index finger to his left pinkie, “a detailed floor plan. Two…” Emerson touched his ring finger. The two conspirators continued in this fashion until the student said, “Finally,” and tapped his right index finger against the tip of his left thumb. “Ma’am, here’s the part you have to arrange yourself. If you can come up with something… we’ll have him.” Emerson explained the gist of an idea. Miss Strupples leaned back in her chair and laughed a shrill laugh. “Now, Ma’am, you can’t go using acid or anything like that,” Emerson warned. “We can’t injure him, remember.”

Leticia Strupples put a hand to her mouth, drummed the fingers of her other hand on the desktop and frowned. She giggled and laughed aloud. “Oh, you dear boy, Emerson, I’ve got just the thing.” She scratched down another note.

“What is it?” the boy asked and craned to see what she had written.

“I’m not telling,” replied Strupples in an obstinate tone and pressed the sheet of paper to her chest. She might have been twelve years old again.

“Actually, Ma’am…” Emerson said and took a breath, “it’s probably best that I don’t know.”

+ − × ÷

Less than a week later, after dinner, Miss Strupples walked to her Science lab to mark assignments. Emerson's binder lay atop the pile. She opened it first. Along with his lab experiment she found a detailed set of instructions, complete with provisos and dread warnings: a virtual prankster's handbook. She read the notes, awed by the detail and the understated elegance of Emerson's plan. She marvelled at the warning not to be the first or last person the mark sees after the prank, not to panic if the plan doesn't work the first time and not to laugh too loudly if it does.

No one saw Strupples carry the brown paper bag back to her lodgings. In her room, the Science master reset her alarm and went to bed. Four-thirty would come all too early. Half past four came but the alarm clock did not ring. An impatient Strupples had been awake for some time, pacing her room. The novice prankster's nerves, like those of the pilot trainee, were jumpy before her first solo. The woman pulled a heavy bathrobe over her flannel nightgown and, minutes later, pressed an ear to her door. Directly, she heard Willoughby-Wallows' whistle as he approached. She listened to him flip-flop past and heard him enter the shower room. Still she waited. After he retraced his steps and she could no longer hear his footfall, she counted slowly to ten and left the room.

The corridor was deathly quiet. Visibility was poor. The only available light entered through a single window at the end of the hallway. On reaching the men's showers, she cracked a door open, peered into the gloom and then stepped inside, easing the door closed behind her. She found the switch and flipped on the lights. The woman conducted her business quickly, doused the lights and retired to her room on cat's paws. She left her door ajar, breathed normally once more and peeked out through the crack.

The morning bell rang and the hall lights came on. "Warneke will be on his way," Strupples said to herself. She gathered her shower bag and towels, took a deep breath while opening her door, then entered the corridor. Twenty feet away, the English master strolled along the hall, in her direction.

"Strupples."

"Warneke."

The two professors had passed and greeted each other at this time, in this place and in this manner almost every working day for twelve years. Neither broke step. Everything went just as Emerson Jenks had said it should. “So far, so good,” said the woman under her breath. In a pocket of her dressing gown she crossed her fingers.

+ − × ÷

Leticia Strupples stepped from the shower when she heard muffled bellowing. The uproar grew louder and louder and then faded by degrees. Warneke’s voice grew distant and was replaced by chatter and loud guffaws. Strupples enjoyed a hearty laugh, picturing the result of her prank. When she recalled Emerson’s admonitions to act naturally and not under-react, she hurriedly dried herself, dressed and went to investigate. In a display of innocent curiosity, Strupples wrapped her hair in a towel as she approached the crowd milling about outside the men’s shower room. Staff members had gathered there in groups of three and four, discussing the affair. The general consensus was that the morning’s events were rather amusing. Strupples did what Emerson Jenks had recommended and blended in.

When told that several men were hot on Warneke’s trail, Strupples hurried into the main building. She heard loud voices emanating from Mr. Fitzroy’s office as she approached.

After greeting Strupples in the hall, Warneke had entered the shower room, turned on the lights, pushed the door of the first shower stall open and, upon discovering nothing of interest, repeated his actions at stall number two. There he spotted a shampoo container and, without hesitation, stepped over a puddle and inspected the plastic bottle. It was still wet. Strupples had remembered to follow Emerson’s instructions to the letter.

Warneke grabbed the shampoo and took it with him to the sink. He inhaled the shampoo’s bracing citrus scent and made a clucking sound. Tossing the bottle into the air, he caught it and congratulated himself on his thrift. “Thank you, my inattentive little friend,” said the man aloud. It was a poor W. C. Fields impersonation.

The English master removed his glasses and set them beside the sink. He hung his towel and dressing gown on a wall hook, entered the third shower stall and turned on the faucet. He waited for the water to reach a comfortable temperature and, after stepping into and out of the spray, he reached for his most recent hair-care acquisition. Warneke raised the bottle above his head, closed his eyes and squeezed. He felt a generous dab of thick, rich shampoo drop onto his head. He placed the bottle in the rack that hung from the shower head and began to scrub.

It took several moments for the gentleman to realize that this new shampoo did not lather well. "Conditioner," he roared. "Drat!" Warneke harboured suspicions about hair conditioner and the men who used it. He peered through the steam, leaned towards the bottle, dragged a hand over his face and, with a myopic squint, tried to read the label. "Blast these old eyes of mine," he grumbled. The man was positive that the label had read shampoo, so, when the fact was confirmed, he reacted with surprise. Strange, he thought and shrugged. "Ah, leave it to that guy to buy the cheap stuff." No matter how hard he massaged his scalp, no suds would form. He tried more shampoo but had no better luck.

With his eyes closed, the English master rinsed his hair while he soaped his facecloth. He lifted his head clear of the spray and looked up at the ceiling, slapping the cloth to his chest. He scrubbed his shoulders, neck and armpits and strained to wash his back. When he reached for his soap again he was dumbfounded. His white facecloth had turned bright orange. Warneke held out his arms. They too had turned orange. His chest was solid orange. His legs were streaked orange. Everywhere he looked he was orange… Orange Lodge orange. He scrubbed more and more franticly at his discoloured skin. The bar of soap had turned carrot orange. His feet were turning a tincture of iodine orange. In a frenzy he quit the shower. Warneke fumbled about looking for his glasses, found them and put them on. He wiped the steamed-up mirror with his towel and stared at his reflection in utter amazement.

It was at that moment that Leticia Strupples and the other staff members heard the uproar begin. The English master, an enthusiast for exactness of expression, a devotee to adeptness in diction, a promoter of proper pronunciation, contemptuous of the common speech, lost in a moment in time, all but the rudiments of human speech. He bellowed, blustered and bawled; howled, hollered and hissed; grunted, groaned and growled.

Warneke was orange. His face was orange. His torso was orange. His limbs were orange. His head and hair were orange. And, insult to end all insults – the mother of insults – his beautiful white moustache had turned bright orange.

Fitzroy ran for his doors as they rattled on their hinges. They were pushed towards him and Warneke, a bull blind with rage, stormed past him into the room. Fitzroy's jaw dropped. His eyes bulged. He looked his visitor up and down. He ran his fingers through his hair. "My word, Warneke!" he shouted, "You're… you're… you're all orange." The fact that the gentleman was all but naked seemed not to enter either man's mind. Warneke stood before the headmaster with nothing but a not very large towel with which to preserve his dignity. He held it in place with his left hand while his right flailed about, a testimony to the man's complete consternation. "What in the world?" continued Fitzroy.

"Some idiot put something in my shampoo," complained Warneke.

"Your *shampoo?*" Fitzroy's face betrayed his astonishment.

"My shampoo, Sir," declared Warneke. "Whose shampoo do you think it was, Sir?" In an effort to exhibit more of the damage, Professor Warneke stretched his right arm over his left shoulder and twisted his body in a vain attempt to display his back. This graceful motion was followed by a crude imitation of a ballerina's pirouette. Warneke attempted to repeat the manoeuvres, but in reverse order: left arm over right shoulder. Maintaining a firm grip on the towel proved more difficult than expected. Warneke stood before his headmaster in a condition commonly referred to as naked as a jaybird. His skin tone, however, was more akin to that of a robin redbreast. Warneke lurched for the towel and did his best to maintain a degree of modesty.

Fitzroy failed to stifle a chortle. Wrath and indignation spread across Warneke's face. The approach of Professors Darling and Fong, with others hot on their heels, spared Fitzroy a tongue-lashing. The headmaster stepped around the all-but-naked man and slammed the office doors. Warneke had been far too busy inspecting the damage and trying to cover himself to notice the visitors. "Ah… ah… you'd better wait here," stammered the headmaster as if Warneke intended to leave. Fitzroy ran to his bedroom and returned with a dressing gown. The big man yanked the all too small garment from the headmaster's hands and covered his body as best he could.

"Sir," stated Warneke with a sputter and then stopped to think. "This is… is…"

The ever-helpful headmaster attempted to assist. "Egregious?" he suggested.

"Egregious!" repeated Warneke as he glared at Fitzroy. "Egregious?"

Fitzroy tried again, "Outrageous?"

"Outrageous! Outrageous, Sir!" shouted Warneke. "This goes way beyond outrageous. And I expect you to do something about it."

Fitzroy paced for a few moments and began to chew his thumbnail. "How could someone have gotten hold of your shampoo?" inquired the headmaster.

Warneke paused before answering. "I don't know," he barked.

"But how did they get into your room?" asked Fitzroy. "You always lock your room and—"

"—I said… I *don't* know," Warneke bellowed.

"But, Sir…" insisted the headmaster and paused to rub his forehead, "if you want me to do something you have to help. Tell me—"

"—I said I don't know, Sir," shouted Warneke. "And I don't know."

"But, who…" Fitzroy raised one hand to his forehead and placed the other on his hip. "Who would ever do such a thing?"

"Good day, Sir," grunted Warneke. "I will not be taking my classes." He strutted to the doors, threw them open, stormed past several shocked colleagues and marched towards his lodgings. He did not even acknowledge Miss Strupples when they passed in the hall.

The woman watched her victim's performance, let him pass and giggled after he disappeared around the turn in the corridor. She thought that Professor Warneke seemed very, very orange. It occurred to the Science teacher that she had perhaps put a touch too much dye into the lab gel.

It was a fleeting thought.

Headmaster Fitzroy, not Professor Warneke, arrived for each of the English master's classes that day. The students were given nothing by way of explanation for the professor's absence, or for the racket some had heard echoing through the building earlier that morning. The ears of the boys who had rooms on the second floor, near the entrance to the faculty wing, had been witness to Warneke's early morning eruption. All the others learned of it at breakfast.

"Is it true that Professor Warneke's got jaundice or something?" asked a student.

Fitzroy shoved his tongue into his cheek and looked at the floor before answering, "No, Professor Warneke does not have jaundice."

It took all that day and most of the next for Headmaster Fitzroy to adequately impress upon Professor Warneke his duty to St. Timothy's and his students and to get the man back to work. They agreed that the English master would return to class the following Monday. "I can't just keep telling them to review the next chapter, Sir," Fitzroy said to the orange man.

"And why ever not?" shouted Warneke. "That's all I'll be doing with them. How..." demanded the English master, rolling back his sleeves and holding his arms out to Fitzroy. "—how am I supposed to stand there in front of those sneering little... looking like this? Can't you see? I... I... I'm all over orange, man."

"Well... not all over," suggested Fitzroy. "The backs of your..."

Warneke's mouth dropped open. He shook his head slowly.

"I know," said Fitzroy as if he had a brilliant idea, "I'll order the students not to laugh."

Warneke, who had gone to the mirror to inspect the damage for the hundredth time, turned and gaped. "You can't possibly be serious, Sir," he roared.

+ − × ÷

Warneke demanded that he be allowed to take his meals in his room. The kitchen staff had strict instructions to leave his tray on the chair outside his door. On Sunday, just as Warneke's breakfast was ready for delivery, Wilfred Willoughby-Wallows arrived at the kitchen. He wrestled the tray from the cook saying, "I'll take it to him—you're busy enough here." With a smiling face and a merry whistle, the dormitory supervisor walked to the faculty wing. He set the tray on the chair, removed an extra large orange from his coat pocket and set it atop the coffee mug next to the glass of juice. The orange had two sad eyes, a downturned mouth and a bushy moustache drawn on it. Willoughby-Wallows admired his handiwork then rapped three times on the door.

"Just leave it and go," ordered Warneke. His voice was gruff, troll-like in fact.

Willoughby-Wallows retreated down the hall and around the corner, then peeked back towards Warneke's door. He hoped to catch a glimpse of the man's face when he discovered the orange. He did see someone, but it was not Cyrus Warneke. He drew himself back and waited.

The shadowy figure stepped out of the stairwell near the English master's room. He looked around, took two carrots from his pocket and placed them on the tray before tapping on the door.

"I said, leave it and go," bellowed Warneke. The man sped down the corridor and, on rounding the corner, bumped into the shocked Greek and Latin teacher.

"Why, Mitch Fong! Great minds *do* think alike," declared Willoughby-Wallows after gathering his thoughts.

"You beat me to the punch though, Wilf," admitted Fong and laughed. "But I just had to get him back for that Stroud Island deal."

"Yeah," replied Willoughby-Wallows as he draped his arm over Fong's shoulder. "And for one or two other things, I suppose. Hey, Mitch, did you notice… on the tray?" added Willoughby-Wallows. "The cook sent him orange juice!"

+ − × ÷

When the English master finally reported for duty, he began talking before he entered the classroom. "Not a word, Gentlemen," he roared. "Not one single word, I say… unless you wish to spend an extra week or two here with me. Do I make myself perfectly clear?" he roared. The English master stood before the grade nine students. He told them to continue reviewing the year's material in preparation for the final exam.

"Sir?"

"Yes, Mr. Callaghan… with what, pray tell, may I assist you today?"

"Well, Sir…" answered Callaghan, hesitating, "it's this here note you wrote on my free verse, Sir. You said, more colour required and I don't know what you mean, Sir?" Callaghan's classmates chortled. Callaghan, remembering that he had to stay at the school to the bitter end anyways, had placed unusual emphasis on the word 'colour'.

"Ah… we have a comedian in our midst, I see," growled Warneke. "Does anyone in the class really feel like laughing?" He drew out the word 'really'. "Mr. Kelly… how about you?"

Kelly clamped a hand to his mouth and focussed on his work. Those nearest the boy heard him mumble, “Feel like laughing, Sir? Oh, no way… not me.”

“Just as I thought,” said the English master. “Now, Mr. Callaghan, I don’t think I quite understood the question, Sir. Would you care to repeat it, Mr. Callaghan?”

“Actually, Professor, Sir, I think I see what you meant, Sir… now that I think about it, I mean, Sir,” answered Callaghan.

“A very good thing too, my boy,” replied Warneke. “Oh… and thank you so much for reminding me about that lovely sonnet of yours, Mr. Callaghan. That had entirely slipped my mind.” Warneke allowed the subsequent chuckling to continue uninterrupted.

+ − × ÷

“Would you like another Nanaimo bar, Emerson?” asked Miss Strupples. A week had passed since she had executed her first prank. “How about more chocolate milk?”

“No thanks, Ma’am,” answered the student. “I’ve had an awful lot already, Ma’am. And I find this stuff too sweet anymore.”

“Oh, but not nearly as sweet as my revenge,” replied Miss Strupples with one of her hearty laughs. Emerson wiped his lips on a serviette and stood to go. “Emerson, I’ve been thinking,” said Strupples. “What if someone else had used that shampoo… instead of Professor Warneke, I mean?”

“That would be their problem, wouldn’t it?” replied Emerson. “And serve them right, too.”

“You know, Emerson, it’ll take weeks for that orange to come off,” Strupples added.

“I can see that, Ma’am,” he replied. “What could do that to him, Ma’am?”

“Oh, I can’t tell you that, Emerson,” answered Strupples. “Why, you might try it on someone else... even me?”

“Ma’am, do you really think I’d do that… to you, I mean?”

Strupples tilted her head to one side, frowned and stared at her young guest. Emerson narrowed his eyes and smirked. “Hmmm, maybe I taught you more than I thought,” he said. “Maybe I’ll have to be more careful around here myself from now on.”

Curtain Call

Strupples overtook Willoughby-Wallows in the basement corridor, just before they reached the student refectory. Together, they continued apace towards the auditorium.

"What's up, Leticia?" asked the Greek and Latin teacher as he struggled to keep up. "Mr. Fitzroy doesn't call these special meetings very often, right?"

"Never, Wilfred. He hates meetings – especially Sunday meetings," replied Strupples and accelerated away from her companion.

The young man had to alternate between a fast walk and a jog to keep up with the woman. His side was burning by the time they arrived outside the auditorium. Miss Strupples halted and stared at the doors. "It's been a very long time, if ever, since he's done anything like this," she stated.

Willoughby-Wallows pressed a hand to his side and wheezed. "Phew… well here we are, Leticia."

"Indeed," replied Strupples. She gazed at the door, arched her eyebrows and turned scornful eyes on her companion.

The younger teacher, unable to comprehend why they were not entering the room, waited several seconds before asking, "Shall we go in then?"

"As soon as you open the door for me, Wilf." Strupples sounded indignant. Willoughby-Wallows blushed, reached around the woman, pushed the door open and held it while she entered the room. Strupples stopped immediately and turned her head to the left. Her eyes and those of Professor Warneke locked on one another.

"Amazing," mumbled Willoughby-Wallows and followed Strupples' lead. The sight of his two peers in silent confrontation gave the man the jitters. With a curt nod, he greeted the English master who stood against the back wall, even deeper in shadow than usual. Warneke sported a wide-brimmed hat pulled down almost to his eyebrows to cover his discoloured facial features. The man acknowledged neither of them.

Strupples turned to Willoughby-Wallows and, in a smoky, playful voice, said, "Or-ange you glad we're on time, Wilf?"

"Humph! Laugh now, Madam. Enjoy yourselves, you two, but I shall have the last laugh... you'll see," warned Warneke. "Proceed with caution, Madam. You too, Sir."

"Caution, huh!" cried Strupples. Her voice dripped contempt. "An orange man speaks of caution, Wilf. There's irony in there somewhere."

Willoughby-Wallows placed a hand on the small of Miss Strupples' back and directed her ahead a few paces, whispering, "We really shouldn't tease him, Leticia." As he glanced into the back corner he noticed that Warneke's eyes were fixed firmly upon him. "He's likely to get really nasty," he added.

"Pshaw, Wilf... pshaw," cried Strupples. "No need to be afraid of him." In a huff, the Science professor made her way to the front row and found her usual seat. Her companion looked about before finding a chair against the side wall opposite Warneke – the better to keep an eye on the gentleman. As Willoughby-Wallows looked around, he could see a questioning look on each face. Throughout the room, people sat or stood in small groups and spoke in whispers as stragglers wandered in.

To everyone's amazement, the headmaster entered the room on time for once. Having stepped through the stage door, he slipped through the opening in the curtains and materialized, spectre-like, at the lectern. "Ahem, Gentlemen... Miss Strupples," shouted Fitzroy. The staff members stared and several double-checked the time. Those who were still milling about found their usual places.

"This shan't take long. Please take your seats... everyone," added Mr. Fitzroy. Every eye rested on the headmaster who scanned his audience pointing from head to head, counting. "Twelve, thirteen, we have fourteen," he announced. "There are three still missing. Tardy!" he mumbled with a loud 'tut'. "Why can we never start these meetings on time?" The teachers looked from one to another, each wondering how the man had the gall to voice such a complaint.

Strupples stood, turned and counted heads. "Professor Bentley and... and Professor Fong..." she announced.

"Here!" cried Fong as he entered the auditorium. "Sorry I'm late," he added. "I got held up… delayed. Sorry," he repeated without once looking at Fitzroy. He quickly took a seat in the back row. Bentley slipped into the room behind Fong, took his place next to Warneke and acted as if he had been waiting there for hours. Fong leaned over and, in hushed tones, asked his neighbour if he had missed anything. Mr. Darling shrugged, frowned and shook his head.

"There's still one missing," complained the headmaster. Impatience could be heard in his voice. He pulled out his pocket watch and checked the time. His eyes passed back and forth over the gathering. He gazed at the wall clock and drummed his fingers on the lectern.

Miss Strupples spoke. "I believe we're all here now, Sir. Have you forgotten to count yourself perhaps?"

The headmaster made as if to dismiss the notion but performed a quick recount and apologized. "Sorry, Madam. You're quite right. Well… let's get started." The teachers sat in anticipation of some momentous piece of news as Mr. Fitzroy loosened his tie and struggled to unbutton his collar. "Well…" he said and looked up at the ceiling. Several teachers looked up too, following his gaze. They saw nothing but the ceiling. "This is very difficult for me," continued the headmaster at last. He dropped his head and stared down at the lectern.

Miss Strupples caught sight of a glimmer in the headmaster's eye. She thought he looked sad. A terrible thought struck her. "Oh, Lord! Cancer!" whispered Strupples. No one sat close enough to hear her words. She looked around in alarm. She could not rid her mind of that word: 'cancer'.

"I… I… want you to be the first to know," continued Headmaster Fitzroy. "At the end of this month… well, Dr. Graham knows, of course, but only he…"

Miss Strupples fished a tissue from up her sleeve, scrunched it in her fist and pressed the fist to her mouth. Tears welled up in her eyes. "Cancer," she repeated in a voice no one else heard. "I can feel it in my bones," she muttered. "Oh, he's so young. Oh, oh, oh! What a pity."

Mr. Fitzroy continued, "What I mean is… I have… I have…" He paused once more. "I knew this day would come. Everything must come to an end. We must all pass on, I suppose… sooner or later. No use fearing the future, is there?"

"And so brave," thought Miss Strupples. Her shoulders a-tremble, she blew her noise and choked back tears, wiping them from her cheeks and chin. Fitzroy did not seem to notice. The others were as mystified by the lady's behaviour as they were by the headmaster's incoherent rambling.

In the end, Fitzroy's words came in a rush. "I'm thinking… I mean I shall be tendering my resignation at the end of term and applying for a position… elsewhere."

"Oh, thank God," shouted Strupples as she leapt to her feet.

In utter disbelief, thirty-two eyes stared at the woman. Seventeen mouths hung open. Fitzroy exhibited only slightly less shock than did Strupples. As soon as he could speak, which was not immediately, he blurted out, "*Pardon me,* Madam?"

Strupples' face burned crimson. She fanned herself with both hands. "I thought…" she replied, turning from Fitzroy to her peers and back, "that… well, I thought you were going to say you were dying, Sir… that you had cancer or something."

The headmaster shook his head, lowered it and spoke softly to the lectern. "Madam, you are positively mind-boggling." To Strupples he said, "No, Leticia, I do not have cancer. I am not dying." After letting his eyes pass over the gathering once more, he added, "Well, that's it… that's all," and took several sideways steps towards the centre of the stage.

"But… but…" cried Willoughby-Wallows as he struggled to his feet and tried to take in what he had heard. "But, Sir… why?" he asked. A humming could be heard. It built into a drone. Soon, other voices asked the same question: why? Mr. Fitzroy stood, centre stage, staring at his shoes. All eyes were trained on him.

"I know you must all think I'm crazy…" explained Fitzroy, stepping back to the lectern, "with this poltergeist business and all."

"Humph… we think nothing of the kind," shouted Warneke. "Nonsense, man! I say… what?" He looked around the room and, in a much louder voice, added, "Well… do we?" A murmur came in response as did a shaking of heads. "Where did you ever get such a… well, such a silly notion, Sir?" the orange man asked.

Fitzroy ran his fingers through his hair. "I… I don't know… exactly," he answered. "But, ever since that… that visitation… I just… well, I just haven't been myself. You all know that." The headmaster placed one hand on his hip and the other over his mouth. "I do not feel able to continue," he added after a moment's pause. "Sometimes I think I'm crazy myself. Lord knows what you people… and the students think. And the parents…" He stopped and then added, "Oh, when the parents find out?"

Willoughby-Wallows spoke. "We think nothing of it, Sir, nothing at all. Neither do the students, Sir. We think someone played an elaborate prank… an atrocious trick on you, Sir. That's all." All heads nodded agreement.

"A trick! A trick, you say?" replied Fitzroy, becoming more animated. "Can anyone explain how a drawer can open by itself, how non-existent chains can rattle, how a book can fly off a shelf… and halfway across my room… by itself, mind? How do you… and don't give me any pseudo-psychological mumbo-jumbo either… how do you explain what happened, eh? Tell me that!"

No one spoke. No one could speak. No one, not even Warneke, had any explanation.

"Ha! Just as I thought," declared the headmaster as if some great victory had been won. "That's why I'll be resigning. Good evening." With an uncharacteristically graceful motion, Fitzroy turned, swept the curtains aside and dexterously disappeared. Once the stage door clicked shut behind him, everyone tried to speak at once.

After the meeting, Strupples paced along the corridor, contemplating Fitzroy's announcement. She started up the stairs. As she passed the chapel door the face of Emerson Jenks and thoughts of his April Fool's Day pranks – those she knew about – flashed in her mind. She stopped, snapped her fingers and then continued on her way.

+ − × ÷

On Monday, a mob of energetic youths, Emerson Jenks among them, spilled into the Science lab. All noise ceased when they noticed legal-sized sheets of paper, face down on their desks. "Pop quiz," announced Strupples. A chorus of moans erupted. "Take your places. Don't look at the questions until I tell you. Ready… you have fifty minutes. Set… remember to read all the questions carefully before you start writing. And go!" shouted Miss Strupples.

The students flipped their tests over. All but Emerson counted the questions. Many poked a finger beside the first question, read it and began writing feverishly. A few began reading through the material. Emerson stared, dumbfounded at his question sheet.

"You may leave as soon as you finish," announced the teacher over the noisy hustle and bustle. "Turn your answers face down on the desk when you're done."

When Strupples mentioned leaving early, Callaghan stopped writing and smiled a sly smile. "Ahem… ahem!" He cleared his throat until he attracted his toady's attention. Kelly looked up to see Callaghan sitting idle, an arm draped over the back of his chair. Callaghan gestured towards the others with his chin, rolled his eyes, raised an index finger to his temple and made circular motions. He feigned laughter, held up his test paper and pointed to the final question.

Kelly let his eyes run to the bottom of the page. When he finished reading, he turned back to Callaghan wearing a quizzical expression. He shrugged again. Callaghan looked at Kelly as if he must be crazy too. Kelly shrugged a third time.

Callaghan picked up his question sheet with exaggerated swagger. He read the final question for himself. It instructed him to describe the process for determining a substance's density. The boy's eyes popped open. Kelly, more puzzled than ever, watched his friend. Callaghan checked the other questions. He suspected the old cliché: instructions to read but not answer the questions. His disappointment turned to alarm… his alarm to panic which showed on his face. The look was contagious. Kelly's eyes widened and his mouth fell open. The two boys wrote franticly trying to make up for lost time.

Emerson was the only student not writing. He looked at the test again. Strupples had asked him only one question: *Emerson, will you please tell me how you did that ghost prank on Mr. Fitzroy? I know it was you.*

Emerson hesitated. He scratched the side of his head and pursed his lips before beginning to write. He stopped to steal a glance at his Science teacher. She gave him an approving nod and then watched him with a bemused smile on her face. His instincts warned him to be on guard. Nevertheless, Emerson described how he had staged the haunting of the headmaster's office. After twenty minutes, he printed across the bottom of the page, *Please do not say anything to anyone until we talk. May I see you tonight? Please!!!*

To the dismay of his classmates, Emerson turned his answer sheet face down on the desk, got up and left the lab early. He felt the need to walk and ponder the consequences of what he had just done. He was afraid to stay lest he tear his answer sheet to shreds. No one else left before the bell rang, certainly not Callaghan or Kelly.

"That's time, Gentlemen," announced Miss Strupples. "Pens down," she added. Boys scribbled even faster. "Gentlemen!" their teacher shouted. "Turn your papers face down, please." An outbreak of moaning and groaning filled the Science lab.

+ − × ÷

As the students settled down to study that evening, Emerson walked to the back of the room and handed a slip of paper to the study hall supervisor. After the assistant head student read the note, he jerked his head towards the room's back door. Emerson left and wandered through the silent halls to Miss Strupples' door. After taking a deep breath and exhaling, he knocked.

"Come on in, Emerson," Strupples called out.

"You really shouldn't answer the door that way, Ma'am," he advised upon entering the woman's lodgings.

"Pardon?" said Strupples.

"You said my name, my first name too, Ma'am," replied the boy. "What would Mr. Warneke or Mr. Fitzroy think if *they* heard?"

"Why would that matter, Emerson?"

"Well, they'd start to wonder why I came here so much and why you've started to use my first name all of a sudden," explained Emerson. "That could spoil everything… let them know who did you-know-what."

When Emerson settled himself at the oak table the woman held an envelope out to him. Emerson took it, examined it, found it sealed and looked up. "I want you to give that to Mr. Fitzroy," the woman told him.

"What is it, Ma'am?"

"Why… it's the information you gave me today," Strupples answered as if the boy should have known. "About the ghost thing."

"What?" he cried and dropped the envelope onto the table as if his hand had been burned. He could not believe what he was hearing. "But, why?" he asked, looking at the envelope again. "I don't understand."

"Listen, Emerson. Mr. Fitzroy needs to know exactly what happened that night. It's driving him crazy, you know. No one but you can convince him it was just a prank. Now, please…"

"What makes you so sure that was my prank, Ma'am?" demanded Emerson. A feeling of desperation swept over him. "Someone else could have…"

"Come, come, Emerson. Who else but you? I ask you," said Strupples. "Who else?"

Emerson continued to stare at the envelope. It dawned on him that his career as a prankster was over. The thought struck him and struck him hard. "Do I have to?" he asked.

"No, Emerson. You don't have to. But I want you to… and I think you need to. You see, Emerson, even though you didn't mean to scare the headmaster as badly as you did, even though it was all in fun, your prank has led to some rather devastating results."

"What kind of results, Ma'am?" The boy looked from the envelope to his teacher and back.

"I can't tell you that, Emerson," Miss Strupples replied. "What I can tell you though, is that if Mr. Fitzroy cannot be convinced that he was not visited by a poltergeist or ghost or whatever… there will be serious consequences for all of us and for life here at St. Timothy's." Emerson said nothing. The Science teacher continued, "If I'm making this sound serious, Emerson… that's because it is. I wouldn't ask you to do this if it weren't."

Emerson picked up the envelope with both hands, tapped it on the tabletop and frowned. "If you say it's that important, Ma'am."

"It is that important, Emerson."

"So, you want to convince him that it was a prank, eh?"

"Yes, Emerson. The notes you've made should do the trick."

"I don't really think so," the boy advised and frowned. "That he'll believe this, I mean." He waved the envelope in the air and then tossed it onto the table.

"Why wouldn't he?" inquired Strupples. A puzzled look appeared on her face.

"What if he figures you made me write it? That I just dreamed this all up for you? I spent months convincing him the place was haunted before I pranked him," explained Emerson. "With a prank like that it takes time to soften a guy up, you know. Mr. Fitzroy'll probably figure Dr. Graham got me to confess." The boy noticed Strupples' questioning squint. "The doctor knows a lot about me," he explained.

She pondered the boy's words. "You might be right, Emerson. Mr. Fitzroy's sure convinced the place is haunted. Hmmm… I see what you mean." The woman stood and began to pace the room. "Lord, I don't know how you get away with all this stuff, Emerson."

"But perhaps there is a way," he began…

+ − × ÷

On Wednesday, five minutes before the end of her next-to-last class of the day, Strupples locked all her cabinets and left her grade nine students, except Emerson Jenks, alone in the lab.

Mr. Fitzroy answered the knock on his office door and waved his Science teacher into the room. While looking at the floor and pinching the bridge of her nose, she asked for aspirin.

The headmaster expressed his concern and then all but jogged to the infirmary. He was on a mission of mercy and did not want to waste time. He was absent for several minutes. On re-entering his office, he saw Strupples behind his desk, tipped back in his leather chair with her forearm over her eyes. "Sorry I took so long, Leticia. These," he held up a bottle of pills, "weren't where they were supposed to be." As he handed the woman the aspirin, the bell sounded. Strupples groaned and told Fitzroy she was feeling too ill to teach and then asked him to take her last class. He consented. Strupples pretended to take the pills and waited patiently while Mr. Fitzroy adjusted his tie, donned his blazer and walked to his door.

"It's so cool here… and quiet," sighed Strupples. "I think I'll just sit here for a bit… if you don't mind." The headmaster opened the door. "Oh, Sir," cried Strupples, "it's my grade elevens. Just have them review for the final?"

"Look, you stay put as long as you like, Leticia," advised the headmaster. "I'll see to everything." He closed the door behind him.

The woman pushed the chair back from the desk and let Emerson out from beneath it. "Get to work," she ordered.

+ − × ÷

Later that evening, Mr. Fitzroy sat at his desk, writing. Every light in the room was ablaze. Bear bells hung upon the door. The headmaster jumped when suddenly there came a tapping, someone gently rapping at his office door. He glanced first at the roll-top desk then at his doors. Rising, he warily stepped to the centre of the room. "Yes?" he called. "Is there someone there?"

"Mr. Fitzroy?" shouted Miss Strupples.

As Fitzroy stretched out his hand the door swung open, setting the bear bells and his nerves a-jangle. Cyrus Warneke, whose skin had faded to a slightly more subdued shade of orange, stepped into the room. "For heaven's sake, Scotty!" he declared as he removed his floppy hat. "You look like you've seen a…"

Strupples poked the big man in the ribs. She and Willoughby-Wallows had entered the room in the large man's wake. The younger man closed the doors behind them. "We need to talk," continued the English master. "And you need to listen." He looked around. "We'll sit over here. Drag those chairs over. That's a good lad, Walloughby-Willers— oh, drat… *Wilfred*."

"You're getting closer, Sir." Willoughby-Wallows chuckled. "You nearly got it right that time."

Miss Strupples took a stunned headmaster by the elbow and led him to the chairs the other two men were arranging. "Sir, we want to talk to you about your decision," she announced. "We would like you to reconsider." Fitzroy's face announced that he had no intention of reconsidering. "Just listen to what we have to say," begged the woman. Mr. Fitzroy listened but with a frown on his face.

Strupples argued and summarized and then argued some more. She persisted, "Sir, please, just hear what we—"

"Scotty, don't be such an ass," cried Warneke and turned to his two companions. "I told you he wouldn't listen. This is preposterous, Sir. We are simply not going to allow you to resign over such… such twaddle. Don't look at me like that, man. I said twaddle and I mean twaddle." Warneke stood and walked to the double doors. He removed the bear bells and studied them. "By the way," he added, "do you happen to have a bottle stashed around here anywhere, Scotty? I could really use a drink."

"A bit of Glenfiddich, Cyrus… in my bedroom," replied Fitzroy and pointed to the door in the side wall.

From the moment the trio had entered the room, Willoughby-Wallows had fixed astonished eyes first on one colleague and then on another. He had never heard the headmaster addressed as Scotty. He had never been told that Warneke's given name was Cyrus.

"Humph! Glenfiddich, eh?" declared the English master. "Glenfiddich it is then. Well… go get it, man."

Fitzroy left the room and returned with a tall, dark green bottle and four glasses. "Leticia?" he asked, holding up the whiskey. "Might be good for that headache, eh?"

"*Headache?*" repeated a quizzical Miss Strupples. "Oh yes—my headache!" She massaged her temples in a pantomime of pain. "Three fingers… neat, Sir," she added.

"Wilfred?" asked the headmaster as he carried Strupples' drink to her. "Anything for you?"

"Oh no, Sir," answered Willoughby-Wallows. He had to pause as he stared at Strupples. The manner in which she threw back her head and downed over half of her whiskey made the young man but not the woman, blink. "I… I… I don't drink, Sir," he added. Willoughby-Wallows wondered what mysteries he might have uncovered had he not spent the entire year in the dorm.

"You're sure?" coaxed Fitzroy. He held the bottle out towards the young man.

"Absolutely, Sir…" replied Willoughby-Wallows. "But, I'd have some cold milk… if it's not too much trouble."

"Rubbish!" cried Warneke. "Pour the boy a real drink… just mix in a little water. Milk! Well, did you ever?"

Fitzroy poured a dram of the whiskey into a glass – he had no milk… or water – and carried it to Willoughby-Wallows. "Just a taste… try it," he advised. "You might like it."

"Ah, I'll just go ahead and pour my own," announced Warneke and set the bells on the headmaster's desk. "You don't mind, do you?" he added as the amber liquid spilled into the larger of the remaining tumblers. "Ah, let me pour a tad for you too, Scotty."

The headmaster returned and gaped at the two glasses. Each was filled to the brim. He looked at his bottle in utter dismay. Fearing spilling even a drop of his precious Scotch whiskey, he bent forward to slurp up a bit before lifting the glass.

"Ah," declared Warneke after swallowing a large gulp. He lifted the glass to the light, studied its contents, closed one eye and gave his head two or three quick sideways shakes. "Not bad… it's not Jameson's mind, but it's not bad," he admitted and returned to his seat. "Go ahead, Strupples… Plan B, if you must. I won't say a word. But, when you fail, I'll handle Plan C."

"I have here…" began Strupples, taking an envelope from her purse, "an explanation… a confession, if you like. It tells exactly how the ghost prank happened." She held the letter out to Headmaster Fitzroy who looked at it but did not take it from her. "You will read it, won't you, Sir?"

"Look, Leticia… I appreciate your concern, really I do… yours too, Gentlemen." Strupples attempted to interrupt. "No, let me finish," Fitzroy demanded, waving his hand dismissively. "I know what I saw and I know what I heard. I know what happened and no phoney explanation is going to change that… okay? So you can just put your envelope away."

"But I… I mean we…" stammered Willoughby-Wallows who had been trying to shake off the effects of his first ever sip of whiskey while puzzling over how the others had all but finished theirs. As he tried to end the sentence, he was struck by an involuntary shudder. It originated in his stomach and spread throughout his entire body. In a state of near panic, he eyed the whiskey. "Is this stuff," he asked, "supposed to taste so…"

"So strong?" Miss Strupples blurted out in an effort to help.

"So vile?" continued Willoughby-Wallows and coughed.

"Listen people… there are no ifs, ands or buts about it," announced Fitzroy. "Mr. Willoughby-Wallows, Sir, I'm working on the final draft of my resignation right… Are you alright, Wilfred?"

Willoughby-Wallows made a fist, placed it to his lips and belched. "I think I'll be okay again in a minute, Sir. Excuse me."

"As I was about to say, I've made up my mind," continued Fitzroy. "I can't stay here with what I know about this place." He was interrupted by a second, quieter burp. "If you only knew what it's like. I can't sleep. I can't eat. I can't concentrate. I jump at every strange noise. I don't know what to think about all this." Fitzroy stopped and groaned softly.

"Enough of this nonsense," shouted Warneke. "I told you two we were wasting our time. He's as stubborn as a mule… always has been. It's time for Plan C." He looked to his two companions. "Is everybody ready?" he added in an actor's stage voice. Both Willoughby-Wallows and Strupples nodded – the former with determination, the latter in defeat. "Okay then, Scotty, just sit back and behold," continued the English master. "Curtain call, everyone!"

Warneke stood and patted his stomach. "Ah, that whiskey really hit the spot," he said. "Surely, you're not going to waste that, Sir." This observation was made to Willoughby-Wallows who had forsaken all interest in whiskey in general and Scotch in particular. Without waiting for a reply, Warneke lifted the glass to his lips. Before he set it down, he stared into the empty glass, a look of sadness in his eyes, lamenting the fact that not a drop remained. The English master drew the back of his hand across his mouth and declared, "How that Glenfiddich grows on one!"

"What's this about, Cyrus?" demanded the headmaster.

"Patience, Sir… patience," answered the English master as he moved about the room turning off lights. "Just to establish the mood," he explained. "Now… what was the first mysterious happening?" he asked.

"A drawer," replied Fitzroy, "flew out of my desk there." He pointed across the room. "And I found my stuff dumped all over the floor."

"You mean like this?" cried Warneke as he swung around, stretched out his arm and pointed at the desk. There was a loud crash. In a state of shock, Fitzroy leapt up but did not quite make it to his feet. His arms flailed about as if he was warding off a bee attack. Warneke continued, "I believe you heard chains clanging… like this." The sound of rattling chains filled the room. Fitzroy fell back into his chair and let his arms dangle over its sides. He glanced about the room. He noticed that none of his guests showed the slightest alarm.

"Oh, that is so spooky. I say! What?" continued Warneke. "Woooo! And I believe the last thing, the *coop duh graw* so to speak, was a book flying from that shelf and landing about here." Warneke moved to a spot between the desk and the wall opposite. "Dickens, my friend, come," he shouted.

A *Christmas Carol* launched itself into the air. All four adults watched the volume turn two or three summersaults, come open and fall to the carpet at Warneke's feet. The big man retrieved the book and handed it to Fitzroy. "How about that, Scotty? Impressive, eh?" he said as he picked up his empty glass and walked towards the desk. Fitzroy did not move, let alone speak. Warneke started to pour himself another drink. "This bottle's empty, Scotty," he added with a longing look towards the headmaster's bedroom door.

The headmaster neither heard the English master's voice nor saw his gaze. "How'd you do that? What just happened?" Fitzroy exclaimed. He examined the book. He rose, walked to the desk and inspected the mess littering the floor. "What is going on?" he demanded.

Warneke returned to his chair and took his seat. The three visitors remained still and silent, determined to let the headmaster stew in his own juices. Fitzroy squinted and massaged his chin. He ran his fingers through his hair and looked imploringly to his visitors. Finally, he took his seat without another word.

After nearly a full minute, Warneke raised his voice and called out, "It's okay, Son."

"Pardon?" demanded Fitzroy.

A soft, barely audible voice drifted out of the shadows and across the room. "Sir?" Emerson Jenks spoke as he stepped out from behind the curtains. "Sir?" he repeated.

"Jenks!" gasped Fitzroy after he turned and looked at the boy.

"It was just me," confessed the boy. Emerson inched closer to the four adults.

"It was just *I*," Warneke corrected. "What in the world is happening to the Queen's English?"

"Sir," said Emerson, "I'm sorry, Sir… really I am. Please, Sir, let me explain?"

"What?" gasped Fitzroy. He looked about the room with a puzzled, glassy-eyed stare. Silently, he pleaded with Willoughby-Wallows, Strupples and Warneke in turn but found no answers. He turned to Emerson. "Where did you… I mean, how did you get… when did…"

Warneke explained. "Scotty… I let him in when you went for the bottle. I held your ridiculous bear bells in my hand so he wouldn't make a racket coming in. No voodoo or anything remotely like that."

"Emerson is a prankster… that's all," declared Strupples. "And a very fine one too as such things go. This was all his work, Sir." Again, Fitzroy directed a questioning glance towards Emerson. Strupples continued. "It's all really quite simple… ingeniously simple, I suppose," she continued.

"That's right, Sir… what Miss Strupples just said, I mean," added Emerson. "The whole thing's simple… just strings and tacks and tape and stuff. I was in the infirmary that night, Sir, with a bunch of strings running from here over there." He pointed to Fitzroy's window. "It's all in the note I wrote for you, Sir. I should have put in the part where you came in to get the aspirin, but I forgot about that." He pointed at the envelope in Strupples' hand. "It's all right there, Sir." The Science master rose and stood next to Emerson.

At the mention of his stopping into the infirmary for aspirin, the headmaster squinted and then eased himself back into his chair. "But that book flying across…" mumbled Fitzroy.

"That's easy, Sir. I used fishing line and sticky tape… up there where no one would see it," explained Emerson and pointed to the bits of clear tape still hanging from the high ceiling. The wave of Emerson's hand drew Fitzroy's eyes up the wall and across the ceiling from the bookshelf to the window.

"So it was you," cried Warneke. "You put something in that shampoo, eh?"

Emerson froze in place. His mouth fell open. He shot a pleading glance towards Miss Strupples.

"No, Cyrus, I'll take credit for that one," announced Strupples. Her audience detected a certain degree of pride in her voice. "But you know you deserved it... after all the dirty tricks you've pulled, Sir." She was quick to forget Emerson's admonitions about admitting nothing until doing so became absolutely unavoidable.

"You!" bellowed Warneke in disbelief. The orange man continued staring at the Science teacher until he pointed a rusty finger at Willoughby-Wallows. "I figured it was him... I mean he... He left his..." Warneke stopped before admitting anything more about finding the bottle of shampoo in the shower stall.

"And the water on the stairs..." added Willoughby-Wallows.

"Whoa! Gentlemen!" Strupples interrupted the accusation session. She stood flapping her arms in protest and then, like an over-protective mother hen, pulled Emerson under her wing. "I promised Mr. Jenks that if he helped us with this little demonstration we'd not hound him about other things he may or may not have done. And you both agreed."

Fitzroy stood and moved towards the exit, speaking softly. "If you don't mind... I think Mr. Jenks and I need some time... and some privacy so we can chat."

The others, except for Emerson, followed him to the door. Strupples gave Emerson the sealed envelope, a quick hug and a knowing wink. "Thank you, Emerson. You're a very brave young man," she declared. Before leaving the room, she turned and said to the headmaster, "Sir, I trust you'll honour our agreement with this young gentleman?"

"Of course, Leticia, of course," Fitzroy replied as he shooed the three adults out of the room. "No harm will come to him. Oh... Leticia, you wouldn't by any chance have a cigarette on you?"

Miss Strupples reached for her case. "I thought you quit," she replied.

"I did. The darn things started tasting really bitter... like sulphur or something," replied the headmaster as Strupples withdrew her silver case from her vest pocket. Emerson had averted his gaze as soon as Mr. Fitzroy asked for the cigarette. When he heard the flick of the lighter he raised his head and looked at Ms. Strupples. The woman's eyes admonished the boy.

The three teachers stepped into the hall. Emerson found himself alone with the headmaster. The man moved towards the doors. With his back to the boy, he said, "Sit anywhere you like, Mr…" Fitzroy stopped in mid-sentence and swung around. "On second thought—" he added, "you best bring that chair over here. We need to talk."

Emerson dragged a chair to where Fitzroy sat and took a seat. "Yes, Sir?" The boy looked straight into the headmaster's eyes.

"Just strings and tacks and tape, Jenks?" asked an incredulous Mr. Fitzroy as he took the envelope from Emerson and turned it over in his hands. His eyes rested on his guest. "No friends? No old men with feathered pens?"

Science Fair: Part Two

Classes ended on the last Friday in May. While the boys ate dinner the headmaster posted lists informing each student of the final exams he would have to write. 'Recommends' was the sole subject of conversation at table that evening. Before dismissing the eager boys, Andrews threatened dire consequences for anyone caught running, pushing or shoving on his way to his classroom. The students sprinted out of the refectory at speeds world class heel-and-toe competitors would have had difficulty matching. Soon, the classroom corridor rang with hearty hurrahs and heart-rending howls. A few boys had their fears and forebodings put to rest while others had their highest hopes shattered. Emotions ranged from joy and jubilation to disappointment and dismay. Some teachers were applauded as angels; others decried as demons. Some boys climbed to the common rooms and celebrated with comrades. Others, dejected, dragged themselves off to the dorms where they languished alone.

Emerson Jenks poked his head and a shoulder through the grade nine scrum and ran a finger down the recommendations list. Opposite JENKS, E. was a single word: 'Greek'. The boy's mood darkened. It grew even darker when he learned that his only final was scheduled for the next to last day of exam week. Later, after failing to convince Willoughby-Wallows that he deserved a higher grade, just three percent higher, his mood turned black. One exam meant he had to stay at St. Timothy's for study week and at least four days of exam week. Emerson was not a happy boy.

+ − × ÷

As always, the school celebrated the end of classes with a final feast and a Saturday evening *soirée*. Food was set out smorgasbord-style in the auditorium. On this one occasion, students and staff ate together, sitting with whomever they chose. The *soirée* marked the end of Andrews' term as head student. He had run the race. He would host the entertainment, then pass the baton. The atmosphere was festive.

After the main course, staff and students returned to their tables with tea, coffee or hot chocolate and dessert. Mr. Fitzroy called Andrews and his assistant forward and thanked them for their year of service. Following the applause, Andrews took centre stage and spoke in the voice of a carnival huckster, "Lady and Gentlemen, it is with the greatest pleasure that I invite you to sit back, relax and enjoy our show. To begin, the students of the graduating class will present a skit. I disavow any involvement in the script."

The players spent fifteen minutes poking fun at members of the staff. When the audience finished laughing – this took an inordinate amount of time – Andrews called on the grade eleven students.

The auditorium lights dimmed. As the curtains opened, the footlights flashed on to reveal an empty stage. The audience heard but did not see the boy who yelled, "He's not ready yet… close the curtains." Moments later, Emerson Jenks appeared on stage carrying a chair and a music stand. The fact that he was only in grade nine was recognized by all. Emerson disappeared and returned with his guitar and some sheet music, propped the instrument against the chair and left again. For half a minute nothing happened.

"Are you ready back there? Are you guys ready?" asked Andrews with growing impatience. A muddle of voices came floating back to him. The audience began to titter. A moment later, Angelo Guardiano lunged from the wings, stumbled, caught his balance and stood stock still, frozen in fear at the sight of so many faces. Laugher and a few hoots rose from the audience before an ominous silence settled upon the scene. He stared out at the crowd. Emerson stepped onto the stage, took his friend by the arm and led him to the chair. Guardiano took his seat. Emerson handed him the guitar, adjusted the score, then leaned forward as the older boy whispered into his ear. Emerson nodded and took up a position at his friend's elbow. A hush fell over the gathering. Members of the audience stared into their laps or coffee cups or covered their eyes with their hands as Guardiano strained to see the notes swimming before his eyes. Everyone, anticipating utter catastrophe, experienced a range of feelings, from personal discomfort to embarrassment by proxy.

Emerson whispered, "It's okay, Angelo," and nudged his friend's shoulder.

The guitar sounded a single, low-pitched, throbbing minor chord followed by five quick-paced higher notes and Guardiano's rich, tenor voice filled the room. "*Ave Maria*," sang the boy, "*gratia plena…*"

As Guardiano's performance continued, Emerson faded into the shadows. Guardiano remained alone in the spotlight. Not until his final chord diminished to silence did he look up. A puzzled expression swept across his face. Not a sound could be heard. The boy stood and, in panic, looked around for Emerson.

From the back corner, near the door, came loud, enthusiastic applause. Professor Warneke stepped out of his favourite corner, clamped his little black cigar in the corner of his mouth and yelled, "Bravo, bravo, my boy," and continued clapping. Here and there throughout the room, softer, more polite expressions of amazement and appreciation could be heard. Like an over-stretched elastic band, the spell Angelo Guardiano had woven finally snapped. The staff and students applauded and slapped tabletops with open hands. One by one, then by the dozen, they stood and cheered. Emerson led his friend off stage, patting him on the back and whispering in his ear the entire way. The grade eleven students celebrated as they returned to the floor of the auditorium. Loud cheering recommenced when Guardiano appeared. The applause lasted for several minutes.

Andrews took the stage to try to continue the program but he found himself at a loss for words. The entertainment that was to follow had been most assuredly upstaged.

The next morning, after mass, Emerson Jenks sat on the top step of the main entrance watching fully recommended students leave for home. He did not hear Miss Strupples' approach. "At last… here you are," said the woman. Emerson did not look up. "Push over," ordered Strupples and sat beside the boy. She drew her skinny knees up under her chin and wrapped her arms around her legs, surveying the scene: departing students, a few cars, several suitcases, moms and dads, brothers and sisters, friends and classmates. "I'm so sorry, Emerson," she whispered. "I know how much you were looking forward to going home today… No sour grapes, Emerson?" she added tentatively.

"Nah… sweet lemons," said Emerson and laughed. "No biggy. I've got the whole summer, I guess."

The Science professor smiled a rueful smile. "Listen, Emerson…" she continued, "I'm getting a bit worried about Fredericks."

"Fredericks?" Emerson's surprise showed. He had forgotten all about Fredericks.

"He's being very secretive… about the Science Fair. He says he doesn't want my help… won't let me even see his work," explained Strupples.

"Oh yeah… that," replied Emerson. "I know… said he wanted to do it all by himself. He doesn't like *me* nosing around either."

"I hate to interfere, but…" Strupples hesitated. "Do you think you could try? If you could just… well… just let me know what you think. I don't want to spoil this for him… but I don't want him embarrassing St. Timothy's—or himself for that matter."

Strupples and Emerson lifted their eyes at the sound of cheering. Someone was just driving off with his parents. "He's been out in that workshop with old Mr. Ellis for weeks now," the Science teacher continued.

"Mr. Ellis? Why him?" asked Emerson in amazement. Ellis, the school's custodian and handyman, was so old the students joked that he was the one who helped von Baumgartner carry his trunk the day he arrived for ninth grade. "I can try, I guess, Ma'am." Emerson stood and stepped into the building.

"Just one more thing, Emerson," added Miss Strupples without standing. "Feel free to say no. I'd like you to come with us to the Science Fair… as my assistant. The other fellows would appreciate the support and we can always use an extra hand."

Emerson shrugged. "We'll see, Ma'am," he replied and climbed the stairs to the foyer. Over her shoulder, Strupples watched the boy trudge off into the shadows.

Emerson found Fredericks and Mr. Ellis in the school's workshop. They had left the door ajar. "Can I come in?" called Emerson as he knocked.

"Stay out," shrieked Fredericks and ran for the door. He popped his head through the opening. "Jenks! What do you want?" he demanded.

"Just to see how you're coming along," answered Emerson. "I won't say a word… cross my heart."

Fredericks gazed over his shoulder into the room for a second, turned back to Emerson, thought for a moment and said, "Just don't touch *nothin'*, okay?"

"Sure," replied Emerson. "I'm curious… that's all." He followed the Science Fair competitor into the room.

"Stuff's still wet," Fredericks cautioned. Emerson stuffed his hands into his pockets. Ellis was busy brushing a coat of shellac onto a three-panel, hinged display screen. The old man looked happier and years younger. Working with Fredericks had proven to be a fountain of youth. Emerson crossed the room to the workbench. Fredericks was all but finished bolting the second of two telephones to a thick board that had been covered in green felt.

"Looks pretty neat," admitted Emerson as he ducked down for an eye-level view. "But, that plank's got to weigh a ton," he said.

"Plank!" cried Mr. Ellis from across the room. "That's no plank, boy," he added. "That's a hollow box. We banged it together ourselves. Didn't we, Raymond? It's got all the wires and batteries and stuff inside."

"Really?" Emerson said and took a closer look. "It's got to be what… eight feet long and a foot wide?"

"Exactly…" replied Fredericks, "and three inches thick… took a whole sheet of plywood, nearly."

Emerson whistled. "Cool," he added. He walked completely around the object examining it. "What's it do?"

Fredericks stopped working and, using a long screwdriver as a pointer, presented an overview of his project. He pulled a few coloured drawings from a portfolio. "These'll go on those panels," he explained, holding a drawing up and pointing to where Ellis was working.

Emerson removed his hands from his pockets and examined the diagrams and Fredericks' contraption again. He used a more discerning eye the second time. "Well, Fredericks… this is pretty cool," he said finally. "If you need any help just ask, eh?"

He stood back and watched as Ellis continued his brushstrokes and

Fredericks started back to work. Emerson called out a farewell which, if heard, was not acknowledged. He stepped outside, closed the door, shook his head and laughed. "And I thought Talbot was a dupe," he groaned.

"Miss Strupples, Miss Strupples," called Emerson as he ran down the main drive after dinner. Strupples stopped, turned around and waited for the boy. "Fredericks let me in this afternoon, Ma'am."

"And?" demanded Strupples.

"Well… he doesn't want any help, except from old man—I mean Mr. Ellis. I had to swear not to touch anything just to get in the door. But everything looks fine, Ma'am," reported Emerson. "He figures the two of them can manage okay… by themselves, I mean."

"So, what did you think, Emerson?"

"Like I said, Ma'am, everything looks great."

"Emerson? Is that a smirk on your face?" asked Strupples.

"Smirk, Ma'am? Why no, Ma'am. Why would I smirk?"

"I don't know, Emerson," replied the teacher. "But when you smirk it makes me very nervous. Fredericks will be ready by Saturday… *right?*"

"I don't see why not, Ma'am." He's just got a few finishing touches to take care of." Emerson wanted to change the topic. "How are the spider boys coming along with—"

The Science teacher was having none of it. "—Emerson! You seem a little nervous or something," she suggested.

"Nervous, Ma'am?"

"Or something," continued Strupples. She was not to be put off.

"No, Ma'am," he declared.

"If you're pulling one of your pranks on me, Emerson…" threatened Miss Strupples. She raised her head, turned it slightly to one side and stared into the boy's eyes before finishing. "I'll be very disappointed in you."

"I'm not pranking anybody, Ma'am. Really I'm not. And I don't plan to either."

"I'll take you at your word," said the woman. "How do you think he'll do, Emerson?"

"Fredericks, Ma'am?"

"Fredericks."

"That's hard to say, you know. Ah… he might just surprise us all…

you know… the way Guardiano did last night," responded Emerson. He still desired a less dangerous topic of conversation.

"Well, let's hope so, Emerson," said Strupples. "Guardiano did do a fine job, eh. Who knew?"

"You've no idea how hard he worked on that, Ma'am," replied Emerson in an effort to keep the conversation off Fredericks. "Bye, Miss Strupples." He turned to go. "Oh…" he added, turning back, "and I'd like to help out at the Science Fair after all… if you still want me to."

Strupples still wanted Emerson's help and told him so.

The boy sighed in relief as he entered the school. "Man alive! I better get used to grillings like that," Emerson muttered, "now that so many people know about me."

+ − × ÷

On the Friday evening before the Science Fair, Miss Strupples organized the participants and supervised as they packed their projects into the school van. She was still nervous about Fredericks' effort but calmed down when she saw his well-constructed display screen and strange looking green box. The realization that Fredericks' efforts outshone those of the boys she had helped nagged at her.

"Well, Mr. Ellis," said Miss Strupples as she approached the old gentleman, "what do you think of young Mr. Fredericks' chances?"

Ellis continued wrapping protective covers on the boy's equipment. "He's gonna win sure," replied Ellis. "First place… you'll see, Ma'am."

"You've no idea how relieved I am to hear that," admitted Strupples. "I've been worried sick he'd make a mess of it. He wouldn't even let me near it, you know. I pictured him embarrassing me and the school and—"

"—Oh, no, Ma'am… no, sir-ee," Ellis assured the woman. "That boy's got real talent, Ma'am. Gonna win sure," added the old fellow as he shuffled off to help Callaghan and Kelly tie down their spider box.

"Well," confessed Miss Strupples when she next met Emerson, "I owe you an apology I guess, Mr. Jenks."

The boy adjusted his glasses and stared back, mystified. "Pardon, Ma'am?"

"When you gave me such a positive report on Fredericks," explained

Strupples, "I thought you might be up to something. I've misjudged you."

"Up to something, Ma'am?" asked Emerson with a grin. "Me? I told you how great it looked, didn't I?"

"That you did," replied Strupples. "That you did, Sir. And I have to admit… you were right. I guess I had nothing to worry about after all."

Emerson's hand rose to his mouth as he turned away. He lowered his eyes and marched off.

At eight o'clock Saturday morning, Strupples, Willoughby-Wallows and eight St. Timothy's students, seven Science Fair participants and one helper, left for town. Upon their arrival at the host school, they registered and checked to insure the posted descriptions of their projects were accurate.

At the bulletin board in the main lobby, Fredericks looked at the outline for his display with pride. The announcement read:

Display # 63 FREDERICKS, Raymond
St. Timothy's Preparatory School – Ninth Grade – Age 14
Telephone Service for the Hearing Impaired:
Raymond's telephone allows the hearing impaired
to make and receive calls,
giving them access to a communication device
heretofore denied them.

"Very impressive," Fredericks mumbled as he stared at the sign, fingers meshed together, hands clamped atop his head. "Hey, Jenks, look at this."

Emerson approached the bulletin board. "They put in the words 'heretofore denied' and everything," Fredericks said, pointing out the words. "Pretty cool, eh?"

Emerson joined his classmate and read the announcement. "That's the easy part, Fredericks," advised Strupples' assistant. "Let's hope you can live up to all the hype. Good luck." Emerson wandered off to check out the competition.

Strupples and Willoughby-Wallows were busy making sure the students were organized and well behaved. Much of their time was spent dodging the other teachers who wanted to discuss recent changes to the Ministry's policies and other issues educators are wont to discuss whenever they get together. Miss Strupples corralled the boys in the lobby at 11:30 and announced that they would go to lunch – at a restaurant – and return before one o'clock. "Where's Jenks?" she asked in alarm and looked all around her. "Wilf, go find that boy... please?" The woman was plagued by thoughts that the prankster was up to something. Turning to the other boys she continued, "Remember, fellows, they let the judges in first, so all of you have to be back here on time and ready to go."

Wilf returned from the display area. He had Emerson by the collar.

Arm twisting was not required to get the boys to eat. Not one had tasted pizza in months. The restaurant manager was happy to see such a large group arrive. He was happier to see them leave. The students had gobbled his all-you-can-eat Pizza Palace to the brink of insolvency.

On returning to the fair, the boys followed their teachers into the building. Miss Strupples made her way through the crowd to the auditorium doors. As soon as she entered the gym, a man wearing a dark suit and carrying a clipboard hurried over. "Miss Strupples? You are Miss Strupples?" he asked while glancing at his clipboard.

"Yes?" replied Strupples. The man looked troubled. "Is there a problem?" she asked.

The man pressed the top edge of the clipboard against his chin. "I think so," he answered. "Is Raymond Fredericks with you?" Miss Strupples called to the boy. They followed the man to the display area. Fredericks looked around as if he had forgotten something and could not recall what it could possibly be.

The Science teacher shouted at Willoughby-Wallows, "Wilf—find Jenks and bring him to me... this minute!"

The Greek and Latin teacher could tell that Strupples was miffed so hurried off without comment. He looked about. Emerson had vanished. After calling the other St. Timothy's students to him, Willoughby-Wallows, like the hunt master when the hounds have the scent, turned the boys loose to run down young Mr. Jenks. When the fugitive saw Willoughby-Wallows go east, he moved west.

Miss Strupples grabbed Fredericks and headed to his display. She let her eyes run over the boy's project looking for signs of trouble; she found none. The display impressed her more than ever. Fredericks' diagrams were well-drawn and neatly labelled. His apparatus, the box covered in green felt with a telephone at either end, was quite attractive. The display screen looked very professional. Its wood shimmered under layers of shellac. She had seen much worse used at teacher conferences. Everything looked fine and Strupples had to admit that Emerson had been totally straightforward with her. Having doubted the boy, she felt a twinge of shame.

"Sorry for the delay," said the man with the clipboard. "I've sent someone to find Miss Marshall. Please bear with us." The fellow grew more and more agitated, pacing and consulting his watch. A minute or so later, two attractive young women arrived from one direction just as Willoughby-Wallows arrived from the other. He had Emerson Jenks in tow.

"Miss Strupples, Raymond… I'd like to introduce you to Miss Eva Marshall," the man announced. "Miss Marshall and—" He stared helplessly at Miss Marshall's companion.

"Trudy Holmes," the second woman chimed in.

Miss Marshall smiled, mumbled something no one understood and turned to Miss Holmes. Her fingers flew into frenzied action.

"Eva says she is very pleased to meet you all." Miss Holmes spoke to the crowd without taking her eyes off her friend's hands.

"Oh," said Strupples.

"Oh," added Willoughby-Wallows.

"Oh," mumbled Fredericks.

"Oh, oh," Emerson Jenks groaned as he tried to back away. Willoughby-Wallows thwarted the attempted escape.

The deaf woman's companion continued, "Eva reads lips. If you just look directly at her and talk in a normal voice… not too fast though, and only one at a time…"

"Is there some kind of a problem?" asked an anxious Miss Strupples. Emerson, having failed in a second attempt to slip away, pushed Fredericks to the fore. Eva Marshall laughed an intriguing laugh. She signed to Miss Holmes who began speaking while watching her friend's fingers flash sign language.

"Let's see," continued Trudy Holmes and began interpreting. "She says she will show you the problem... if you'll just go down to that end, Miss..."

"Strupples," replied Miss Strupples, "Leticia." She stepped up to one of the telephones. Eva Marshall walked to the opposite end of the box and signed again.

"Okay," instructed Miss Holmes, "let's assume you want to call Eva. Right? So you pick up the phone and dial her number. Go ahead, Leticia." Miss Strupples lifted the receiver and had it halfway to her ear before she asked Fredericks for the number.

"There's no number, Ma'am," explained Fredericks. "You have to push the white button on the side there and kinda pretend." Fredericks, despite being absolutely confident his phone would work, chewed on his lower lip. He had tested the device several times just before leaving for lunch and it had performed flawlessly. It will work great, unless somebody messed with it, the boy thought.

Emerson used a hand to cover his mouth – to hide a gasp, not a smile on this occasion.

Strupples held the receiver to her ear and depressed the white button. The large red light on Miss Marshall's phone lit up. So did Fredericks' face.

"See!" declared the young inventor and stared from one face to another. "Told yuh!"

Eva Marshall ignored the light and Frederick's commentary. When Miss Strupples released the button, the light on Eva's phone stopped blinking. Fredericks smiled proudly. Miss Strupples repeated the procedure. She held the button down and again the light flashed.

Fredericks grinned at his companions. "It works," he whispered to Emerson. "See... told you it'd work!"

After a few moments, Eva Marshall looked at the light, pressed a hand to each cheek, opened her eyes in wonder, smiled and picked up the phone. When the light instantly stopped blinking, Fredericks puffed out his chest and smiled the smile of the accomplished.

When Eva placed the receiver to her ear, Strupples said, "Hello." She received no response. The teacher repeated her greeting. "Hello? Hello?" she shouted. Fredericks' smile began to fade.

The hearing impaired woman looked puzzled. She took the phone away from her ear, held it two feet in front of her and repeatedly signed the word 'hello' with her free hand. With the receiver held to her ear and her free hand resting on her cheek, Miss Strupples stood with her mouth hanging open. In confusion, the Science teacher stared blankly at Eva Marshall, trying to fathom the purpose of the demonstration.

Trudy Holmes took Eva's receiver and spoke into it. "She's signing to you, Leticia. She says she still can't hear you." Slowly, the awful truth dawned on Miss Strupples. Panic showed plainly on the Science teacher's face, a face that turned pale then flashed candy apple red.

"I believe you understand now," suggested Miss Marshall's friend.

"Jenks!" cried Strupples. "Stop right there."

Emerson had begun backing towards the exit. During the demonstration, Willoughby-Wallows' mind had wandered from his guard duties.

"Fredericks, you clear this… this… this junk out of here," ordered Miss Strupples. "Oh my goodness! Go get that project description first. Go, go… run!" Strupples walked towards the woman at the opposite end of the display. "I am so sorry, Miss Marshall," she muttered. "I don't know what to say."

Eva signed to her friend. "She says not to worry," said Trudy. "She says she needs a laugh every now and then and hasn't had one this good in a very long time." The two women crossed the gym. Twice they stopped and turned towards Fredericks' display and laughed. When they reached the exit, Eva covered her mouth as she stepped into the lobby. Her very distinctive chuckle was muffled by the doors as they swung closed behind her.

Fredericks returned with a crumpled sheet of paper in hand. Willoughby-Wallows had started to disassemble the display. Emerson stood, staring at the floor with his hands clasped behind his back. He ground the toe of his shoe into the hardwood floor. Miss Strupples put her hands on his shoulders, spun him around and marched him, quick step, to the far corner of the room. "How could you, Emerson? I mean how could you do that to me?" chided Miss Strupples. "I've never been so humiliated in all my life. Oh, how could you?"

"What did I do?" asked Emerson, all innocence. "I didn't even touch the thing. It's all Fredericks' fault."

"But you looked it over. You must have known…" cried Strupples. "Oh! How could you? I'll never live this down."

"All I said was it looked good… and it did, too," declared Emerson in his own defence. When he saw the look on Miss Strupples' face he wished he had kept his thoughts to himself. For the moment, Emerson was spared further reproach by the arrival of the man with the clipboard. He tapped Strupples on the shoulder.

"Madam, there are a couple of people outside… in the lobby, I mean. They asked to speak with you," he told her.

"With me? Are you sure?" asked Strupples. "But who are they? What do they want?" demanded the woman. The man pursed his lips and shrugged. "Oh drat… tell them I can't… tell them I'm too busy," she said. "No, wait! Tell them I'll be right there." The gentleman turned and headed for the lobby.

"Okay… let's get this stuff out of here right away," demanded Miss Strupples. "The doors will open any minute now… we need to hurry." The boys picked up all of Fredericks' material and carried it towards the lobby. They stopped in front of a set of double doors. Strupples and Willoughby-Wallows blocked their path. The Science teacher checked to insure that no trace of the fiasco remained. "That's everything," she announced. "Let's get it out of here… straight to the van. Okay, everyone…"

Willoughby-Wallows, with a good hold on Fredericks, put his back to the left side door. Miss Strupples, with Emerson Jenks in tow, did the same to the door on the right. Together, they pushed backwards into the lobby. The other boys, with their bulky load, advanced.

"That's her," cried the man with the clipboard and pointed at Miss Strupples. "The one in the long black skirt," he added.

The woman spun around. Her eyes popped open. Her jaw dropped. Willoughby-Wallows lunged for his companion but they were shoved apart by several strangers who barged in between them. The double doors swung closed with the six students who had retreated in the face of the enemy safe behind them. The crowd pinned the two teachers and the two students to the wall. The captives could neither advance nor pull the doors open and escape. Not a couple of people, but a good dozen or more had surged forward. Some held note pads and one man carried a TV camera on his shoulder. Flashbulbs popped. People waved microphones about like batons. Before the first finished a question, a second and third were beginning theirs.

"Miss Strupples, I'm with the *Tri-County Gazette*. Is it true?" asked a short, fat man wearing a floppy fedora.

"Is what true?" demanded Miss Strupples. Flashbulbs exploded in her face. She blinked and held her hands up to protect her eyes. When she looked at the reporter again his face was obscured by a dozen or more bright yellow spots that swam in her field of vision. She blinked and clamped her eyes shut then pinched the bridge of her nose. When she tried to see her assailants again the spots still danced before her eyes. The woman squinted and blinked at the crowd.

"I represent C.H.U.B. radio. Will this invention really allow the deaf… I mean the hearing impaired to use the telephone?" asked a woman as she shoved a small tape recorder into Miss Strupples' ever more startled face.

Another woman poked a microphone over the C.H.U.B. representative's shoulder and announced, "C.B.C. TV, Ma'am. Look straight at the TV camera for us, Ma'am? Is it fair to say that Alexander Graham Bell's dream has finally been realized?"

"What?" cried Miss Strupples. "What on earth…"

"This here's Fredericks then?" demanded a tall, thin man as he grabbed Emerson by the shoulder and dragged him forward.

Emerson failed to maintain a grip on Miss Strupples hand. "Not me, not me," shouted the boy. "That's Fredericks," he exclaimed, pointing towards his friend. The man shoved Emerson to one side and advanced upon a frightened Raymond Fredericks. The boy with the funny round glasses might have been so much gift wrap on Boxing Day. The crowd behaved as if Fredericks was a rock star. Fredericks was not cut out for the rock star life. He cowered behind Willoughby-Wallows. The reporters pushed forward for a better look at the young genius, finally cutting him off from Emerson and his two teachers.

In the confusion, Emerson slipped through the milling, muddled maze of humanity and made good his escape. At a safer distance, he stood and watched, thinking he had discovered why these strange people were called the press. Fredericks, Strupples and Willoughby-Wallows were not so lucky. They were caught up in the scrum for more than ten minutes.

Miss Strupples could well have used her pointer and metal chair but alas, she could but flail her arms over her head and cry for order. After expending unprecedented amounts of energy jumping up and down and shouting, she managed to quiet the crowd long enough to explain the situation. Like air escaping from a poorly knotted balloon, the frustrated fifth estate dispersed. Willoughby-Wallows took hold of Fredericks and fled as if for his life.

Miss Strupples ran after the man in the old fedora, clamped her hand on his forearm and dug in her heels. "Wait, wait, please," she begged as the reporter tried to pry his arm loose. "Why did you come here? How..."

"Look, lady... I just do what I'm told, eh? And the boss told me to get over here, pronto. Said a big story was brewing... something 'bout a telephone that deaf folks can use. That's all I know. Hey, lady... you're hurting my arm there, eh."

Miss Strupples released her grip. The reporter began massaging his forearm as he backed away. "But how did your boss find out?" asked Strupples, pursuing the gentleman across the lobby, she in forward, he in reverse.

"How should I know?" answered the man. "But them other guys – he pointed through the window at his departing colleagues – they said some feller called the story in jus' before noon... just before they – he pointed to the cars speeding away from the school – were headin' out fir somethin' to eat." The reporter looked at his watch. "Look... I'm sorry, lady, but I ain't had no lunch. I gotta go."

"But who on earth knew about..." The woman paused in mid-sentence. A loud banging distracted her. She glanced about but found the lobby all but empty. She turned back to the reporter but he had taken to his heels.

"Oh, wait... just a second... please... Sir." Miss Strupples ran after the escapee. When she realized she would never catch up, she shouted, "This won't end up in the paper, will it?"

The man, on gaining the safety of the doors, stopped and spun around. "Hey, lady, I ain't Caesar, so that ain't up to me, eh. I just do what the boss tells me, see. But... come to think of it... it might make a pretty funny general interest story."

Miss Strupples could not find her tongue. She stood with her head tilted back, her eyes closed tight and her mouth opened wide. She held one hand to her forehead, the other rested on her hip. The reporter stepped outside and jogged towards the parking lot. He did not look back.

Strupples turned and trudged towards the display area. As she reached the doors, she again heard loud knocking. Somewhere, someone was banging on glass. She scanned the length of the lobby. Cyrus Warneke stood outside, shading his eyes and looking in. He waved to Strupples, winked and blew her a kiss.

Repercussions

"And don't you dare get out of this van… either of you," threatened Strupples. Shamefaced, silent, with their hands clamped between their knees, Emerson Jenks and Fredericks stared at the floor. "Some helper you turned out to be," the woman said to Emerson, spitting out the words. She slammed the door. The Science professor returned to the Fair where she suffered hours of real or imagined humiliation before the exhibit closed for the day. She was sure that people were looking at and talking about her all day long. Every laugh had to be a response to retelling the telephone-for-the-deaf fiasco. The two boys spent the afternoon cooped up in the vehicle. Neither dared disobey. They knew doing so would bring about the most serious repercussions.

+ − × ÷

Early on Sunday evening, Emerson responded to a summons from the headmaster. Nothing had been said about the Science Fair debacle even during Saturday's drive home. In fact, Miss Strupples had spoken not a single word to Emerson since dragging him to the van. The boy had hoped the matter was forgotten but now feared he was being called to account. He approached the oak doors with trepidation.

"Come," commanded Fitzroy on hearing Emerson's knock. "Ah, Jenks, good! Your mother called—" the man checked the time, "—twenty minutes ago. She'd like you to call… said not to worry though."

"Sir…" Emerson replied and eyed the phone. "May I?"

"Oh, of course, Jenks." Fitzroy rifled through the papers on his desktop. "Wait and I'll give you some privacy." The headmaster carried a stack of files to his sleeping room. "Don't forget to reverse the charges, Jenks," he added and closed his door.

"Hi, Glenda?" said Emerson when his sister answered. "Mom there?"

"Nope… Dad and her went out," answered Glenda. "She told me

to tell you Dad has to go to Hamilton next weekend. Big meeting or something. Prob'ly won't get back 'til late Saturday."

"But he's supposed to come get me on Saturday!"

"That's why Mom called," explained Glenda. "They'll be down there Sunday or maybe Monday… all depends on—"

"—Oh! Just great!" groaned Emerson. "Man alive!"

"Sorry… but that's why she called," added Glenda. Emerson made no response. "Still there, Em?"

"Yeah, I'm still here. I'm thinking." Emerson continued, "Listen, Sis—" the boy glanced towards Fitzroy's room, cupped his hand over the mouthpiece and lowered his voice, "—I need a favour." After some hard bargaining, Emerson had to promise – cross his heart and hope to die – to take Glenda's turn doing dinner dishes for the entire time he was home. "Okay then… here's what you've got to do. Got a pen handy?"

Minutes later, Emerson knocked on Fitzroy's bedroom door. He thanked the man and delivered the news about the change of plans.

"Ah, listen…" said Fitzroy. "No promises now… but I may be able to get you a ride home on Saturday morning. You'd have to be up with the sun though."

"That's great," replied the boy as his face lit up.

Later, Fitzroy met Emerson in the corridor. "I've arranged your ride. Be on the front steps with your things by 6:45 at the latest, understand? Your parents know you're coming. Will you need an alarm clock, Jenks?"

Emerson declined the offer.

+ − × ÷

The headmaster spent Monday evening vainly trying to reassure Miss Strupples that St. Timothy's would survive in spite of the irreverent review under the headline, *Telephone for Hearing Impaired Misfire* that appeared in that day's *Tri-County Gazette*. How the woman went on about the picture of her with her face partially hidden behind her hands. How she cried despite Fitzroy's best efforts to assure her that she did not look like a convicted criminal being led from court.

On Tuesday morning, Mr. Fitzroy looked up from his desk and frowned. Someone was pounding on his door – again. "Come," demanded

Fitzroy. The door opened and an animated Wilfred Willoughby-Wallows burst into the room, chattering and waving a two-page document in the air. The headmaster remained seated, his elbows on his desk, his chin resting in his hands, staring morosely down at a budget sheet.

"Look at this, Sir. Just look at this," exclaimed the dormitory supervisor as he crossed the room. "I can't believe it, Sir. It's such wonderful news."

"Can't believe what?" asked the headmaster without looking up.

"It's an invitation, Sir... to speak to The Tri-County Classics Club. This is so exciting, Sir. I didn't even know the club existed. Imagine!" Willoughby-Wallows read from the letter, "*Dear Sir*—it's addressed to me, Sir."

"I gathered that," replied Mr. Fitzroy as he leaned back in his chair. "Go on."

"*I apologize for being so forward but time is of the essence...*" read Willoughby-Wallows aloud. He skipped through the note. "*A former teacher of yours, a very old and dear friend of mine, Dr. Kenneth Reardon, stopped by my home on Saturday. In the course of our conversation your name was mentioned. Ken spoke highly of you and suggested that you might favour us with a presentation at our next meeting.*" Willoughby-Wallows turned the letter towards his superior to show him the Club's logo. "It looks like an old Roman standard, see?"

"Go on," groaned Fitzroy without paying the logo or his visitor much attention.

"Let me see," continued Willoughby-Wallows. "Ah, here it is. *Our last meeting of the year et cetera...* Wait a sec... ah, here it is. *We are serious students of classical and New Testament Greek...*" he read, "*as well as ancient and medieval Latin*. How about that, Sir?" Willoughby-Wallows read on: "*I mention this only because Dr. Reardon indicated that you might be altogether too scholarly and erudite for us*. Imagine that, Sir... me... scholarly and erudite... and from Dr. Reardon no less," boasted Willoughby-Wallows. "He's the head of the Classics Department at—"

Fitzroy's yawn curtailed Willoughby-Wallows' explanation. "Yes... just imagine," Fitzroy mumbled as he tried to disguise a second yawn.

Willoughby-Wallows flipped to the next page. "*But we shall endeavour to prove Ken wrong. You will find us more knowledgeable than he sup-*

poses... et cetera, et cetera. It's signed, J. Benjamin Stokes, Ph.D." The Greek and Latin professor ended his spiel with a question, "Now, what do you think of that, Sir?"

"Wonderful news, Willing... Wilf. I think you ought to get started... *quam primum* as it were."

"*Quam primum?* So you remember your Latin, Sir," replied the young teacher with a laugh. "Very good, Sir."

"Sounds like they might be a match for you," added Fitzroy.

"Do you really think so?" asked Willoughby-Wallows in all seriousness. Fitzroy sat up, his pencil poised over his papers, and stared into the young man's face. He said nothing. "Well then, I'd better be off, Sir."

"Indeed," replied the headmaster.

St. Timothy's Greek and Latin man stepped lively across the carpet and entered the corridor. It was a full minute before he poked his head into the room and said, "Sorry, Sir... guess I forgot to close the door. Perhaps I'll get to be a member... of the Classics Club, I mean."

Willoughby-Wallows closed the door and skipped down the corridor, whistling loudly.

+ − × ÷

Emerson Jenks finished his Greek exam at 11:15 on Thursday, left the classroom a free man and loitered in the corridor until noon, waiting for the mail. He waited in vain. He returned to the mail basket on Friday and breathed a sigh of relief when he found a parcel bearing Glenda's handwriting. In the trunk storage room he tore away the wrapping paper. "Oh, Glenda, absolutely perfect," he cried aloud. The boy looked around to insure he had not been overheard and then locked the parcel's contents in his suitcase.

At dinner on Friday evening, the new head student made an announcement. "Most of us leave tomorrow. But some will be here a bit longer. Am I right, Mr. Callaghan, Mr. Talbot, Mr. Kelly?" Those three boys and several others had had their sentences commuted from up to two weeks to just three days at hard labour. St. Timothy's had to be thoroughly scrubbed and polished before closing for the summer.

Andrews' successor continued, "Mr. Meddows is off to Boston tonight. Right, Meddows?" Since Easter, it was common knowledge that Meddows' parents had moved to the States.

"Earlier if I can manage it," replied Meddows in a successful effort to amuse his mates.

The head student announced the departure of four other boys. Each was given a chance to say a few words – something short and witty was customary.

"We'll have to shake Mr. Jenks' hand tonight too," the new head student announced. Emerson stood at the mention of his name. "You're off at the crack of dawn—right, Mr. Jenks?"

"Off to the crack of doom?" Emerson asked in mock dismay. Only one boy got the joke. "Frodo? Samwise?" he added. Still, only the one boy understood. "Ah, come on, you guys, surely you've read… Ah, forget it." He slumped down in his chair.

After dinner, Emerson climbed the stairs to say good-bye to Meddows. "No hard feelings?" he said to the older boy.

"Nah," replied Meddows. "You got me good a couple of times. But I figure I sort of deserved it. What with the licking that old lady laid on you." Emerson winced at the memory. "You know, I didn't plan to get you beat up like that, eh, Jenks? I just wanted to scare yuh's all," added Meddows.

"Yeah, I know," Emerson replied. "Water under the bridge… until next year, eh?"

"Listen!" said Meddows. "During the summer, think this over… us two'd make a great team."

"I'll think about it," answered Emerson. "Promise. But listen, if you need a hand… you know…" He pointed at Meddows' luggage.

"Thanks, Jenks… maybe you and Guardiano can lug that trunk downstairs for me. It's pretty heavy."

"Be right back," promised Emerson. The younger boy ran off and retuned in short order, his friend in tow. "You get that end, Angelo."

"Whoa up, guys," exclaimed Meddows as he leapt to his feet. "Not so fast. Not that I don't trust you, Jenks… but how 'bout we all go together, eh? I don't want you and that trunk outta my sight at the same time."

"Whatever," replied Emerson and glanced down the hall. "Willoughby-Wallows, guys," he announced in a harsh whisper.

"Come on, Meddows, you're going to miss your train," called the dormitory supervisor as he approached the cubicle. "The van's out back." Emerson squatted at his end of the trunk, grasped the carrying strap with both hands and lifted. The trunk rose an inch and fell back to the floor.

Guardiano tipped the trunk on end and gave it a bear hug. "Just watch this," he bragged.

"No!" shouted Willoughby-Wallows, Jenks and Meddows in chorus.

"Guardiano, you take one end. Meddows, you get the other," ordered Willoughby-Wallows. "Let's move it. Jenks, you grab that suitcase or whatever you call it." The caravan moved along the corridor and down the stairs. The dorm supervisor, empty-handed, led the way. Guardiano and Meddows followed with the trunk, the bigger boy bearing more than his fair share of the burden. Meddows grunted and groaned under the weight of his end of the trunk and Guardiano's teasing. He kept looking back anxiously over his shoulder, urging Emerson to keep up. Emerson, who used both hands to lug Meddows' medium-sized carry-on, lagged behind.

"What you got in here anyways, Meddows, bricks or something?" Emerson shouted. When they reached the van and the baggage was stowed, Emerson approached Meddows as if to give him a hug.

Meddows jumped away. "Oh, no you don't, Jenks. You want to stick a 'kick me' sign on my back or something, right?"

"I'd never do anything like that to you, Meddows," replied a crestfallen Emerson. The younger boy extended his hand. "Shake?"

"Sure," replied Meddows. "Remember... think about what I said, eh?"

A crowd milled about the vehicle. Meddows kept a close eye on Emerson. The farewells ended when Willoughby-Wallows looked at his watch and cried out, "Oh goodness, we're late! Into the van everyone." Meddows dove into the vehicle with the four other departing boys and waved goodbye.

"Well, Em," said Guardiano as the two boys watched the van disappear in a cloud of dust, "I guess you won't get him back 'til next year, eh?"

"Well, Ange... you never can tell. Strange things happen sometimes."

"Yuh should've let me fix 'im right away, Em," replied Guardiano.

Meddows and four other St. Timothy's students waved to Willoughby-Wallows from the window of the eastbound train. They talked and laughed about Meddows' many pranks the entire way to Montreal. The boy talked his audience into lugging his trunk to U.S. Customs so he could continue his trip home. Meddows grew increasingly nervous as he stood in line. He attributed his apprehensions to having never crossed a border.

In the long queue, he advanced like a box on a conveyor belt towards three customs officers, all of whom, unbeknownst to them, intimidated the boy. Meddows noticed that the fellow to his right smiled... once. The other two wore grim expressions and appeared altogether too officious. As he waited his turn, Meddows counted heads and calculated the time each inspection took, trying to determine to which guard he would have to report. "Lucked out," he mumbled when the border guard who had smiled waved him forward.

"I.D.," demanded the officer who had noticed Meddows' nervousness. He had seen the boy swaying left and right, evaluating the inspection process. The sweat from Meddows' palm had smudged the ink on his train ticket. The officer noticed the smudges. After the customary questions about destination, purpose of visit and length of stay, the man asked, "May I look inside your carry-on, please?"

Meddows looked down and pointed at his bag. "This one, Sir?"

"You have two?" replied the man. Meddows laughed at his mistake. The officer did not laugh with him.

"Ahem... ah... no, Sir... I mean, no, I only have the one, Sir... not no you can't look in my bag, Sir" said Meddows and heaved the small but heavy case onto the counter.

"What's in here, Son?" demanded the guard, hefting the bag. "A bit heavy, isn't it?"

"Just a few books, Sir," answered Meddows. "And some comics and a change of clothes, Sir. That's all, Sir.

The officer noticed that the boy used the word 'sir' a lot. "Should be no problem then," he responded. "Please open it for me."

Meddows unzipped the bag. His hands trembled. The guard noticed. The boy flipped his carry-on open and made a quick survey of its contents: books, comics, clothes. He drew a deep breath, sighed and turned the suitcase towards the customs officer. The officer noticed the sigh. Meddows kept a close eye on the man's face as he rummaged through the bag. The officer's expression never changed. Meddows jumped when the guard looked up quickly and flipped the bag closed. The officer noticed that the boy jumped.

"Everything seems to be in order," announced the man. He noticed Meddows' raise his eyebrows, saw his chest heave and heard the boy's long, slow sigh of relief. Well-trained, experienced eyes, suspicious eyes, focussed on the carry-on. The guard realized there was a pocket on the front of the bag.

"Do I have your permission to take a peek in here?" asked the man, pointing at the zipper.

"Oh, there's nothin' in there, Sir," claimed Meddows. "I didn't even know..."

"Nothing?" asked the customs man.

"Nothin'," repeated Meddows. "Nothin' at all, Sir."

"Then you don't mind, right?" suggested the officer.

"Why no, Sir... ah... of course not, Sir," stammered Meddows. "Why would I mind, Sir?"

The man opened the pocket, leaned forwards and peeked inside. When he looked up, he flashed an amused smile. "Don't go anywhere, okay," he warned with a wag of his finger and a wink. He tapped the suitcase, leaned towards Meddows and whispered, "And, ah... don't touch, okay? I'll be back."

"Okay, Sir," replied Meddows. The boy's eyes followed the retreating border guard. As the man passed his fellow officers he stopped and whispered to them. The two men turned their heads towards Meddows and smiled for the first time. They stared at the boy, excused themselves and, while travellers waited impatiently in the lengthening queue, moved down to Meddows' place at the counter. They leaned against the wall with their arms folded across their chests.

Meddows stared at the sign over the door to which his customs officer had gone. *SUPERVISOR*, it read. Momentarily, the guard and a short, fat, bald man stood before him.

"Officer Mitchell here—" the supervisor jerked his thumb in Mitchell's direction, "—says we've a problem with the contents of your bag, Son."

"But it's just school books, Sir, and comics and stuff," replied Meddows. The supervisor eyed the boy and upgraded his assessment of the teenager's condition from nervous to panicky.

"Not that," interrupted Mitchell. "These!" Mitchell pulled a pair of women's panties – pink silk panties – from the bag. "And this," he added, plucking out a matching, lace-trimmed brassiere the way a magician plucks rabbits from a hat.

Meddows blinked and then blanched. His mouth fell open. A look of horror swept across his face. A feeling of nausea washed over him. He tried to speak but only managed to sputter. Mitchell's two brother officers sniggered as did the people in the queue. They waited more patiently now.

"Get back to work, you two," bellowed the supervisor. "Check that trunk, will you, Mitchell? You!" he said to Meddows. "You come with me."

When Meddows' interview ended, he was given instructions to wait while the supervisor went to call St. Timothy's. It was only when he sat alone that a light flashed in Meddows' mind. "Jenks!" he grumbled and jumped to his feet.

+ − × ÷

Angelo Guardiano helped stack Emerson's gear outside the main entrance then stared at the ground, kicked an imaginary tin can and struggled to make small talk. "Well… I guess that's it for this year, Emerson," he mumbled. "You're comin' back, right?"

"Sure, I'll be back. Of course I'll be back. You can count on it."

The bigger boy's lower lip began to quiver. He rushed to his friend, threw his arms around him, then backed away, turned and retreated into the building.

"Next year for sure," called Emerson into the darkness of the foyer. "See you next year."

At what must have been midnight, Emerson, who could not sleep, dressed and left the dorm. Throughout the long night, he walked around the circle drive countless times and to the river twice. He sat on the front steps and strummed his guitar but found no pleasure in it. He thought about his year at St. Timothy's and the people he had met. Recalling his pranks, he smiled. He walked to the eastern border of the property and stared into the old woman's orchard. He cringed at the thought of little green apples. Before old Sol rose over the horizon, Emerson had drifted into sleep with his head resting on his knapsack.

The sound of tires on gravel roused him. He opened his eyes to see Professor Warneke staring at him over the steering wheel of the car. "Up and at 'em, my young friend," the English master called out as he exited the vehicle. "Jenks, my man," he added, "let's be off. I have promises to keep—"

"—And miles to go before I sleep," responded Emerson with a yawn.

"And miles to go before I sleep," Warneke repeated. "Fine brain in there," he replied and patted the boy's head. "Exquisite workmanship!"

They stowed Emerson's belongings on the rear seat and climbed into the car. Before the rose window was lost to view, Emerson was lost to the world. Warneke arranged his well-worn suit coat over the boy and drove on.

"What time is it, Sir?" said Emerson as he sat up and looked around. Warneke answered by pointing at the clock on the dash. "Five after ten already," said the boy as he yawned. "Wow!" he added as he stretched. "Will we be stopping soon, Sir?"

"Hungry, are you, Jenks?" asked Warneke.

"Ah… no, Sir," answered Emerson. "It's not that."

"Oh!" replied Warneke. At the first opportunity, he exited the freeway, swung south and entered a village. "There's a gas station just ahead," announced the driver.

"Good," replied Emerson.

When Emerson came out of the washroom, Warneke tossed him a bottle of pop and a bag of chips. "Enjoy," the professor said. "If we keep this pace, you'll be home by noon." They climbed into the car. Warneke checked the fuel gage, hemmed and hawed for five seconds and then drove to the pumps. After paying the bill, he pulled out of the service station and drove north, back towards the freeway.

"You and I are cut from the same cloth, I think," suggested Warneke after a long silent spell.

"Sir?"

"Pranksters," explained the English master. "We both like pranks, Jenks." Emerson said nothing. "That masterpiece you pulled off in Fitzroy's office—" Warneke made a low grumbling sound, "—was a corker, my lad… top drawer that. I've never seen anything like it." Emerson persisted in his silence. Warneke gave him a quizzical stare. "You're reluctant to talk about our little predilection, I see," he added.

"Sir… well, with you being a professor and all…" replied Emerson.

"Forget that," cried Warneke. "The year's over. We know each other's styles. Why, we're practically comrades in arms. Besides… now that you've been exposed, I'm on my guard. You won't be pulling any of your fast ones on me. No, Sir."

"Yeah," mumbled Emerson as he exhaled, "I know. But, I'm sure going to miss it." The boy turned and gazed out the side window. "The pranks, I mean, Sir." The boy fell into a gloomy silence. Warneke had seen people exhibit less sadness over the loss of a family pet. After a moment, the boy made a loud huffing sound and added, "Oh, well!"

Eventually, the talk about pranks continued. Warneke and Emerson swapped tales. They talked of successes and failures, even about pranks in which they had been targets. As the travellers opened up to each other, they began to establish a stronger bond. A veritable mutual admiration society sped westwards.

"You know, my boy," suggested the English master, "you should seriously consider writing a book. You have no lack of material. That's for sure."

"A book, Sir?" replied a shocked Emerson Jenks. "Oh, I don't think I could be a writer, Sir." After a moment's thought, he added, "Anyhow, I'd want to be a lot older and a lot further from St. Timothy's before trying anything like that, Sir. There could be serious repercussions." They continued down the highway in silence.

+ − × ÷

"I'm here to see Dr. Stokes. My appointment's at 10:30," announced the young man at 10:25 on Saturday morning.

The person he addressed had dark circles under his eyes and wore jogging pants and a coffee-stained singlet. He stared back across the counter at the neatly-dressed gentleman who had just roused him. "Stokes, um? A doctor, yuh say?" He rubbed his bristly chin. "Niver 'eard of 'im. Appointment, yuh say?"

"He's probably in the conference room. He's…" The desk clerk's reaction stopped Willoughby-Wallows dead in his tracks. He stared at the sickly looking gentleman with alarm.

The man's rheumy, bloodshot eyes filled with tears as he began to laugh and then cough. "Conference room?" sputtered the man after he regained his composure. "Why we ain't got no conference room here." To the red-nosed fellow dozing on the lobby's couch, he called out, "This here feller's lookin' fir the conference room, Ike." Ike blinked then opened his mouth, revealing his vacant eyes and then his toothless gums.

"Dr. J. Benjamin Stokes is…" stated Willoughby-Wallows, "the secretary-treasurer of the Tri-County Classics Club." Even Ike and the desk clerk could tell their visitor was indignant.

"Benjamin? Benjamin? Oh, yuh must mean Benny? Why the heck didn't yuh say so? A doctor, yuh say? Nah!" The man waved his arm in the general direction of a rickety staircase. "They's in 2-12," he announced. Willoughby-Wallows did not move. "One floor up… third—no fourth room on the left," the desk clerk added in an attempt to placate his perturbed guest.

The young teacher glowered. His face grew red. The clerk ran his fingers through his sparse, oily, unkempt hair and rubbed his bristly chin. He reckoned that Willoughby-Wallows wanted him to do or say something but he could not, for the life of him, think of what it might be. The man scratched his potbelly and the back of his neck simultaneously. He looked past the professor towards Ike. Ike was no help. Ike had gone back to sleep.

"Third door's the garbage room, eh," the desk clerk explained, hoping to satisfy the strange little man on the other side of the counter.

"I would like you... to inform Dr. Stokes... that Mr. Wilfred Willoughby-Wallows is here to see him." Willoughby-Wallows spoke slowly, articulating his every word. The man opened his mouth to protest, thought better of it and exited what passed for an office. Willoughby-Wallows heard mumbling and muttering as the clerk climbed the stairs. The words 'conference room' and 'Dr. Stokes' were all he could make out.

Alone in the lobby – save for Ike who snorted and snored in his repose – Willoughby-Wallows began to notice how very shabby the Blue Bayou appeared. He thought it an odd location for people of Dr. Stokes' calibre to hold meetings. The Greek and Latin professor paced, rehearsing his speech. He became aware of an offensive odour that several air fresheners did not quite obliterate. His thoughts strayed to the frayed couch cushions and the initials carved into the arms of chairs. His anxiety grew by the moment. He wanted to make a good first impression on the club and perhaps be nominated for membership. He ran through what he hoped would be a stirring finale to his address

Willoughby-Wallows turned at the sound of approaching footsteps. A roly-poly little man, wearing soiled blue jeans held up by a belt with a buckle the size of salad plate, entered the lobby. He removed a ball cap, which in a former life had been white, and wiped his bald head with the sleeve of his red and black mackinaw. "Dang hot in here, ain't it?" the man asked no one in particular. His eyes swept the lobby before staring straight at Willoughby-Wallows. "You the feller lookin' fir Benny Stokes?" he asked.

"Yes, yes, I am," answered Willoughby-Wallows.

"You are? Well now?" said the man as he smirked and looked the teacher up and down. "Well... you found 'im, friend," the man in the ball cap announced. "I'm him." Willoughby-Wallows' surprise blossomed into full-blown shock. "Well, Son, let's git to 'er. The boys and me's bin a-waitin' on yuh."

Willoughby-Wallows followed the man obviously impersonating J. Benjamin Stokes, Ph.D. across the lobby and up the stairs. They passed the grinning desk clerk on the way. Willoughby-Wallows was having difficulty picturing Benny reading Pindar or Juvenal. He was having a hard time picturing him reading the *Tri-County Gazette*. 'Yet the letter...' pondered Willoughby-Wallows in an effort to reassure himself, 'said this slovenly fellow was a close friend of Dr. Kenneth Reardon.' "How very, very odd?" he said aloud and shrugged.

"What was that?" asked Stokes as he threw the door to 2-12 open. "Age before beauty, my man." When Willoughby-Wallows passed through the doorway, his full-blown shock turned to dismay. The room was filled with Benny Stokeses.

Three Benny clones lounged on the bed. Another sat on the window sill with his legs crossed at the ankles and stretched halfway across the room. Another Benny sat on a chair in a corner, arms folded. His head rested against the side wall. Without looking up, the man touched the brim of his ball cap in greeting. A Benny, who had to be the first Benny's twin, wore a green mackinaw. His chair leaned against the end wall. Only its two back legs rested on the floor. The fellow's chin rested on his chest. Willoughby-Wallows reckoned the man was asleep. The final Benny entered from what was apparently a bathroom. He zipped his fly and belched as he nodded to the guest speaker.

"Let's have at 'er!" shouted the first Benny. The other Bennys, except for Green Mackinaw Benny, mumbled and muttered.

"Go fir it, Mister..." added bathroom Benny. "We's all ears." He kicked Green Mackinaw Benny's chair, gaining the man's attention and all but dumping him on the floor. Everyone but Willoughby-Wallows and Green Mackinaw Benny thought the joke was hilarious.

During his inaugural year at St. Timothy's, Wilfred Willoughby-Wallows had made many questionable decisions and let many bad situations worsen by acting before thinking things through. He had demonstrated an uncanny ability to burry himself in troubles by allowing others to tug, turn and twist him like saltwater taffy. He was about to make the same mistake. He tossed off his doubts and suspicions, cleared his throat, threw back his shoulders and surveyed the eager faces before launching into his speech.

"I have with me some pictures you'll no doubt find interesting," announced the M.A. in Greek and Latin as he looked for a safe place to display the photographs. "I cut this one out of a calendar my mother gave me for Christmas," he explained.

Quiet chuckles rising from his audience caused the scholar to hesitate. When he found no place to display the picture he handed it to one of the on-the-bed Bennys and instructed him to study it and pass it around. The other seven Bennys leapt up as one and huddled over picture-holding Benny. They peered and pointed in astonishment. They turned the picture right and left. They turned it over to see what was on the back. Contrary to all appearances, their curiosity was evident. These gentlemen definitely appreciated classical architecture.

Bathroom Benny glanced up and cried, "Well, dang me! Looks like a dozer wint clean through somethin'. What tuh-heck was it b-fir?"

"That, Sir," explained Willoughby-Wallows, seizing the teachable moment, "is what remains of the great citadel of Rome."

"Golly," whispered J. Benjamin Stokes, Ph.D. and whistled. He turned his ball cap around so that its peak pointed straight back. He leaned in closer for a better look. "Is that where yuh picked up that there '27 Reo of yours?"

"What?" demanded Willoughby-Wallows. "I'm in the right place, am I not, Sir? This is the Tri-County Classics Club… right?"

"A-course," replied two or three Bennys in unison.

"And you're J. Benjamin Stokes… the secretary-treasurer?"

"One 'n the same," replied the first Benny. "Dang tootin!" He removed his hat and scratched his head. "Though there ain't niver been no 'J' in it that I knowed of."

For many months afterwards, Willoughby-Wallows wondered why he had not simply excused himself at this point, before a minor misunderstanding turned into a full-scale calamity. But, alas, the thought did not cross his mind at the time. Inexplicably, Willoughby-Wallows had somehow or other gotten caught up in the thing.

The guest speaker rescued his precious picture of the citadel and held it up. He pointed to the pile of rubble in the centre of the photograph. "This, gentlemen, is the spot, the very spot," he explained in his most dramatic voice, "about which that great Roman historian wrote these immortal words: *Ibi a Gaulis, visi sunt senes, qui ceteros cives in roma-*

num non sequti." He paused and looked from one stunned face to another giving each Benny time to translate.

The floor of Room 2-12 was carpeted from wall to wall, except where the underlay showed through at the foot of and along either side of the bed, at the main entrance, in front of the closet, at the bathroom door and under the writing table. But when Willoughby-Wallows finished his quotation anyone in the room could have heard a pin drop. No pin dropped. What dropped was the lower jaw of each and every Benny.

"What tuh-heck did he just say, Phil?" asked a Benny: not the first Benny or his twin and not bathroom Benny.

"Sorry, Willie, I missed it," answered Phil.

The questions fell fast and furious on Willoughby-Wallows' ears. He raised his voice, knocked loudly on the writing table and called for order. In confusion, Willie, Phil and six Bennys stared at their guest.

"Can anyone here tell me the Greek for… let me see… for the word… 'fear'?" The members of the Classics Club gaped. Each deferred to the others rather than shouting out the right answer. "Benjamin, how about the Latin word for 'a wall'?" demanded the teacher.

J. Benjamin Stokes, Ph.D. removed his ball cap and scratched his temple. Anyone would have thought the answer teetered on the tip of his tongue. He struggled in vain to pluck the answer from his all too deficient Latin vocabulary. The man looked about in desperation, pleading for assistance. Wide-eyed, he searched the faces of his astonished friends.

Green Mackinaw Benny laughed at his twin brother whose reaction hinted of a propensity for violence. "Okay, wiseacre… that's it," shouted the first Benny and leapt up from the edge of the bed.

Willoughby-Wallows' raised one hand, traffic cop style, and cried out, "Now, now, gentlemen, I'll not have you calling each other names, okay?"

"I ain't talkin' to him… I'm talkin' to you, smartass," continued the first Benny – this to Willoughby-Wallows not Green Mackinaw Benny. "You're so smart, eh? Tell me… how much horsepower they gettin' outta a stock 350 Chevy, eh?" There was no need to give Willoughby-Wallows time to think of the answer. His face confessed to knowing nothing whatsoever about the 350 Chevy or about horsepower in general.

"Or how 'bout the torque from that there Dodge 318 Hemi?" demanded Phil.

"This is a... a... *car club?*" cried Willoughby-Wallows. "A classic car club?"

"What the heck did yuh think it was, you donkey?" replied the first Benny. "Your letter said you'd tell us about that Speedwagon of yours, eh?"

"What's a Speedwagon?" asked the bewildered teacher. The room filled with derisive laughter. Upon pondering the words 'wiseacre', 'smartass' and 'donkey', Willoughby-Wallows realized it was well past time for his departure. "There's been some kind of mistake, I guess," suggested the Greek and Latin man.

"Yuh think?" replied two or three Bennys.

"He don't know nuttin'," declared chair-leaning Benny. "If he's the guy who rebuilt that Speedwagon then I'm the guy who built them there pee-ree-mids over in E-jip."

Before the situation worsened, Willoughby-Wallows turned on his heel and bolted from 2-12 and the Blue Bayou. As he sprinted to the school van, he heard six Bennys, a Phil and a Willie hoot and holler, giggle and guffaw, chuckle and chortle as they squeezed together at the second story window. He noticed the desk clerk and Ike joining in the fun from the hotel's main door.

Once Willoughby-Wallows was sure he was not being pursued, he pulled to the side of the highway and leaned his head against the seatback. A single word escaped his lips.

"Warneke!" he screamed.

+ − × ÷

Warneke, with his young passenger on the edge of his seat, pulled up to the Jenks' home at 11:45. "Could you back in, please, Sir?" Emerson requested. "So I can unload my stuff easier, Sir."

Without comment, Warneke reversed into the driveway until the car's rear bumper was about six feet from the garage door. "How's that, Jenks?" he asked.

"A bit further back, please, Sir."

"Okay," replied Warneke and rolled the car to within a foot of the building.

Before Emerson could step out of the vehicle, it was mobbed by Mrs. Jenks and her two youngest sons. Emerson's father exited the house but stood well back taking in the scene. When he beckoned to the driver, Warneke stepped out of the car and joined him. Glenda raced between the two men as if they were not there and joined the throng, jumping up and down and shrieking.

"Hail the Conquering Hero," declared Warneke.

Emerson's father stared at the big man. "Pardon?" inquired Jenks senior. This was the first time he had laid eyes on Warneke and already he was wondering if not just the headmaster, but all of St. Timothy's people said strange things.

As if Mr. Jenks could not possibly misunderstand what was meant, the professor repeated himself. "Hail the Conquering Hero!"

"Hmmm! Oh, I know…" replied a relieved Mr. Jenks, "that old Sturgis movie?" He frowned trying to make the connection between the wartime farce and the scene playing out before him.

"No, Sir," corrected Warneke, "I refer to Handel, Sir… George *Frideric* Handel?"

"Well, anyway… the kids have actually calmed down a bit." Mr. Jenks tried to ignore his guest's haughtiness. "It's been a madhouse since I got home. Meeting got cancelled, eh."

His siblings dragged Emerson's belongings from the car into the house while Mrs. Jenks, with her hands on her son's shoulders, directed him inside.

"Judy's just fixing lunch," explained Emerson's father. "You'll eat with us, won't you, Sir?"

Warneke pulled out his watch, stared at it for a few moments and grimaced. "No. Sorry, but I can't. I have to be in the city early."

"You'll come in for a moment… a little something to drink, maybe?"

At the word 'drink', Warneke pulled out his watch for a second look. "I guess I can spare ten minutes or so." The two men passed through the kitchen into the parlour.

"Judy doesn't have her feet on the ground yet. I'll see what I can dig up," advised Peter Jenks.

As his father exited the room, Emerson entered. "Mom says you have to stay for lunch. She's cooked something really special... just for you," explained Emerson and sped off before Warneke could object. "He's staying for lunch, Mom," the boy yelled as he hurried past her.

"Emerson," cried his mother as he bolted past. "Come here, please." The woman lifted the lid from her soup pot, stared at the contents and massaged her forehead, as Emerson waited.

"What, Mom?"

"Oh... never mind," she replied. "It's alright. Say, Emerson—" she looked towards the parlour and whispered, "—is Mr. Warneke okay? His complexion doesn't look very good to me." Emerson shrugged and ran off to the family room.

Alone in the Jenks' parlour, Warneke looked at his watch for a third time and thought of bolting. But, he really needed that stiff drink.

Ten minutes passed before Mr. Jenks returned walking very slowly and carrying two cups. "I hope you like Earl Grey," he said. "It's all I could find." He did not see Warneke turn up his nose.

"You call that a drink, you nincompoop," mumbled the English master.

"Pardon?" inquired Mr. Jenks. "What was that?"

"I said Earl Grey will be just fine, Sir," answered the family's reluctant lunch guest.

After the meal, Warneke slid his chair away from the table and heaped praise on Mrs. Jenks' bland and, mercifully he thought, not very plentiful meatloaf. He imagined chunks of tomato-topped burger bobbing about in a pool of watery soup and tepid tea.

After a few more pleasantries, Cyrus Warneke broke his bonds asunder. He collapsed behind the wheel of his car and tried not to scream. The clock on the dash told him it was almost two o'clock. As the car rolled forward, Emerson ran from the house and stopped in front of the vehicle waving one hand wildly in the air. Warneke knew he should stop.

"Drat!" he muttered as he applied the brakes and rolled down his window. "Now what?"

"Dad asked me to give you this... for driving me home," explained Emerson. "I hope I remembered right... that it's the right kind, I mean."

Warneke opened the prettily wrapped box and smiled a warm, loving smile. Appreciation oozed from every pore of his ample jowls. "Your memory is impeccable, Mr. Jenks," he said. "Im...pec...ca...ble!" After checking to make sure no one had tampered with the bottle's seal – comrades in arms or not, Warneke did not trust young Mr. Jenks one little bit – he tucked the quart of eighteen-year-old Jameson's under the front seat, wished Emerson a good summer and drove off.

Emerson watched as Warneke's car sped off westwards. He walked back to the kitchen door, nodding his head slowly. "I'm home!" Emerson shouted and entered what had once, but no longer seemed such a large kitchen.

+ − × ÷

Once Warneke reached the highway, he breezed by every vehicle he came upon. Forty minutes later, he accelerated down the ramp and merged into much heavier freeway traffic. Fearing a ticket, he slowed his pace to just under the speed limit. A steady stream of cars passed him. Drivers tooted their horns, gave him dirty looks and raced on. Warneke, unperturbed by their impatience, turned up the volume of his music and ignored the people and the noise outside. He was a free man at last. Thoughts of a fine steak dinner, a comfortable hotel room, a good cigar and the exquisite taste of fine Irish whiskey soothed his nerves.

"Oh, to have nothing but sweet thoughts in one's head," mused Warneke aloud. "*While visions of sugarplums...*" he added, recalling the words of the Christmas poem. Not even the heavy traffic with its blaring horns dampened Warneke's spirits. The English master was more relaxed than he had been since the day before the start of first term. He was not about to let anyone rain on his parade.

He had not counted on the thunderheads towering above him. A motorcycle cop pulled up beside the car, emergency lights flashing. Before the officer could activate his siren, the driver glanced to his left and, in wide-eyed, open-mouthed wonder, stared out the window. The cop was no mime but his frenzied finger pointing and manic mouthing of the words 'pull over' left Warneke no doubt about what he was being ordered to do.

"Oh Lordy, Lordy," Warneke moaned as he applied his brakes. Before coming to a stop, a shiver ran up the man's spine and his face flushed. "Blast your eyes, Jenks!" Warneke bellowed upon realizing that he was not out of Emerson's prank range *quite* yet.

ABOUT THE AUTHOR

At age 13, Mel Anthony left his home in Peterborough, Ontario to attend St. Mary's College in Brockville, Ontario. After graduating in 1968, he attended Holy Redeemer College and the University of Windsor (B.S.W. '72, M.S.W. '75). Mel Anthony is a retired social worker (2004). He lives in Sherwood Park, Alberta but spends most of his time aboard his sailboat, the *Talisman IV*, in Sidney, BC. He has three sons living in Alberta. He enjoys sailing, reading, playing guitar and spending time with friends and family. Recently Mr. Anthony has devoted his energies to writing and to Christian relief work in and around Puente Piedra, Lima, Peru.

LaVergne, TN USA
08 October 2010
200141LV00004B/4/P

9 781897 435434